ROBBIE JAMES
A Life in Football

Gary Wharton

lushington PUBLISHING

For Joan, Roy, Samantha, Hannah and Luke.

ISBN 978-0-9542187-8-2

page design: gary wharton

quadmodbook@yahoo.co.uk

Printed and bound by
Aquatintbsc
48 Weir Road SW19 8UG
www.aquatintbsc.co.uk
sales@aquatintbsc.co.uk
020 8947 8571

lushington **PUBLISHING**

CNTENTS

BORN IN GORSEINON, some six miles from central Swansea on Saturday 23 March 1958, to parents Roy and Joan, Robert Mark James was from a family of four, including sisters, Wendy, Susan and Kay and brother, Alan. The family relocated to city the town centre area and Robbie would return to the Sketty some years later, following his second spell with Swansea City.

Often professional footballers will say that they would happily have played for nothing but what a thrill to turn 'pro' and actually be able to make a living as a professional. Robbie James, forever remembered simply as "Robbie" or "Jamo" (by his team mates), was one such person to do so. He made his way up through the usual channels, playing for Mayhill school and then in both the under-13s and under-15s whilst at Bishop Vaughan, in the Morriston area, where an ex-school pal remembers him as being a very nice guy, very unassuming." He also played for Swansea Schools whilst attending Bishop Vaughan and joined the Under-15s squad initially as a Reserve during 1970/ 71 season. He was in their team that won the Welsh Schools Shield in the following year, with Robbie scoring a cracking goal in the second leg final at the Vetch. It was whilst involved with Swansea Schools that Gareth Williams remembers him. "I was the one who said to Harry Gregg (then Swansea manager) that he should speak to Robbie's parents about signing him," recalls the former school teacher. "When he did sign, it was the best thing that Robbie ever did," he adds. "When I look at what happened to other names that were far more talented than Robbie, I believe that a boy who has got talent and works, will achieve more than somebody who is highly talented but who won't work. I have seen so many boys fall by the wayside and that's why I have the highest regard for boys like Robbie. No one would have a bad word to say about him."

Young Robbie progressed to apprentice status at Swansea City F.C prior to signing professional terms with them. Although, as a ten-year-old his potential had already been recognised when he was picked to play for Swansea Schools Under-11s: when even then he dreamed of becoming a footballer.

But his career could have taken him down a different path, if Cardiff City had offered him terms. It looked likely that he might drift away from the game before the Swans took him on after he was released by the Bluebirds. Ever the pragmatist, Robbie got himself a job down the docks and was all set to become an electrician after having started an apprentice.

The acerbic Harry Gregg, a "tough, no-nonsense personality that you didn't answer back too," as a former Swans player Nigel Stevenson recollects, had offered Robbie amateur terms in March

1973 and this former keeper was someone who Robbie credits as being his biggest influence. "You didn't argue with Gregg. He would go on the offensive to get you on the defensive," adds Williams, once heavily involved with Swansea Schools football, when they played their games at the Vetch Field. Gregg believed that at sixteen, a boy was too young to leave home to join a big club such as Arsenal, as would be in Robbie's case later, or Manchester United. Williams was at the Vetch after one particular game and recalls the manager addressing the parents of the young players. "I promise you this, if a boy signs for Swansea City, I will look after him. I will make sure that he is taught good habits. There will be no nonsense, he won't be going out in the afternoon with the senior players and playing snooker or having a drink. There will be strict discipline, I will work the boys hard and I make you a promise; if they respond, I will give them the opportunity to play, at whatever age they are, if they are good enough, for a Football League club." Robbie and his parents Roy and Joan were there that day at the Vetch to hear Gregg create such a lasting impression.

Robbie began as an amateur with the Swans before advancing to playing for the club in both the Welsh League and Football Combination before being given his full League debut in an end of season game with Charlton Athletic in front of 1,880 spectators. That occurred at the Vetch Field on 28 April 1973 and was the final game of that particular season, when the club would finish their campaign in twenty-third out of a possible twenty-four in the Third Division. It meant that along with Scunthorpe, Brentford and Rotherham, that Swansea would start the 1973/ 74 season in Division Four. Robbie featured in a much-changed side against opposition that had hammered them 6-0 at their place back in late-August. Selected in the number seven shirt, he played a part in his side's 2-1 win that broke a run of defeats and at last gave the 1,880 crowd something to cheer about. Gregg had made a dramatic statement to the press that the sporting world might not hear anything from his club for a couple of years as it was undergoing a state of major reconstruction. "This is a bleak moment for Swansea and for the whole of Welsh football," he wrote in his programme notes for the Charlton game. "I am convinced, however, that it is not a disaster (relegation). The job on which I must now launch myself is no different from the job I would have done had we stayed in the Third Division. We start back at the foundations."

Robbie was given a role of playing out on the right wing, with Alan Curtis out on the left. The season had seen a managerial change at the club with Roy Bentley departing in October 1972 prior to former Manchester United keeper Harry Gregg coming in after a caretaker spell under both Roy Saunders and Harry Griffiths. Curtis and Robbie would become great mates and although the former did not play much this season, he remembered seeing Robbie in past trial matches and school boy fixtures before lining-up alongside his future pal.

Swansea Evening Post reporter Bill Paton was complimentary

about the new boy's endeavours, "...the most heartening feature was the highly promising debut of 15-year-old Robert James, who seemed to have an old head on his slender shoulders." With the Swans going 2-0 up, his praise continued, "There was no trace of nerves from this ex-Swansea schoolboy, whose delicate touches and subtle passing were an object lesson to more experienced players." The Swansea team line-up for that momentous match was: Davies, Jones, Evans, Davies G, Williams, Thomas, Robbie, McLaughlin, Screen, Johnson, Curtis.

Known for his ferocious shot, skilful use of the ball and for being difficult to dispossess, Robbie also had a great turn of pace that left opponents in his wake. Of course, he would make his name with his home town club but he also did well elsewhere, including Bradford and Cardiff City, where the fans remember him fondly. This book details his long and illustrious playing career and also records his time as an international player with Wales. We also look at his later years when he moved into the player/manager mode at Llanelli A.F.C and his tragic death whilst playing for them at their Stebonheath Park ground in February 1998.

His legacy as the consummate 'pro' whose body took many knocks, lingers. He was a man that resembled more a P.E teacher or rugby player rather than the fancy young peacocks playing today. Married twice, with three children remaining, namely Samantha, Hannah and Luke, to whom along with parents Roy a and Joan,this work is dedicated. Ultimately, this project is about a life in football of a true Welsh sporting great.

Swansea City

"Robbie was shy off the field but totally different on it but he was always approachable and friendly towards the fans."
Team mate Nigel Stevenson

Having been relegated down into the bottom tier of the Football League for the 1973/74 season, Swansea City found itself competing against the likes of Lincoln, Northampton and Bury across forty-six fixtures in a division containing twenty-four clubs. Known for its rough physicality, Division Four would prove a challenging baptism for life as a professional football player for the seventeen-year-old Robbie James. As a club, the Swans also entered teams in both the Welsh League and Football Combination this year. Manager Gregg was keen to express that his team was on the up but he wasn't foolish enough to offer an immediate fix and promise promotion. Quite the contrary, Gregg stressed that it would take time to build from the foundations being laid into place at the club. In amongst the heavy side-burns of his team mates in the traditional team photo, shown above, a cherub-looking Robbie, back in the days when he was minus his trade-mark moustache, can be seen seated front row, fourth from left, next to Wyndham Evans in amongst seventeen players. This season saw the Swans wearing a plain all-white kit which was set-off by a large dragon on the left of the chest, with over-sized 'S.C.F.C' lettering underneath.

There was no sign of the familial swan nor was there a manufacturer branding and of course, this was back in the days when there was no such thing as shirt sponsorship.

Since registering his full debut back in April, Robbie joined the squad for a tour of southern Ireland arranged by Gregg, who was intent upon making changes before the start of the season. Fixtures were met against Limerick, Waterford and Hibernian on the week-long trip before they returned to Wales on Saturday 18 August, in readiness for the 1973/ 74 football campaign.

A gate of 2,500 watched the opening game of the season against Chester on 25 August and saw Robbie in the number eight shirt in only his second appearance in the first team at the Vetch. He would also pull on the numbers nine and eleven jerseys during the season.

Other new arrivals in the squad included Pat Lally, Danny Bartley and Paul Bevan. Bartley had joined this season from nearby Bristol City and his son, Kevin, became a professional at Cardiff City in the early-1990s when Robbie was there. Bevan was a former Shrewsbury Town defender who had scored against the Swans at the Vetch back in the 1972/ 73 season. Whilst in goal, the club tried a number of names, with usual number one Tony Millington leaving by the close of the campaign and on-loan names Jimmy Rimmer and Dai Davies would return in future seasons, too. Known affectionately as 'Millie', Tony was struggling in his final season with the club and the Wales international was dropped from the national squad scheduled to meet Poland at the end of September.

A fledgling Robbie would score twice this season; against Rotherham and Mansfield, both away from the Vetch. Their goal scoring away from home was poor; with seventeen scored but thirty-one conceded, whilst on their own patch they would strike twenty-eight times and let in fifteen.

An under-strength Chester side had not enjoyed a prosperous pre-season and by the final whistle, things had not improved: they were beaten 2-0. Played on a blisteringly hot afternoon, the Swans offered much on a healthy victory that had seen an anxious City side go in at half-time 0-0. With both teams heavily altered since the previous season, Robbie put in an admirable performance that added to his burgeoning experience whilst Lally proved useful in offering the teenager much of the ball.

The Swans proved poor in cup competitions this season, going out in the early rounds of the F.A Cup, Welsh Cup and via a replay, in the League Cup. Usually, cup games draw a lower attendance than League fixtures but the late-August meeting with fellow-Division Four counterparts Exeter City proved the opposite. A healthy 3,036 attended the Vetch to see a 1-1 played out and temporarily improved their form from last year's competition, where they had been put-out by Newport. It was Robbie's one and only cup appearance and he did not feature in the subsequent replay which the Swans lost 2-1. The lower divisions were notorious for the often crude battering given out to the young, creative players and both Robbie and team mate Alan Curtis suffered this season. The duo would become firm friends at Swansea and 'Curt' who at twenty-one was a little older than his mate, played in many of the fifty games fulfilled by the club this season. In a match watched by a decent gate, supporters saw a spectacle strewn with free kicks coupled with a negative approach favoured by the visitors. Tony Screen scored the winner and he would be top scorer with nine collected this year. Lacking in goals, by May when the team had completed its fixtures, the season proved to be an underwhelming one.

With an adherence to an ethos of outright attack demanded by Gregg, the Swans travelled to south Yorkshire to meet the Millers, also relegated from Division Three back in May. They had taken the honours, both home and away previously, and continued with a 1-0 victory at Millmoor which saw Robbie substituted in the first-half, a consequence of a below-par team performance. Replaced by the tall Herbie Williams, the second-half saw lots of pressure being applied by the visitors but no goals.

Robbie was absent for the 0-3 defeat by Gillingham at the Vetch but returned for the 0-0, mid-September visit to Crewe whilst another unsuccessful encounter came in a 2-1 defeat at Mansfield, within a game that again saw Robbie subbed.

In a season when a home programme cost 7p, supporters could show their devotion by buying Swansea car stickers for 9p, a key ring for 15p and a fringed pennant for 20p from the club shop situated in a terraced house close to the ground (it has since returned to private ownership). With seven games completed; five in the League and two in the League Cup, Robbie had featured in five of them and only enjoyed a single win (the Chester game). He was absent from the first team for the next fourteen League matches but would return on 8

December, for an away trip to Bury. Without him, the Swans recorded five wins, three draws and six defeats.

However, upon his return in the twentieth League fixture of the campaign, he retained his place in the team in all but three of the twenty-six remaining games. In between, Robbie played for the Combination side, as did Alan Curtis, who was in and out of first team contention. The Combination League was very strong and numbered Spurs, Q.P.R, Arsenal and West Ham United in its midst but the Swans did not do very well in it. They finished twentieth out of twenty-two, winning eleven out of forty-two games whilst rivals Cardiff procured the exact same points tally in a League won by AFC Bournemouth.

October proved to be a depressing month for those with an interest in the affairs of Swansea City Football Club, when Chairman Malcolm Struel revealed a loss of £50,000 being recorded by the club in the previous season and an overdraft peaking at £70,000 this term was also a "cause of great concern." Struel, an opinionated personality, often spoke about what he wanted for the club, despite their lowly status. He publicly pleaded for fans to turn out and support the Swans but it failed to galvanise them and across the whole season 63,629 made their way through the turnstiles. In stark contrast, Welsh rivals Cardiff City revealed that they had made a profit as a working football club in the last twelve months.

Gregg acknowledged that his planned team progression scheme might not be seen to be working for at least five years and he knew that he might not be at the club to reap the projected rewards. Manager at the Vetch since November 1972, this former goalkeeper was also capped at international level for Northern Ireland. The Swans job was his second managerial position, coming after four years spent with Shrewsbury Town.

Advancing to October 1973, his current team had registered six points from a possible eighteen. (The team photo below shows Robbie second right in the top row of standing players).

Although their away record was poor, scoring seventeen but conceding almost double that, the Swans did play some attacking football. They might not have always won but the team remained resolute in sticking to this style of play and would continue to do so. At home, the club was struggling to attract support across many fixtures played out in wet and windy conditions.

Robbie was selected in a thirteen-man squad that made the long journey north to visit Bury at Gigg Lane in the second week of December. Possible injury concerns to Lally and young Wyndham 'Windy' Evans meant that Robbie was joined by Williams as cover. Their hosts had recently lost to Newport County but were a strong side in the division, suffering a blip in form but remaining in the top four for some time. Goals from Ronnie Rees and Tony Screen completed a Welsh 'double'. Rees was a current Welsh international, signed from Nottingham Forest in January 1970.

Following the win at Bury, Robbie was in the Wales Youth team side that met the Netherlands, at the Vetch Field, on 12 December. He was joined by team mate David J. Davies. Known as Dai, but not to be confused with the goalkeeper of the same name, this Mr. Davies was a youngster who would make six first-team appearances for Swansea City this season (he started in League games alongside Robbie through February-March 1974). The two had featured in the Football Combination side from the previous season. Confusingly, Dai made his full League debut as a professional footballer against Reading, in a game that saw the other Dai Davies in goal! The Wales game was a group qualifier for the U.E.F.A youth tournament being staged in Sweden during the coming summer. Wales, managed by the popular Mike Smith, found themselves in a tough group with England and Holland, from which one team would go through. Smith voiced his belief that his young side must continue with its attacking mode of play when they next met England, twice. He had been involved with the Welsh set-up since 1967 and had worked tirelessly. A subsequent 3-0 win against the Dutch delighted him; in a match which Robbie played in. He had also featured in the goal-less draw with them back in November. Davies put Wales ahead and two quick goals from Powell and Stevenson sealed a convincing win. A subsequent 1-0 loss to England was concluded with a 1-0 win at Ninian Park, in March 1974 and meant that Wales went through to the finals. Both finished on five points whilst Robbie played in the game at Cardiff.

After his exertions in a Wales shirt, Robbie did not play in the Swansea side which exited the Welsh Cup via 1-2 loss at the Vetch on the Saturday following the midweek international. The game with Stourbridge, then situated in the Southern League, was loan keeper Jimmy Rimmer's seventh appearance for the Swans after Manchester United had granted permission to allow him to play in the fixture against a side that also beat Wrexham this season. He would eventually leave for Arsenal but returned to the Vetch in the 1983/ 84 season and later ending up running a golf shop in the city! Jim was succeeded by Everton's Dai Davies before Tony Millington returned to keep goal for the final nine League games. Being an ex-keeper, Gregg had good links with his old club Man United and tried out a few men in the position this season.

Lucky Torquay United enjoyed the spoils of a 0-1 win played out on a terrible Vetch Field surface after scoring in the first minute. Switching to a purely defense-minded game plan, the visitors completed their own double over the Swans, after a previous 3-1 at theirs back in September. They had won that game despite a strong display from a City side missing Robbie and only let down by goal-keeping errors. Robbie was recalled for the game watched by 1,889 at the Vetch.

With no Cup commitments to concern themselves with, the club could focus its attention on League matters with two festive away trips to Reading and Rotherham concluding a busy December. Screen contributed all the Swansea goals across both games; a 1-2 on Boxing Day at Reading and a 1-1 a few days later. Robbie and his team mates would enjoy completing a double over Reading in March but had previously lost to Gillingham back in September. The latter fixture found the Swans up against the top scorers in Division Four and was a point won rather than lost, taken from a club that would be promoted as runners-up. Gregg selected an unchanged side to face them and would do so again for the significant New Year's Day visit to Wales for Rotherham. It proved to be a valuable point as the Swans fell behind before Robbie was switched to midfield and Herbie Williams into attack for the second-half. The change worked as they equalised in front of a crowd totaling close to 10,000. Two players were sent off, five others booked and both managers received cautions. Gregg was booked for urging Robbie to move away from an on-field incident and was bemused as to why he was the one being penalised! In a match that Gregg felt was ill-managed by officials, both he and Evans had their bookings rescinded at a disciplinary hearing.

Life in Britain back in 1973 was a lot different from today; a three-day working week had been introduced due to a national power crisis. This had a direct effect upon football as it meant that the use of floodlights was prohibited and consequently the Swans could not play the Friday night fixtures that they previously enjoyed. Games had been scheduled for this day so as to avoid the televised Saturday international rugby matches. Kick-off times had also been moved an hour forward so as to utilize the natural light. The year saw electricity cuts and a fuel crisis resulting in panic buying at the petrol pumps which consequently produced shortages for motorists across the country. Another hot topic this year was the gentle introduction of Sunday soccer, with the impetus of it possibly attracting higher attendances for those clubs involved. Some fixtures had already been staged by December, mainly cup ones and the option was being presented on a broader basis. It does seem like another world now, but back in the 1970s the expansion was a big deal. I think many of us still believe that 3pm on a Saturday afternoon is the right time for all League games to kick-off. The F.A. gave the choice for clubs to schedule Sunday games and Swansea took this up.

It has been broadly acknowledged that although its attacking philosophy was admirable, the playing mentality under Harry Gregg was one of physicality. Players such as Evans, Bevan and Mickey Conway were three of many that received suspensions this season across which period fifty-four cautions were dished out to Swansea players. This was something that Harry Griffiths, who would replace Gregg, immediately sought to redress. However, Division Four was a ruthless League and teams sought to stifle creative sides such as Swansea by any means available: Gregg would call them 'cloggers'. As they sought to begin an eventful climb up the divisions, it would prove most frustrating for many working hard within the football club.

A gate of 4,962 made their way to the Vetch for the Tuesday 1 January Rotherham United match and they were rewarded with a six goal thriller: four coming from the Swans, including one by Robbie. The visitors would eventually finish 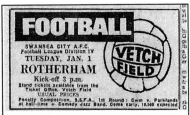 one place beneath them in the table but managed to speed to a 0-2 first-half lead in the largest attended match of the season, so far. Coming back to win 4-2, Robbie had a terrific game, being imaginative and tenacious in his accurate passing whilst also showing his strong defensive capabilities.

The team put in a show of great prowess, with the talented seventeen-year-old shining brightly. United contributed much but a dipping Robbie shot from twenty-five yards out beat the unsighted keeper and signaled a revival from the home team. It was his opening goal for the first team although he had scored on a number of occasions for the reserves. Kudos must go to double penalty king Dave Bruton and Tony Screen for providing the other goals. Bruton a midfielder signed during the close season from Bristol City converted five pens this season in a role that Robbie would later fulfil.

Gregg, in conjunction with his coach Jimmy McLoughlin, Harry Griffiths and Herbie Williams realized that they had to develop a team around local young talent and Robbie was one of their first success stories. More followed. Gregg utilized the experience from professionals such as McLoughlin and Williams, both with well-established links to the club. After the 1973/ 74 season had been concluded, the Vetch would furnish a testimonial match for Herbie played on Tuesday April 30. A true pro and a humble man, youngsters such as Alan Curtis held him in high esteem as did his fellow professionals. In all, he made 500 League appearances in a Swans shirt and many more in various cup competitions. Mike England, Francis Lee, Jimmy Rimmer, John Mahoney and others played in the game which probably featured Robbie.

However, returning to January, this proved to be a fruitful month for the Swans, producing four wins with nine goals scored against three conceded. Still with a big chunk of games remaining, Gregg was playing down all mentions of promotion but would have been delighted with the spirit shown by his team which culminated in a sixth place spot in the division. They showed a vast difference from the previous month when the team was near the bottom. Duplicate 2-0 victories against Brentford and Mansfield Town, away and at home, respectively, followed. Another decent attendance against a Town side that had beaten Swansea at their place, back in September, was also memorable in that it gave sixteen-year-old local defender Stephen Thomas a run-out. Back in the 1972/ 73 season, along with Robbie and others like Curt and Davies, he was playing in the Combination team and looked set to follow Robbie in the Vetch production line but would only feature in seven first-team games this season. The Swans continued their rich vein of form and gathered nine, from a possible ten, points in a deserved win with Lally and Robbie combining well in the heart of the midfield.

After beating them 2-0 at the Vetch on the opening day of the 1973/ 74 campaign, Chester failed to capitulate at Sealand road in a 1-0 victory for the Blues against a Swansea side unbeaten in their last five games. Our Mr. James was overshadowed by match winner John James, who scored via a disputed first-half penalty in a game which their visitors had a goal disallowed but looked unlikely to win. Chester concluded their season in seventh.

The visit to the Vetch Field by strugglers Workington on Sunday 27 January was the first-ever fixture to be played on the Sabbath across its 60+ year history. Welsh rivals Newport County were also staging a game at Somerton Park, too. Swansea City wanted to avoid competing for spectators directly with rugby internationals being played on a Saturday and so the experiment was welcomed by those at the club, if it boosted attendances. An impressive 6,712 watched the match against visitors with an atrocious away form. Needing to seek re-election at the close of the season, Workington lost 1-0. Struel was disappointed that the match failed to draw a higher gate but decreed that the club was happy to play additional Sunday games, so long as the Football League offered some flexibility. The crowd might have been more expansive but the Swansea team performance was not one of their best. They had played better and lost but the two points proved welcome.

Proving consistent in the number nine shirt, Robbie featured in the next Sunday game at home, against Bradford City. Coming a week later, the Bantams took away a 0-1 win in front of a crowd slightly less than the previous weekend's game. Regrettably, the Swans team seemed to play as if they were unfamiliar with each other and not having notched up thirty-three games. Bradford, a club that Robbie would spend two seasons with later, had been enjoying a good recent run of form but failed to gain promotion this year. However, they managed a League double over the Swans.

After the sluggish and unimaginative team showing against Bradford, a poor 2-0 defeat at Colchester United produced an under-par team showing from an ill-disciplined Swansea side which saw bookings and a sending off. Only on-loan keeper Rimmer, Bartley and Bruton were worth their wages in an insipid result played on a wet pitch against an opposition that itself would seal its promotion come the end of April. That disappointment was soon followed by another Sunday afternoon home fixture, now with Stockport the challenge. A

**Vetch Field,
Swansea.
Phone: 42855.**

goal from Curt had taken the points back in October and strikes from Evans, Lally and Robbie sealed victory here. It was his second League goal of the season.

Robbie was played in a much-deeper midfield role in the preceding goal-less meeting with Scunthorpe United in the last week of February; that was a well-marshaled by the defenders of both sides. Attempting to feed his two forwards and rarely succeeding, Robbie saw that the fixture was played predominantly in the middle of the park. Neither side could put the ball in the net, whilst Robbie also missed an opportunity from close range. The 2,238 gate for the game was one of their lowest attended matches of the season: even less had bothered to watch the corresponding encounter in Wales (1,743). Also this month, Anthony James, Robbie's cousin, signed for Swansea on schoolboy terms and would feature in the reserves before playing alongside his illustrious relative next season.

After some efficient defending in the recent Swans-Scunny match, the promotion race stepped up a pace on 3 March with the visit of Reading. One of seven fixtures in this hectic month, it was the fourth scheduled Sunday game at the Vetch of the 1973/74 campaign, presented to dwindling gates. Dai Davies was playing his second game, on loan from Everton, where he had been unable to get into the first team. Rimmer had joined Arsenal after his eighteen games loan spell whilst registered as a Manchester United player and Davies played in the next five games for the Swans. 'Millie' returned for the final nine fixtures, as previously stated. Big Dai would sign for Tosh in 1981 and was to let in nine goals during his uninspired loan period. The clubs were rivals, with the former winning 1-2 on Boxing Day.

Peter Abbott, another loan player at the Vetch, spotted by Gregg in a Central League game for Man United, scored both the goals against Reading in Robbie's nineteenth appearance in a first team shirt. The latter picked up a booking in amidst a game that kept its referee busy and also saw a caution for the mercurial Robin Friday.

There was little glamour involved in playing on pitches in the Division Four whose grass had virtually been trodden away by October, back when butter cost 9p, a bag of potatoes, 26p and a loal paper, 3p

At Northampton, a club that had suffered relegation alongside Swansea, half of their pitch was used as a car park to accommodate the summer cricket!

Consecutive March losses to Barnsley, Peterborough and Bradford were curtailed by a trio of draws in a disastrous run-in which saw the Swans net three times in six games. A 2-2 away at Sincil Bank, to Lincoln City, and an entertaining draw with Brentford, and another with Doncaster, extended a feeble run of form that continued on in to April via a woeful 1-0 away defeat by Workington. Robbie was missing from the next three League games but would return for the last three fixtures commencing with a trip to Newport County. Bury then came to the Vetch before a final away visit to Exeter City on 27 April, against a side that played "neat, attractive football."

A goal-less affair with Darlington at home, in the season's lowest-attended match at the Vetch, saw a rare 1-0 win away at Hartlepool before back-to-back derbies with Newport. Robbie missed the first one, a 1-1 at the Vetch but was in the side that travelled to Somerton Park a day later, only to lose 1-2. He wore the number eleven shirt in that match before Bury provided the test for the Swans in the final home game of the campaign which resulted in a surprising 0-1 win for the visitors. Robbie was subbed during a game watched by 1,821.

After defeating final day opponents Exeter 1-0 back in December, Swansea completed their fourth encounter with them this season via a 2-0 loss. Having played fifty games in both the League and Cup competitions, Swansea finished a mediocre fourteenth in a table of twenty-four; five behind Newport. They had won sixteen games, drawn eleven and lost nineteen in the League in contrast to winning fourteen, drawing nine and losing an astronomical twenty-three in the previous season. In the Welsh League, they were twelfth out of eighteen and in the Football Combination, twentieth out of twenty-two.

Selected for twenty-nine games (including the League Cup), the campaign proved to be an underwhelming first full-season for the new professional, Robbie.

Above: the Swansea squad for the 1975/ 76 season.
Robbie is immediate right, top row.

"At first he was shy, slender and not sure of his ability. Now he is a strapping athlete, confident of himself and not afraid of taking on the responsibility of scoring." That was the summation provided about Robbie from Sunday Express sports reporter Michael Boon in October 1974, as the latest season progressed.

But back on 17 August, a trip up to Darlington had kicked-off the 1974/ 75 season for the Swans in what would transpire as being a long and traumatic campaign for everyone involved with the club. The financial crisis became acute, resulting in the football club withdrawing its team from the Football Combination, mid-season and a change would occur resulting in a managerial reconfiguration; and all before the final day fixture at Rochdale on 26 April 1975. Various money-making plans were proposed to seek to combat some of the £150,000 debts; one scheme was headed by former Swan Roy Saunders, father of future Swansea player and Wales boss, Dean. Roy was one of a number of ex-pros wanting to get involved in helping their old club out. He would soon return to the Vetch as assistant manager and coach following the eventual departure of Gregg.

Robbie did not feature in the opening match of the new campaign, a game which saw his side give away a 0-1 lead and have its youngster Stephen Thomas dismissed. The seventeen-year-old would be seen in three additional games before being released by the club in October 1975.

Meanwhile Robbie James was playing in a Reserves side that put in a dogged showing in a 1-1 draw against Birmingham City at the Vetch. Also noteworthy in that match was the inclusion in the visitor's side of new signing Gary Sprake. For the Swans, their selection between the sticks alternated between Derek Bellotti and Stephen Potter, both new arrivals this year.

The pesky Exeter City once again put Swansea out of the League Cup thanks to a mid-August, 3-1 win at their ground. Elsewhere, in the F.A Cup the Swans also flopped but in the Welsh Cup, they would advance to the sixth round this season.

In his first appearance in a white shirt of the campaign, the third game of the season for the club, Robbie played in the opening home game against Barnsley. It was watched by a crowd of 2,421 who saw their side well beaten via a 0-3 final score. Coincidentally, the Tykes would do the double over the Swans, beating them at Oakwell in the penultimate match of the season. Substituted in the game, Robbie did not play in the next three League fixtures which were against Darlington, Brentford and Newport County; games which they won 1-0 lost 0-1 and 0-3, respectively. They might have lost to County but a twenty minute spell proved a great spectacle and showed how effective the Swans could be at times.

Wyndham Evans, who got the winner at the Vetch against Darlington, would find his name cropping up in six other games as would both Robbie and Geoff Thomas. The away trip to Brentford found no place for Robbie but it did for Alan Curtis. Curt had proven inconsistent during his early career with the Swans, a claim often muted about Robbie, but the 1974/ 75 season saw Alan play in thirty-five League fixtures. Oddly though, he did not score a single goal.

Whilst Curtis, the nephew of ex-Swansea player Roy Paul, played in the 1-0 defeat with Darlington, Robbie was back in the Reserves at the Vetch and selected to face Norwich City. They would run-out on a Saturday whenever the first-team was scheduled to play away. In the squad was a young man that would soon contribute much to the Swansea cause: Jeremy Charles. He was the son of Mel and nephew to John.

A 3-0 defeat at Newport was the first of four meetings between the Welsh cousins this year, twice in the Welsh Cup and the two League fixtures. A third successive drop in home attendances came when the team played-out a miraculous 3-3 with Doncaster Rovers watched by 1,532. The plea from the

Chairman for supporters to come and watch the Swans simply flopped. In fact, gates for games away from the Vetch often proved higher (such as Rotherham, Lincoln, Doncaster and Mansfield). The marvellous Geoff Thomas, a successful convert from midfielder to striker, completed a Swansea hat-trick, and was followed by a two game run of no goals after this game. Those fans that were there saw a plethora of strikes as the Swans shared the points. A goal apiece in the first-half, the action saw Robbie linking effectively with Thomas in attack and also began an impressive, ever-present run in the team for Mr James for the remainder of the season. Wearing the numbers six through to ten and twelve, he was tried in various positions on the pitch and would be substituted on three occasions and selected as a sub in one other game (Chester, away). With less than a quarter of the game remaining the Swans found themselves 1-3 down before the talented Mr.Thomas completed his hat-trick some nine minutes before the final whistle.

At the end of the second week of September, a visit to Shrewsbury Town, formerly managed by Swans boss Harry Gregg, came next. With his current team looking for their first away victory of the season it would not arrive here. Town had new player-manager and former Welsh international Alan Durban and the Swans were unfortunate to lose a scrappy, uneven match in which Curtis shone on the left wing. Herbie Williams also played, in this his final season with Swansea City, and both he and Curt had narrow misses. Robbie and former Gay Meadow favourite but now a Swan, Paul Bevan fizzed around the pitch but both proved unable to control the game.

A brace of cracking goals from Workington, a club successfully re-elected back into the Football League from last season, perpetuated a dire run of results for the Swans. Robbie continued his usual ratio of shots but could not hit the net within a re-jigged Swansea side that proved unfruitful in its endeavours. All the while Welsh rivals Cardiff City were being beaten in Hungary in the European Cup Winners' Cup; qualification coming thanks to winning the last Welsh Cup.

With a 1-1 draw at home against Bradford City recorded Gregg acknowledged the poor run of recent results but remained optimistic that his players could improve. Points had not been forthcoming because the Swans were simply not scoring enough in the League. In the nine matches played so far they had found the net seven times, the exact same total as last season, and conceded twelve (as opposed to sixteen at this stage last time). Probing the Bantams, Robbie and Curt showed great effort but again the Swans would garner more bookings. Conversely, a Bradford player was booked for a foul on Robbie.

The draw was enhanced four days later by another game at the Vetch, this time against Lincoln City, in a cluttered September fixture list. Kicking-off at 7pm so as to help fans work around the local bus service strike, the game was played against a troublesome wind and in rainy conditions, with the Swans equaliser in the second-half found Robbie linking well with Mickey Evans. He had made more than three hundred appearances for the club by this time. The duo combined for a free kick that saw the second goal of the season for the other Mr. Evans, Llanelli-born Wyndham. Super sub Pat Lally proved an invaluable addition in deciding the fortunes of the game, too. The final game of the month saw a long coach journey up to Hartlepool rewarded with a brace from thirty-four-year-old Herbie Williams. It was not uncommon for the players to travel to an away fixture on the morning of the actual match day, despite the often-long distances involved. The win saw a total of nine points chalked-up by the club so far. Swansea would advance to completing a double over their opponents whilst this game saw a demonstration of determined runs at the defense by Robbie which helped to seal a good win. It was tainted a little by further bookings for the team.

October saw Robbie collect his first goal of the season in an ultimately unrewarding 2-1 defeat at home to Mansfield Town, where the Swans played well. The eventual Division Four champions took advantage of the disharmony in the Swansea defense in a game which saw Robbie noted as man of the match. The 'midfield schemer' as Evening Post reporter John Bergum termed him, netted the opening goal a while into the second-half. It came via a Williams pass from a pounding Wyndham Evans volley which concluded with Robbie lumping the ball in off the post. Collectively, the team were strong but they clearly had a problem at the back. Robbie's burgeoning reputation was enhanced but his Swansea team had no excuse as to why they capitulated. The boss was furious and called them a disgrace; adding that he thought that the attitude of the players was all wrong.

Robbie's ninth League appearance this season saw him collect his second goal of the campaign, and the third in his first-team career. A gate of 2,183 attended the Vetch only four days after the Mansfield defeat and watched a poor demonstration of lower league football here provided by

Swansea v Crewe. The game was marred by fouls, bookings and complaints to the referee from its participants.

Another defeat by Mansfield, whom they had now played against twice in the course of a week, spoilt a promising start made by the Swans. Unfortunately they failed to produce an end product i.e. a goal and succumbed to a 3-0 loss, with Robbie replaced by Lally.

Affairs off the pitch proved most serious: proposed redevelopment plans for part of the North Bank at the Vetch which included offices, shops and parking facilities were dropped. Struel bowed to pressure from local residents opposing the scheme within the tightly-knit streets around the small ground. The Chairman rescinded his statement that the redevelopment scheme was imperative if the club was to remain in business. Reports of the club being £200,000 in debt and struggling to pay off the interest accrued marked the situation as being the greatest financial crisis in its history. Gates for the 1974/ 75 season had seen a significant drop on the previous one and the likelihood of the club folding was a real possibility. A plan involving the local council to purchase the Vetch Field was subsequently to be made which allowed Swansea City to continue. With its market value set at £500,000, this was not the actual amount paid: as £50,000 would be given to the club and a £150,000 grant.

With his team lacking consistency, Gregg was at least able to take the time to work behind-the-scenes with his staff in guiding local youngsters like Robbie, Nigel Stevenson, Stephen Thomas, and Anthony James, up through the ranks. He had no funds for transfer fees so such a working scheme, common to clubs like Swansea City and Newport County, proved apt. Scouts from the bigger League clubs could cherry pick Welsh youngsters, John Charles being a prime example from the past, but this was much-reduced in recent years. Both Robbie and Curtis were regularly watched by the likes of Arsenal, Southampton, Manchester United, Spurs and others.

The Swans had leaked half-dozen goals from their first two games this season in games which they had initially led. The defense was in disarray, and changes in goal between Bellotti and Lewis did not stabilise things and so in mid-October, Don Murray arrived on what transpired as a five-game loan to bring his experience and hopefully, steadying influence to the jittery back four. Traditionally a centre-half, twenty-eight-year-old Murray came from rivals Cardiff and had a debut against Newport at the Vetch. The tasty 2-0 win made it sixteen collected from a possible thirty-two after a recent 2-1 away victory at Exeter marred somewhat with arrests to some travelling supporters after a thrilling match which had seen a Mickey Evans header put the Swans a goal up.

Dominant and confident against County before a surging 3,372 gate, the largest of the season and much-needed, it was hoped that the fans would continue to come for the Friday evening visit of Rochdale. The Swans had been bottom of the table in September but had steadily improved. Another Friday night fixture played under difficult climate conditions at the Vetch produced an action-packed match finishing 3-3. The result was a fair outcome as the Swans had slipped to being 0-2 down before an admirable fight-back against a much-fancied team. A cross from winger Dave Roberts was met by the head of Robbie and put in by captain Wyndham Evans for the second goal. After seeing the game, supporters could have dashed to the-nearby Castle cinema whilst trying to avoid the rain to see the 'XX' bill of Line Up & Lay Down/ Nurse on the Job!

Robbie's third goal of the campaign, before he went on to score seven more, came as the equaliser on sixteen minutes across an encounter producing another Man-of-the-match performance from one Robert Mark James. Down 3-1 before half-time, Robbie had easily seen off a defender before creating time to slot the ball in low past the keeper and defender. It made little difference to the final score: a resolute 5-1 to a Northampton Town team that would conclude their season a mundane sixteenth position. Gregg had replaced ex-Southend keeper Bellotti, who had seen twenty-four goals go in past him so far this season, during the game, with Potter in what was an unprecedented swap at the time. It failed to fix things, as the team lost their next four matches.

November proved to be a hugely affecting month in the fortunes of Robbie James as it would see him leave the Vetch. He was to go on loan to First Division Arsenal for a month, in advance of signing fully for the Gunners. However, before this news was revealed, he had an away game to play with his Swansea team mates at Stockport County. The prospect of playing at Highbury in comparison to Edgeley Road must have been hard to contemplate for the teenager, where once again, a faulty defense saw Swansea give away an early lead before losing the game 2-1. Thomas got his penultimate goal of the season, thanks to a move that involved Robbie laying out a pass to the unmarked striker following a corner.

With financial concerns reaching epic proportions, the players could not have failed to be affected as they welcomed promotion-aspirants Rotherham United to a muddy Vetch on 8 November. City pulled out of the Football Combination this season due to the costs involved in another cash-saving venture. It had an adverse affect on those not in the first team with only the Welsh League to play in. A frustrated Alan Curtis would ask for a transfer but was persuaded to stay by Harry Griffiths. Plans to reduce staff numbers at the club were also being implemented. Life seemed a million miles away from reaching the semi-finals of the F.A Cup back in the mid-1960s. Robbie had scored in the corresponding fixture with Rotherham, also relegated along with them last season but had no luck this time as the Swans held out for eighty minutes in a nasty game which saw numerous clashes. A second for the Millers came via a Womble, Trevor Womble, with four minutes remaining of normal time.

Much-changed, the Swansea team that faced Chester before an impressive 4,641 crowd found Robbie as sub. Their Mr. James nabbed a brace against a terrible Swans side. Robbie made it onto the pitch just before the hour mark but he could have arguably replaced any one of six under-performing team-mates that day. But to be fair to both teams, an unfavoured Chester had recently beaten Leeds United in the League Cup.

A full Wales international was staged at Robbie's home ground this month, and it was hoped that the F.A.W would select the ground for future fixtures. It did but the Racecourse at Wrexham tended to be favoured. A gate of 10,500 attended the match, a figure higher than recent Wales matches played at Ninian Park, Cardiff. Luxembourg provided the opposition against a Wales side that featured Gary Sprake, John Mahoney, Tosh and Leighton James, each continuing the Swans connection past and future.

Under-pressure manager Harry Gregg was acutely aware of the fragility of his squad and its faltering levels of confidence and so took them for a few days break at a country club partly-owned by the club's directors. It was hoped that the change might help before an upcoming visit from Scunthorpe.

Keen to reap the financial rewards of a good Cup run, a testing encounter with unknown Kettering, of the Southern League, had seen a 1-1 at the Vetch Field before the fixture with Scunny. An encouraging 3,175 came out to see if the Swans could recover from their recent spell of poor form. Managed by Ron Atkinson, whose brother, Graham, scored a surprising goal to put his side 0-1 up. Defined by their heavy defensive stance, it was clear that the Poppies would be happy to see a replay back at their place. Robbie came on for the second-half replacing Pat Lally, the scorer of a cracking equaliser. The youngster's ankle took a battering in a game which also saw knocks for three of his team-mates.

Having failed to seal a victory in the first encounter, a replay on 26 November concluded with seeing Swansea put out of the F.A Cup by a non-League team for the second occasion in the past three seasons. Atkinson and Robbie raced for a loose ball and a tackle from behind by the Swansea teenager led to a snap in the leg of the defender being audible. The accident occurred shortly after the half-hour mark and it led to 'Big Ron' rushing on to the Rockingham road pitch to confront Robbie and exchange words with his manager who had intervened. Curt seemed to think that Robbie would quite easily have dealt with the situation himself. The distressing incident stopped play whilst some of the Kettering players demanded that Robbie be sent off whilst others understood that it was not done with malice aforethought. He received a booking only. In a game played through the rain, the Swans slipped 2-0 behind and did not look like they were going to take anything from the match which was attended by 5,973. They didn't and lost 3-1. Such was the furor that after the final whistle that an incensed Ron Atkinson was adamant that young Robbie should have been dismissed. Gregg deemed it unfortunate but agreed that it was not premeditated, adding that he knew that "Robbie just isn't that type of lad." As a precaution, a couple of police officers guarded the Swansea team bus against the wrath of the Kent-based supporters. John Toshack's Liverpool won the final.

November had closed with two goals by Robbie away at Scunthorpe, with the League double attained in January. It brought his tally to five and more would follow.

The American cop show Kojack proved a popular Saturday night television event in December, a month with four scheduled League fixtures including a Boxing Day visit to high-flying Shrewsbury Town. Gregg had contemplated a start for teenager Nigel Dalling against Lancashire side Southport and subsequently selected him as sub, from where he did make a late appearance. Not-quite-sixteen, Dalling became the youngest Swansea player to make a League debut. It was one of his three appearances this season in the first-team. Nigel had featured in the Reserves and so was not an unknown quantity to his manager. The Swans drew the match 2-2 with goals from their Evans duo: defender and captain-cum-striker, Wyndham and West Bromwich-born Mickey. A low Vetch Field crowd enjoyed the hearty endeavours from a Swansea City side trying various runs involving Robbie and Curt, working in worrying the Southport defense. Their scheming did not produce a goal but a point was won, despite a late winner being disallowed as Robbie was seen to have impeded the keeper. Also in this month, Robbie was playing in the reserves, as well as first team and by the following May, he was in the Swansea team pitted against Briton Ferry in the West Wales Senior Cup final.

Malcolm Struel had known Aston Villa counterpart 'Deadly' Doug Ellis for some years when it was revealed in mid-December, that a match had been arranged in the Midlands for the then Second Division side to take a closer look at Robbie and Curtis. Acknowledged as the best players at the club, Robbie had returned to the Vetch after just two days spent in north London with Arsenal whilst Curt had caught the attention of numerous clubs. Robbie's brief sojourn at Highbury with manager Bertie

Mee, who had watched him play back in October alongside his chief scout, was said to have been curtailed due to his homesickness and upon his return, a rejuvenated Mr. James picked up his form and he soon re-established himself as a striker. Ironically, this would bring further scouts to watch him play. Later commenting about the affair, Robbie had no regrets about returning to the Vetch and although ambitious, he saw Swansea City as the place to advance his career. He had played in various positions in the team; as a forward-running midfielder, winger and striker. "I really don't mind where I play," he told Reporter Michael Boon, "Whatever the boss says is right by me. I know I am enjoying the game more as I learn more about it, I love it all." Gregg was not keen to sell his prize assets but with a £100,000 fee for the duo touted, it seems his objections were nullified. Nothing transpired from the Villa episode and it was followed by a bid for Robbie from Bristol Rovers being rejected by his club. Another Second Division club, Rovers offered a delusory £10,000 added to by a further £5,000 once he had established himself in the first team at Eastville. Gregg acknowledged publicly that a number of clubs had enquired about his star duo but in Robbie's case, he valued him somewhere in the region of £50,000.

A 2-1 home win against Reading, some four days before Christmas, produced another Man-of-the-Match performance from Robbie and a second-half equaliser. Coming so close to

Christmas Day, an encouraging 3,693 gate, the largest of the campaign, crammed in to the Vetch to watch their team absorb a great deal of first-half pressure in what transpired to be an action-packed and well-fought encounter. Robbie had failed to beat Death; the Royals goalie, Steve Death, early in the second-half but he netted following a set-piece: a subsequent shot by Paul Bevan was concluded with Robbie scoring. Bevan had previously scored against the Swans at the Vetch, whilst a Shrewsbury player and struck the winner with two points deservedly taken in a match with many missed chances. Gregg was pleased with his up-front pairing of Robbie and Wyndham Evans prior to Robbie moving into midfield with Lally taking up his attacking position.

The good news about the council purchase of the Vetch revealed back in November, was not continued by any Boxing Day goodwill demonstrated by Shrewsbury Town who beat the Swans 1-4 in front of 3,501 at the Vetch. Swansea possessed the poorest defensive record in the Football League and the battering added to the total of forty-nine goals conceded in twenty-five League matches (plus seven more in the cup games). By the close of the season at the end of April, the total would have risen to seventy-six; a startling statistic when contrasted with the 1973/ 74 final total of forty-nine. Gregg must have issued the hairdryer treatment to his players as they trooped out early for the second-half, already 0-2 down.

Usual keeper Derek Bellotti was dropped for the final game of the year, away at Torquay United, and would not be selected again for the remainder of the season. The nineteen-year-old Stephen Potter replaced him, being one of two changes made for the ensuing 0-0.

After twenty-six fixtures produced only eight wins, Robbie, Evans, Curt and others, missed a hat full of chances against Workington; including numerous long-range efforts ably saved by the keeper. It came after a recent draw and defeat and was followed by an unconvincing 3-0 loss away at Haig Avenue with Southport. The game was one best forgotten and left the club fourth from bottom in the table on twenty-one points; twenty behind leaders Mansfield. Southport finished a respectable fourteenth in the Division at the season close. Robbie played in the game despite suffering from a stomach upset and saw his unlucky side fall behind on two minutes. The defeat was the third in their last four and the situation was hardly to improve.

The managerial style offered by Harry Gregg might not have been liked by many but in January, with the club in danger of falling out of the Football League, he asked his players to tell him how they felt about their collective plight. Many of them did and it was clear that the younger ones had seen a dip in confidence levels: the opposite being imperative at any club.

Despite their dwindling numbers, the supporters made their feelings known to the players at the Vetch. The atmosphere at the ground, where the fans were close to the pitch, allowed their comments to be directly heard by the players: the unfortunate Bellotti barracked at the end of games.

The New Year also revealed that Gregg had been interviewed for the vacant managerial post at fellow Division Four side Crewe. However, at this stage he had not been involved in direct negotiations with the club that had been beaten previously at the Vetch in October. Although he still had fifteen months remaining on his contract, Struel acted swiftly by appointing Harry Griffiths as caretaker boss in the interim. Many in the game thought that John Charles would step up from his role as Youth Team coach but it was not to be. Griffiths had spent twenty-six years at Swansea, in various roles and this locally-born, former defender had made 421 appearances for the club. He was also pretty impressive as a goal scorer when playing for the Swans back in the mid-1950s. Defined as being "tough but fair" by a young apprentice, Harry had an enormous task ahead of him, if he was to save his beloved club from the drop. But first, plans had to be made for a fifth round away trip to Southern League side Kidderminster Harriers in the Welsh Cup. They were an English team made up of part-timers, allowed entry for the first time in to the competition and having worked hard to reach this stage. Attended by their highest gate of the season, Kiddy did well against the Swans, minus Robbie James and held their visitors to a 0-0. In the preceding season, Swansea had lost to eventual-finalist Stourbridge and had a dire record against sides from the Southern League.

An underwhelming gate of 1,002 braved the elements on a wet and blustery evening to see the replay on 20 January at the Vetch. Played under odd circumstances, Harry Gregg had been made an offer by Crewe to become their new manager but was at the ground helping with preparations for the game in his usual manner. Again played on a muddy pitch, a Robbie header floated wide just before half-time and the visitors also missed an early penalty. But the game belonged to Hank Marvin look-alike Herbie Williams, who struck a hat-trick in his last game as a

Swansea player. The Swans ran out 3-0 winners in spite of the terrible conditions. Herbie, off to Australia in a new player-manager role, would enjoy an emotional testimonial at the Vetch after the close of the season, played forty games this year and scored six times. A product of Swansea school boys, he had been captained by Wales at all levels. His and Robbie's careers echoed one another. Williams made his first-team debut aged seventeen back in the late-1950s and both established themselves as internationals. Victory meant that the club advanced into the quarter-finals stage with a February tie at Somerton Park with Newport their next destination.

News of the local council purchase of the Vetch Field might have been disclosed back in November but what was not known was that the club directors had been paying the players salaries from their own pockets! The money being given to the club for the purchase of the Vetch, a nominal £50,000 with a further £150,000 being paid, was challenged in court but the temporary injunction was lifted and the club was given the payments. Struel immediately set about paying-off their overdraft and to facilitate the day-to-day costs of running the football club.

The second month of 1974 did not start favourably for Robbie and his team mates, as they lost 1-0 away at promotion-favourites Rotherham United. With Harry Gregg now gone, Harry Griffiths was in direct control of team affairs. He was already familiar to the squad, as he was the club physiotherapist and was involved with training before Gregg departed. The Swans had beaten United 2-0 at home back in November but the team would not take away any points in the return fixture. Robbie was switched to attack but was still to be found helping-out in defence where he battled with that man Womble again. A tactical change into the second-half saw Robbie seeing more of the ball before the home side struck their first goal: this despite a Robbie shot from an earlier strike by Lally had been pushed away by their keeper. Griffiths enjoyed the improvement in his side and considered them unfortunate in not taking anything from the game.

Completing twenty-six League appearances so far this season, Robbie won the first of his two Wales youth caps against Malta this month in the qualifying stages of the U.E.F.A junior tournament to be staged that summer. For an account of his international career, please see Chapter 13.

Most young men would jump at the chance to become a professional footballer but not David J. Davies. Mentioned in the previous season, Dai chose to keep his job at nearby Port Talbot steelworks rather than sign full-time with Swansea City. He played in three League games and four Cup matches this season, most of which included Robbie in the starting XI and spent two seasons at the Vetch. Robbie was also joined by another promising young talent, Glen Davies, a defender from the Swansea Welsh League team. That side was doing well and progressed to the quarter-final of the local Cup and the youngster made it through to the final of the Welsh Youth Cup.

In between League fixtures, the Swans made the long trip to Aldershot for a friendly. Attended by a sparse crowd, those who were there got to see a sparkling performance from Robbie James. He was joined in the side by fellow teenagers Nigel Dalling and Nigel Williams. And funnily enough, a match report identified Robbie, known as Robert in his early days, as 'Bob James'. Similarly, a teenaged John Toshack whilst establishing himself at Cardiff City was briefly named 'Shack' and that never caught on, either.

Meantime Harry Griffiths urged local people to show their support for the club by coming to see the game with fellow-strugglers Stockport County at the Vetch in the second week of February. They did, and an additional 247 saw a 1-0 win provided by a rare goal from Tony Screen, one of the players that had featured in Robbie's debut back in April 1973. The month was always the most difficult in the football calendar due to the disintegration of the terrible pitches found in the lower leagues. Mr. Griffiths, who joined the Vetch ground staff as a fifteen-year-old, acknowledged that he had only a small pool of players and staff to work in improving the present situation at the club. He laboured tirelessly at the ground and arrived there at 9 am each day, combining dual-duties as physiotherapist and acting manager. A dedicated, devoted soul that loved football, Harry was well liked by the players, including Robbie, despite inflicting runs on the nearby beach and back complimented by further work at the Vetch! Admirably, he ploughed on despite some shoddy treatment by the club during a period when the managerial post was advertised.

Returning to matters on the pitch, Robbie collected another goal, this time away at Newport in a Welsh Cup, Sixth round tie. He had featured in previous League fixtures against them and enjoyed a deserved win for his team on a "swamp-like" Somerton Park pitch. Forgotten man Ronnie Rees returned and was involved in the goal when his deflected cross shot between two defenders, allowing Robbie to score, at close range. It proved a strong game for many in the visiting team including Robbie, maximised up front, and Curt, Lally and Bruton, most noticeably. Newport equalised in a line-up that saw their player John Relish booked. He would later work with Robbie as a coach at Weston-super-Mare F.C, when the former was still playing.

In their last six games, the team had scored only twice and before the kick-off with Stockport, Robbie joined in with his team-mates by smashing a number of souvenir footballs into the North Bank. But some wits at the Vetch joked that they would be better served in some scoring practice instead! A goal-free first half was only saved by a strike in injury time by Screen to take the points. A trademark Robbie shot flew high over the crossbar following a first-half pass by the teenager reaching the head of Lally, who directed it wide. The Swans may have won but ample goal-bound chances were not seized upon and it was clear the team needed a new, all-out striker.

A Welsh Cup replay with Newport County, the fourth meeting between the cousins this season, proved difficult for Griffiths to select a full line up. He had all fifteen professionals make their way to the Vetch before kick-off so he could decide who to play, dependent upon injuries and so forth. Robbie and Tony Screen had each been suffering with flu but were both selected in a game that saw the Swans lose 1-2. Former Wales player Rees returned but could not prevent another elimination from the Cup; pushing the last time that they had won the trophy, in the 1960s, as an even-greater memory. However, Robbie would play in successive teams that won the beautiful Cup in the years to come and whilst still as Swansea player. The problem remained the same: there was no clear-cut goal scorer available to link-up with balls in from likes of Thomas and attacking full-back Evans. Robbie, who by this time was being applauded for his progress in amongst a terrible season, came close to scoring in a match that saw the Swans trail 0-2 at one point.

Successive defeats against Cambridge United, Chester and Brentford, respectively, saw out a deflated February. A twenty-three-year-old Jan Bekker played well in the Chester game but the loss to Brentford showed that Griffiths' ploy of often asking players to play out of position was not altogether successful. The manager had concluded his extensive search for a new centre forward by looking in the Welsh League and that was where he found the Cardiff-born Bekker. Signing amateur terms with the club, as used to happen, someone like him was needed in a hurry by Swansea City and the manager admitted that it was a gamble on his part in selecting the youngster. Bekker had played on four previous occasions at the Vetch Field, including scoring a hat trick and it was that which brought him to the attention of the club. He did okay this season, being selected a total of thirteen times and scoring three goals. Robbie played well in the 0-1 loss to League Cup finalists Chester, in a game played the same evening as future Wales team mate David Giles was making his Cardiff City debut. The former proved significant in the best chance for a goal for the Swans as well as proving effective supporting the defence. With a dozen games left, the defeat against a Brentford team that had won only once away from home in more than a year, proved an excellent, if sad, barometer demonstrating the problems at the club. With no money to spend on bringing in new signings, the need for which was now brutally acute, there was little that could be done to

avoid seeking re-election as the Swans looked likely to finish in one of the bottom slots. Ill-discipline on the field by some of the players was still a problem, and so a new penalty scheme for the guilty players, many of whom had succumbed to dissent during a game, was implemented. Griffiths was pragmatic about it all but needed to be able to select from a squad able to combat the drop. But to do this, he would need to have a full quota available.

With a dozen League games remaining, seven to be played in March and the remainder in April, the Swans players were intent on rectifying their recent loss at the Vetch with the return match against Cambridge on 4 March. The U's were making their first visit to the ground but had recently been defeated by Swansea 0-2 at their place only three weeks ago. United did well this season and narrowly missed out on promotion as well as being in good form when they came to Wales. Bekker continued to play up-front but it would be goals from Thomas and Bruton that brought a 2-0 win for the Swans. March was a significant month for the country as it saw Margaret Thatcher become the new Conservative party leader.

The club were severely reprimanded by the F.A.W about their disciplinary issues by present Secretary Trevor Morris, a "prim and proper" former manager with them across seven years in the late-1950s. The 1973/ 74 season had seen the club collect fifty-four cautions and in the following season, after Harry Gregg had left, a change of approach made a difference. Cardiff City also disclosed that they were in debt this year, in part, due to dwindling attendances and poor showing in Division Two.

Form was turned upside down with a shock 1-2 win for the Swans against Lincoln in a result that surprised many in the game. Goalkeeper Stephen Potter became the first signing made by Harry Griffiths, as his Swansea team put in a trio of goals at Sincil Bank against a side that had not been troubled there since the previous December. Robbie scored a straight-forward goal, their third, after previously causing a nuisance in the opposition half. Man of the match, Geoff Thomas took a free-kick which found Robbie rising well to score.

A well-earned 1-0 victory at the Vetch against Hartlepool, a game staged for the first time on a Friday evening, produced the third consecutive win after three defeats and it manifest the second of three goals scored by Jan Bekker this season. Seventeen-year-old centre half Phillip Evans made the first of his eleven appearances in a Swansea shirt. Five different players had scored the last six goals for the Swans whilst the attendance was up to 2,303, a strong rise from the 1,520 that saw the Cambridge game.

In an incident-filled match away at Doncaster Rovers on 21 March five goals went in but, unfortunately, three of them were against the visitors. Doncaster had been playing well recently and dominated proceedings for most of the first-half, going 2-0 up thanks to a struggling Swansea rear guard. A goal from trusty Wyndham Evans, his sixth of the campaign, was one of two that he got in the game but it came before Peter Kitchen, a past thorn in Swansea's side, put the home side 3-1 up. Robbie was directly involved in the second goal, after his corner kick was spilt by the keeper. Finally, in what could have been a grandstand finish, his twenty yard rocket was subsequently pushed over the bar. Two further attempts by Bekker also went close, but alas, the Swans lost.

With eight fixtures remaining, the first of them a visit by Torquay United, this particular game bucked the trend of an afternoon full of draws in Division Four. With the Swans losing 0-1 via a Willie Brown goal, the winner highlighted the fact that professional football can be a small world. The striker extended his impressive record of scoring against Swansea City for three different clubs. Robbie worked hard, again coming close to scoring.

Obligated to shell out for two games in the space of forty-eight hours, a gate of 1,833 Swansea supporters paid to see their team lose 1-2 to Reading. With the fixtures coming at a ridiculous pace, two days later, an improving team showing by the Swans saw Robbie put them ahead at Bradford City via a swiftly-taken free-kick. His team seemed much more confident and put in a splendid offering in front of the 2,525 gathered at Valley Parade. Coincidentally, years later, Robbie would score a stunning goal for the Bantams against Rotherham, the merits of which are still talked of today by their supporters.

But returning to 1975, he shone in a Swansea team full of distinction. His goal against Bradford proved to be his final one of the season, his ninth League strike. And it put him top of the club goal scorers list followed by Geoff Thomas on eight and Wyndham Evans on seven (League and Cup).

However, the campaign was not over yet, as the Swans had five remaining games to play in April: Northampton at home, Crewe (A), Exeter (H) and aways at Barnsley and Rochdale.

A gate totalling 1,591 came to the Vetch to see a dominant Swansea side bully the entire first-half against a Northampton team that had let in more goals than it had scored. Sketchy home form was a distinct problem this season: Griffiths, as honest as ever, summed up the predicament. "When we do create chances, we miss even the simplest." Robbie was guilty there but oddly, the winner arrived by way of an own-goal. Not that the new manager minded. Officially acknowledged as such on 5 April, Griffiths became the ninth, post-war manager at the Vetch and soon set about adopting a more flowing style of play. His team accepted the much-needed two points and now had two remaining home games. Funnily enough, the 'O.G' had decided things after innumerable chances for the Swans had gone begging. Robbie's miss-kick came directly in front of goal; then his immediate follow-up shot flew over the bar. It was compounded by seeing his shot smashed off the goal-line, too. Into the second half he was unable to control a ball whilst on the edge of the opponent's penalty area.

The 2-2 draw with Harry Gregg's Crewe was followed by a poor home display on 19 April against Exeter City which both embarrassed and infuriated the Swans manager. A 0-2 defeat against them was distressing as he could see some of his players had slipped back into old habits accrued earlier in the season. Oddly, a lack of professionalism seemed to pervade in the display by many in the team. All apart from Bekker, ironically the only amateur in the Swansea City side, who played well in the final home game of the season which was watched by a crowd totalling 2,000. It proved to be a shocking team effort with repeated opportunities to score all going astray.

Three days later saw a visit to Oakwell and an encounter with a Barnsley team that would finish fifteenth in the division. Swansea had previously beaten them at the Vetch but lost here 1-0 with the final fixture of the campaign arriving four days later; on 26 April at Rochdale.

A lively 3-3 in mid October added to a hugely-significant match of a poor season, against a team also struggling at the foot of Division Four. "It's win or bust," decreed Harry Griffiths to the Swansea Evening Post. One club from either Rochdale, the Swans or Stockport would be joining Darlington, Scunthorpe and Workington at the bottom on this April day. Griffiths still believed that his team could produce a result and so expectations were intense for Robbie and the rest of his team mates. But they did realise that their away record was slightly better than their home form although the recent 1-0 defeat at Barnsley did not bode well. So it had come down to this, the forty-fifth League fixture of a zapping campaign to decide the fate of Swansea City Football Club and its association with the Football League. A total of 1,548 souls turned out to see a 1-0 victory for Rochdale after which Griffiths conceded that his present squad was not good enough and so the humiliation of seeking re-election back into the League during the summer was now a fact. He recommended that wholesale changes would have to be made if this was to happen. Robbie had missed a chance to score during the game but despite the Swans having a better second half, their lack of a potent striker proved glaring: oh for a Bob Latchford! It was the first time that the club had sought re-election but Griffiths did not foresee any problem in achieving this. It was inevitable that they would have their status reinstated as other clubs would be foolish to veto them as they might find themselves in a similar predicament at some point. The Swans Secretary Gordon Daniels was required to go to a meeting attended by all Chairman in the Football League where a vote by each would be cast. Neighbours Cardiff City suffered relegation from Division Two; so it wasn't all doom and gloom for Swansea supporters! Wrexham maintained their Division Three status and Newport their own, in the Fourth.

Worryingly, total attendances at the Vetch peaked at 47,595 in the League, down considerably from 63,629 in the previous season. The Swans closed their League campaign with thirty-six points gathered from fifteen wins (nine home and six away), scoring forty-six times against sixty-seven conceded;

with Cup games added it would be fifty-four against seventy-seven. Robbie had played in forty-two of the League fixtures plus five of the six Cup games and scored ten times.

"The Vetch was a compact ground. The fans right on top of you but the atmosphere was incredible. I don't think other teams relished coming there." That was a quote from Nigel Stevenson in a correspondence with the author but back in the 1975/76 season, it would mark the first, full campaign in charge of team affairs at the Vetch for Harry Griffiths. As a player, he had featured in the same Swansea team as Ivor Allchurch, Cliff Jones and Terry Medwin after joining the ground staff on the same day as John Charles. Amazingly, Ivor, whose memory is honoured by a statue at the Liberty stadium, was still playing football in the Welsh leagues in 1976. Harry and John had now been reacquainted, professionally-speaking, with the 'Gentle Giant' now acting youth coach, assisted by player-coach Gil Lloyd. Roy Saunders also returned as coach and assistant to his former Swansea team-mate this season. Known as 'Benny' in the dressing room, Roy played for the Swans and Liverpool during his career and had previously been at the Vetch as a coach and served as caretaker manager before linking up again with Mr. Griffiths.

A pre-season friendly saw the Swans entertain First Division side Coventry; Robbie scored an equaliser against the Sky Blues who had a certain Tommy Hutchison in their starting line-up. The two would be associated much later into their respective careers but more of that soon.

The opening game of the season came with a visit from freshly-relegated Tranmere Rovers, on 16 August, back when a season ticket cost between £10.35 and £18, depending upon the part of the stadium. In 1975, a loaf of bread cost 13½p, the local paper 5p and in the first week of the season, the Albert Hall in the town centre, had Clint Eastwood starring as The Outlaw Josey Wells, whilst on the telly Seaside Special was the dubious highlight of a Saturday evening schedule.

A half-dozen faces had since departed from the club and the remaining fifteen-man squad was the smallest in the whole Football League. George Smith, from Cardiff, ex-Orient defender Paul Harris and Geoff Bray, from Oxford came to the club via free transfers and each made an immediate impact alongside the likes of Robbie within a group that Malcolm Struel termed a "team of hope."

In his third full season as a professional footballer, eighteen-year-old Robbie would be a virtual ever-present in the team across the 1975/76 campaign. In fact, he would only miss a single game; away to Scunthorpe, in April 1976. He had already amassed seventy-six League and Cup appearances and 1976 would by commemorated by his hundredth game, against Torquay, on St Valentine's Day. Robbie surpassed this figure by the season end on 28 April after playing in fifty games across the season: totalling 120 League/ Cup games in his short career. Wearing their all-white kit with the Welsh dragon emblem on the chest, the team would be well-supported away from the Vetch, a fact appreciated on behalf of the players by Harry Griffiths.

The Tranmere game was attended by 2,886 but the resulting 1-1 proved a disappointment to the manager. Robbie had a goal in the second half ruled off-side, as the Swans reversed their positive first half showing Mr Struel, club Chairman from 1972 - 1983, asked supporters to volunteer their time to help raise funds for the club, after it had safely attained re-election back in to the Football League during the summer recess. New board members coupled with a fresh start for Harry Griffiths made the August start a much-anticipated event.

This year saw the League Cup being played on a home and away basis and so it was on 19 August that familial foes Exeter City came to the Vetch Field for their first encounter. United, just like the Swans, had conceded more goals than they had scored in the previous season. However, in the Cup games, they got it right. Griffiths included Robbie in an attacking 4-4-2 formation, with the emphasis on scoring goals but a 1-2 defeat followed three days later by a 5-3 away loss was probably not quite what he had in mind! Some consolation came with Robbie being involved in the headed goal from Bekker in the 1-2 reverse, following some smart interplay between the youngster and new skipper George Smith. He was a surprise new signing from rivals Cardiff and was a midfielder that would serve them well. Aged twenty-nine when he came to Swansea, his Bluebirds exit had come following a petulant display after being subbed in a game. However, Griffiths was a fan, describing the former Portsmouth and Middlesborough player as "...a battler every inch of the way: a man who takes every game as a personal war to be won." Nowadays, he runs a coaching academy in the North East. The subsequent League double completed by the Swans went some way in restoring their early League Cup exit. Bekker, a prolific scorer when playing in the Welsh League, would soon return there but not in a Swansea shirt.

The second leg, played at Plainmoor, was regarded as an entertaining match to watch, with some decent football being exhibited by both sides. Unfortunately, Robbie managed to arrive late at the Vetch and missed the departure of the team bus as it made its long journey to the English Riviera. His manager must have been miffed after the events on the pitch did not go well for a James-less Swansea across an incident-strewn, eight-goal thriller. They lost 5-3, saw a player dismissed and suffered the inconvenience of their bus breakdown on the journey home.

A day after their departure from the Cup, Robbie had a place on the bench in the second game of the 1975/76 Division Four season, away at Rochdale. Losing 2-1, it was a match that the Swans might have easily won if not for the mixed form of their keeper Stephen Potter. This noteworthy encounter between the sides saw Swansea City leak an early goal and found recent history repeating itself. The second Rochdale goal came from Bob Mountford; the same player that scored the winner against the Swans in the final game of last season. Bekker and newcomer Andy Leitch combined well in the game and worked in scoring a consolation goal. It was the first strike of the season for the 6'4" beanpole Leitch, an amateur footballer scooped from the Southern League after being spotted by John Charles. On the same day, an incoming nationwide ban on hosepipe usage and the washing of cars was announced across the region.

Ron Atkinson returned to the Vetch with his Cambridge team, in the third home game of the season for the Swans. Robbie was recalled in the starting XI after the recent coach debacle and he showed good form in a combative encounter. His start meant that Swansea-born Glen Davies dropped down to the bench. Signed when Roy Bentley was manager, Davies played in all out-field positions for the team after originally signing for Cardiff City as an amateur. Giving away leads in the first two games of the new season, the Swans took the first victory at the Vetch by a 1-0 score line; with the winner from Leitch. He and Bekker had been selected to join Robbie up-front, in a re-jigged line-up. Griffiths recognised that the defence needed tightening up and would have plenty of time to address this issue.

Having signed professional terms, Bekker found the rigorous training a hard adjustment. Eddie May, Robbie's team mate and later, manager at Cardiff and Barry, could vouch for this as he too had made the exact same step up some years earlier. The superfit Mr. James of course, came up through schoolboy and apprentice ranks so for him, he was more acclimatised to the rigours of training as a full time 'pro'.

With five League games to be packed in to September, a point was added to the previous three for Swansea in an away draw at Southport. It proved to be a blinder of a game for Robbie against a lively opposition that created many chances. A wonder blast from Alan Curtis put them ahead, thanks to pressure put on the keeper by the lanky Leitch after a piercing Robbie James-inspired cross. Against his namesake, Joe, Robbie hit a number of telling balls including a sly, bending shot and a powerful rocket which sneaked under the goalie, only for him to recover in time to smother the ball.

"Scoring goals is the best insurance policy," declared Harry Griffiths. And so he proved right as in the six games within which Robbie scored this season (not including a Cup game), the team went on to win the match. In total, he would hit nine across the season. The first of which arrived as the winner against Workington at the Vetch at the close of the second week of September. Robbie switched to outside-right from midfield, as the Swans adopted a 4-2-4 formation. His goal came on thirty minutes from a header in a game which showed the Fourth Division as its best. He put it in from a cross by utility man Danny Bartley, after combining effectively in a fresh combination with Alan Curtis. His endeavours saw a booking come in injury time, also accompanied by one for his opponent. The Swans, proving to be a much better side with a plethora of goal opportunities going begging, should definitely have finished on a higher final score line. The game found Robbie continuing to do what he did best; putting the ball in to the box for others to connect with. Elsewhere, future Swansea and Wales team mate David Giles scored one of the goals for Cardiff in their impressive victory against Division Four champions Mansfield.

Northampton Town, eventual runners-up in the division, was a club producing impressive home gates this year, including the 5,428 that attended their game with Swansea City. Robbie and Geoff Bray were preferred in a well-competed affair which concluded 0-0 but showed promise in both teams. The 'tache-tastic Potter had a strong game in goal whilst the twenty-four-year-old Bray was about to get into his stride in a season that saw him finish top scorer on nineteen. He would collect the £200 that had been offered within the club to whoever scored the most across the 1975/ 76 season.

Plans to utilise the Vetch ground for other things were muted also, with the suggestion of opening a social club one of the ideas put forward. A music festival had been held at the stadium previously but it failed to draw a large audience. That all changed in the long hot summer when a rock concert by The Who took place on Saturday 12 June 1976.

With the club having withdrawn from the Football Combination League, their Welsh League side would do very well this season and finish as Champions. Young Jeremy Charles was progressing nicely and regularly scoring too. His coach, Uncle John, also saw the development of a number of fledgling talent including apprentices such as Nigel Stevenson, Nigel Dalling and Stephen Morris, each of whom would enjoy priceless run-outs in the first team this year. The Reserves offered starts for players unable to get into the first team mixing in. The club joined the South Wales and Wessex League this season and many of their youngsters listed, did well there. Both Charles and Anthony James, cousin to Robbie, both signed apprentice forms this season and continued their mutual family tradition. Jeremy would later play and score for Oxford United against Robbie's Q.P.R in the 1986 League Cup final. Anthony faded from the Vetch but would later reconvene with Robbie in a playing capacity. Dalling, Stevenson, Morris and Davies all found themselves selected to play for Wales Youth during this year, continuing on from Robbie's previous appearances and their collective progress proved very satisfying to John Charles, who was adamant that such players were the future of the club. Stevenson, known as 'Speedy', was unlucky to only collect four full Wales caps after making his name at Swansea City, the lanky central defender spent more than a decade with the Swans and was rewarded with a testimonial from them later (which Robbie played in). The two would remain friends even after both had left the Vetch club. During a Swans/ Cardiff match, with the latter now a Bluebird, Robbie would accidentally break his former colleague's nose. "Playing against Robbie was a great challenge," remembers Nigel, "we were both driven to win."

League scouts had been recorded monitoring the progress of both Robbie and Curt this year. Alan had been inconsistent with his form when under earlier managers at the Vetch but this season saw him realise his true potential; much to the benefit of both club and country.

With the team on a definite upward projection, the Swansea manger and club board introduced a bonus system linked to attendance and results. The players were already on a basic wage and appearance money, so if the fixtures reached a gate of 4,000 then they would be rewarded by a little extra in their pay packets. Only the recent Welsh derby with Newport County had topped that figure whilst the opening game of the season at the Vetch had reached 2,866. They would either meet or be in advance of this in four further home games.

Team form was an improvement on the same stage last year and the Swans had also acquired slightly more points, too. Robbie found himself playing in the Reserves, as well as the first team, in a 1-0 win against Newport alongside Pat Lally, returning from injury. Admission prices for school children had been cut to 30p, with a father and son package into the West Stand costing £1.20. Whilst the new Inter-City 125 train service was introduced costing £9.78 for a Swansea-London return. The Swans squad travelled via their own bus and made the first of two away forays in October, firstly to meet Lincoln City and then, Doncaster Rovers. City, runaway leaders of Division Four this season, beat the Swans 4-0 in a final score that flattered the Imps: last season their visitors had completed the double over them. Regrettably, the result included another goal conceded from a set piece which had recently occurred in the Newport game last month. Robbie's continued endeavours into the second half came to no avail. Griffiths and his coaching staff immediately sought extra training with the squad to deal specifically with their weakness in dealing with free kicks but the pattern continued with more goals conceded this way.

A visit from another relegated side, Huddersfield Town, came next, and a dire 1-1 seemed appropriate for a bitty Vetch Field battle. The Swans struggled to break down their visitors who were renowned for their stalwart defensive qualities. With a disallowed goal for Swansea, it was another physical scrap which saw a mammoth forty free kicks awarded during open play. In fact, there was little to commend it as a spectacle until two late goals allowed a brief spell of interest afterwards. An off-kilter performance by Robbie resulted in him being substituted near the hour mark. The draw proved unfortunate in seeing the visiting players engage in all kinds of shenanigans to stifle the creative Swans. This infuriated both the home manager and his Chairman, who were furious after seeing their tactics.

For the second consecutive game, Robbie was subbed: coming in the game with Doncaster, a 2-1 defeat noticeable for the debut of Tommy Tynan in a Swansea shirt. Despite scoring, the twenty-year-old was unable to add to his team's two points gathered from a possible six, in recent games. A Liverpool player at the time and untried in the League, the

Reds allowed him to come on loan as they had a large playing staff made up of thirty-five professionals and fifteen apprentices. Tynan, remembered for his prolific goal scoring days with Newport County, stayed with the Swans across six games. Fortunes turned for Swansea City in the remaining games of the month, at home to Darlington and Bradford City. Geoff Bray struck in both matches; a 2-0 and 3-1 win, respectively. Played on a Tuesday evening, with Robbie back in at number eleven, he and his team mates managed to keep their cool whilst under duress from the crude mentality adapted by Darlington. Its defence proving solid, Swansea players Smith, Thomas and Robbie combined well in a fraught 2-0 affair. Griffiths was angry that many sides coming to the Vetch would employ a cynical approach aimed at stifling as much of the Swansea open game as possible. It seemed that word had gotten around the division on how to combat them.

As a business, Swansea City Football Club lost almost £27,000 this year; an improvement from the £79,000 of 1974. Recent cut-backs had proven to be effective in their quest to address the

deficit and visitors Bradford also had their own financial concerns this season. The second game in a week played at the Vetch saw the Swans let in a goal from a free kick and they struggled in the first half against the improving Bantams. Robbie got in a couple of punchy shots; one easily saved but the other, forcing the keeper to make a full-length, diving save. Swansea improved in the second half with on-loan Tynan equalising before a brace from Bray sealed a 3-1.

The 1975/ 76 campaign was a peculiar one to study, as by Christmas Swansea had won eight times, scored twenty-eight and conceded the same amount. It proved to be a mediocre showing, seeing the team finish in eleventh position come the season close.

November saw a first-round exit against Division Three side Southend United, defeats by Reading, Exeter and Stockport with only a 3-0 home win against Torquay United offering some solace. Harry Griffiths decried the Cup loss, after having changed his line-up to include the return of the Leitch - Bekker partnership, with Robbie moving to his favoured midfield role. Again the Swansea defence failed to combat the dead ball and trailed 2-0 at half time. Robbie's shot on goal was brilliantly tipped over the bar in a game wherein both keepers shone; particularly Potter, playing with multiple injuries in the Swansea goal. Played out on a sunny afternoon, the trip to Essex was marred by terrace problems involving away fans. This was no isolated incident, as Wrexham, Crystal Palace, Chelsea and Cardiff City saw similar disturbances.

The Swans did earn themselves a well fought point in a testing away fixture with Barnsley. Incorporating an uninstructed defensive style against a Reading side containing Robin Friday was not going to defeat a team in fourth spot in the division, against a tenth place Swansea. And so the Royals sustained their perfect unbeaten home record, against their visitors now fielding an unchanged starting XI across four games.

Back at the Vetch, three days after the loss at Reading, Robbie provided a scintillating, man of the match offering in a super 3-0 win against Torquay. A brace of goals inside nine minutes saw him having a field-day against United keeper Terry Lee, repeatedly putting in lobs that caused the number one many problems. One comedy moment saw an unintended cross by Robbie fly over Lee's head, bounce via a defender on to the post and eventually spin back from the goal line. Torquay had already beaten Swansea twice in the League Cup back in August but faired badly in their League encounters. Both Robbie goals arrived in the first half, each floated above the despairing keeper and his hat-trick almost came early in to the second half, via a header. Robbie had developed a knack for scoring at key times and still a teenager; he was a work-in-progress of whom his only criticism was his inconsistency.

At this stage of the season, the top of the Division Four table displayed a narrow divide between it and a number of clubs beneath. A feeble 3-0 defeat by Exeter City away, mirrored the exact same score line to be repeated at the Vetch in February. Robbie, switched to striker after the departure of Tynan, put in a challenging cross deftly dealt with by the teenaged keeper in a game with much possession attained by both teams but won by Exeter taking its chances.

The highlight of the campaign arrived in the unexpected form of a rudimentary visit to Stockport County on 28 November. Coming a week after the F.A Cup exit, County was a side near the bottom of the division, whilst the Swans were mid-table. Robbie found himself competing against an overweight George Best, who managed to score the winner and showed that he still had much to offer as a player. A gate of 9,220 boosted by the appearance of the former Manchester United and Northern Ireland super star, saw the home side 3-0 up and seemingly set for victory. Curt, Leitch and Robbie all failed to connect on repeated occasions until a brace of goals proved too late for the Swans who lost 3-2. Griffiths was flummoxed as to why they didn't win, "We murdered Stockport. Their goals came from a goalkeeping error, a shot that could have gone anywhere and a moment of pure Best magic. For all the rest of the time, we were a different class." This was an amusing summation of a game that saw Georgie attempt to resurrect his once glorious career. Incidentally, he had made his international debut at the Vetch back in 1964.

Hartlepool had recently battered Newport 4-1 when the Swans entertained them at the Vetch at the end of the first week of December. Swansea had not lost at home all season, and they were able to soak up a lot of pressure until well-after the hour mark. Robbie and his team mates mounted many attacks and he missed a clear chance by heading wide with only the keeper to beat. The second phase saw lots of bookings and four goals: three of them for Swansea in a match where Robbie and others constantly badgered the visitors.

For Harry Griffiths, getting his team out of the Fourth Division was his ultimate objective. He was a player back in the club's Second Division days of the 1950s and wanted to see them returned there. However, his current team had a terrible away form which was hampering his plans at the outset. His players were as frustrated but none wanted to change their attacking style of play which worked so effectively at home.

The mouth-watering prize for seeing off Welsh League side Cardiff Corinthians in the fifth round of the Welsh Cup was a derby match with rivals Cardiff City on 17 February at Ninian Park. But that would have to wait; firstly, they had to travel down to the capital not to Ninian Park but elsewhere in the city. Robbie played up front against a Corries side that was walloped 0-6 on a horrible, rock-hard surface. He finished off the scoring after a brace from Bray and Leitch and one from Curtis. Their hosts admirably held off their illustrious visitors until twenty-two minutes when the first of two first-half strikes.

British Rail may have been advertising a "Mystery Tour" day trip in the local paper but the Swansea team bus knew exactly where it was going next: Crewe. Wales boss Mike Smith was in the crowd, rumoured to be watching the players in the number eight and nine shirts: Curt and Robbie. The Swans went down 2-1 in an action-filled meeting which again repeated seeing the visiting side giving away an early goal.

Boxing Day fell on a Friday this year and sports fans could watch Dickie Davies presenting World of Sport on ITV before heading off down to the Vetch Field to see Watford. A gate of 4,091 viewed an enjoyable encounter won 4-2 by Swansea. Twice battling back from being behind, the game was played at a high tempo with both sides enjoying much of the play. Gate receipts for the day brought in close to £2,000 profit for the club, a figure proving more than twice the amount generated for Crewe's ensuing visit on 3 January.

Ridiculously, the Swans were obliged to make the journey to Bournemouth on the following day, in an opportunity to record their first away win of the season in their twenty-second League fixture. They failed. The 2-0 defeat came in the eleventh game played away from the Vetch which shockingly had seen only three points collected all season.

January 1976 was precisely half way through the 1975/ 76 campaign and it saw the return to the Vetch for ex-boss Harry Gregg, with his new team, Crewe. A training ground move reaped its rewards as the Swans marched 2-0 ahead, against a visiting side which had collected twenty-six bookings this season. Celebrating his and wife Brenda's twentieth wedding anniversary, Mr Griffiths selected new signing Mickey Conway for what transpired to be a pleasing 4-0 win. The Alex fielded a number of former Swans, namely the pacey Mickey Evans, Paul Bevan and big David Davies. After snatching the first goal, Leitch headed in his and Swansea's, second, via a Robbie free kick which gave great satisfaction to their watching manager.

The dismal away record was added to at a wet and windy Abbey Stadium via a 3-1 loss watched by a strong away support against Cambridge United. Three goals down by half time, Robbie got his fifth goal of the season at the close of the first half: pushing the ball through a crowded penalty area following a free kick.

Northampton had drawn 0-0 with the Swans back in September and played out another draw with them, this time after a Friday night 1-1 at the Vetch. Attendances rose to 3,655; an improvement on the recent Crewe fixture. Welsh supporters saw their side acquit themselves well against the promotion-favourites. Robbie was directly involved with the goal that put the home side ahead, a well-delivered free kick and clearly another training ground trick. He passed the ball wide of the defenders for Smith to set up Bray, who made no mistake in collecting his twelfth goal of the season. The match proved another physical skirmish for the Swansea team, competing with a sturdy Town ensemble. Meanwhile Cardiff

City saw out a 1-1 with Halifax Town, with their goal scored by the vastly experienced Mike England, in a team which included ex-Swans striker David Gwyther. There then followed a long haul up to face Workington in a gale force wind at Borough Park. The subsequent 1-1 saw the Swans amass four points from a possible eight this month and demonstrated their annoying habit of being unable to win a match after dominating the second half. The final weekend of January found the postponement of a League game with Darlington and so an unexpected run-out for many first-team players came in a Welsh League match with Llanelli. Two goals from Robbie and Alan Curtis contributed to a 9-0 win.

Games were coming fast by this stage of the season and any possibility of the players enjoying a romantic Valentine's evening flopped due to an away trip to Devon that day to play Torquay. But before that, Reading came to Swansea on 6 February and played the supporting role in a 5-1 drubbing. Bugs seemed to abound amongst the Vetch playing staff, as a trio of lads fell victim to a bout of the flu and added to the selection woes faced by Griffiths. Matters on the pitch progressed beautifully as Robbie put in another Man-of-the-Match performance against the third place Royals. The visitors eventually gained promotion but at the Vetch they were second best to a Swansea team led by sparkling showings from both Robbie and the experienced George Smith. A Robbie shot was followed up by an early strike from Bray superseded by two further goals, including a memorable goal by Robbie from the edge of the area. Curtis came on late and added a brace whilst Robbie saw his name go in to the referee's book; an occurrence repeated on a number of occasions for him this season.

February proved to be an exciting month if you were a Swansea City supporter: six goals in two League games came before a Welsh Cup battle at Ninian Park with a certain Cardiff City. However, three days before that exciting spectacle, Robbie made his hundredth League appearance in their Valentine's Day match at Torquay. Nineteen in March, the trip was also memorable for seeing the Swans win their first away match of the campaign: after thirteen attempts! Indeed fact-fans, the last time they had taken away points was in March 1975, via a 1-2 at Bradford where Robbie scored the opening goal. His century of appearances, more if Cup games were counted, saw the Swansea-born star's name entered into the record books as being the youngest player to attain such a feat. A juggernaut run down the right of midfield by Robbie saw a diving Geoff Bray just miss connecting with his cross before the hour mark. Curt scored his second goal on sixty-two minutes and the Swans held firm to take the points. Griffiths felt that a win would come at some point as he believed that his team had recorded some decent performances away from home. A tactical switch proved effective and a number of Swansea players played well in the game. To commemorate his achievement after the match, young Robbie received an autographed match ball from bespectacled Malcolm Struel.

Harry Griffiths had known Robbie since the latter was a child, back when the penchant for using younger players was grasped by League clubs; the opposite of which was the case back in the 1960s. "Local talent is our lifeline," espoused the manager to Evening Post reporter Bill Paton, "we cannot afford to pay big fees and consequently we cannot compete in the big time." By 1976, Robbie's aptitude as a new professional had seen him improve greatly; he was now more aggressive in winning the ball and had worked hard at improving his inconsistency.

Swansea and Cardiff had not met in recent seasons and so their Welsh Cup derby was much-anticipated by fans of both clubs. The Bluebirds were now in Division Three after a recent relegation and had brought in Spurs player England and the equally-talented Doug Livermore to bolster their squad. Doug, whose son Jake is now a professional footballer, later coached at both clubs (and Wales) and filled in as caretaker boss after Toshack's initial departure from the Vetch in October 1983

Arriving three days after his landmark appearance at Torquay, Robbie pulled on the number nine shirt and ran out on to the Cardiff City pitch for the first time as a Swansea player. Coach Roy Saunders had compiled a report on City for Griffiths and although the Bluebirds were in poor recent form, they had won 6-0 in the previous round. Their manager Jimmy Andrews was keen not to underestimate the Swans as he knew that League status counted for little during this type of encounter. Supporters at the match accounted for a 5,812 gate which enjoyed a well-fought game within which the visitors

 showed themselves as the better team on the night. The rivals ended the game at 1-1 and would reconvene at the Vetch ten days

later to conclude matters. Acting Swansea captain Dave Bruton, who joined the club in 1973, contributed both goals: an O.G as well as the equaliser. "If we didn't know it, it would be hard not to say that Swansea were the Division Four side. Such was the brand of football." That summary was from a fan who had attended the match, recounting their thoughts in a local newspaper. Extra spice was added to the mix upon knowing that winning the Welsh Cup presented an opportunity to participate in the European Cup Winners' Cup. And like Wrexham this season, acquitting themselves admirably against Belgian giants Anderlecht, the possibilities were enticing.

That would have to wait, as a busy League timetable meant that Swansea would welcome Exeter to the Vetch and then travel to Newport County, inbetween time. The Swans had not lost at the Vetch all season: across fifteen games, including Cup matches. It was their third tough fixture within a week. Skipper George Smith felt that it was probably too much to ask for his side to win promotion this season but he was convinced that come the following year they would make the step-up. However, it was Exeter who took away their impeccable home record thanks to a 0-2 victory watched by an impressive 4,252; the second highest of the season

The short trip to Somerton Park gave the Swans their second, and final, away win this campaign against an opposition that would be required to seek re-election back in to the Football League during the close season. The win was their first at Somerton in six years and added the second defeat in as many days for their hosts. Robbie combined artfully with Bartley and Bray in tormenting a limp County side.

A season's best gate of 10,075 crammed in to the Vetch to see the quarter final replay with Cardiff but was a far cry from the 32,796 that saw the F.A Cup visit of Arsenal in February 1968. But it was a meeting that generated excitement. Supporters had been advised to arrive early, to allow easy access in to the tight, little Vetch Field ground but the majority of them would go home disappointed thanks to a 0-3 defeat. Smith was back from injury to face his former club but he could do nothing to avoid the defeat. In spite of their victory, a swarm of hooligans terrorized the town centre with acts of vandalism and assault, much of which passed unaddressed by police, due to its hit-and-run strategy. A makeshift holding area at the Vetch saw eleven of the twelve held acknowledged as Swansea fans.

Obliged to complete an elongated trip up to Bradford the next day, not surprisingly the game at Valley Parade finished 0-0. It was Robbie's thirty-six appearance of the season and was played out before a brimming 6,672. A defence-minded affair, Robbie hit the post with a low drive in the second half.

The Swans were scheduled to play four home games and two away fixtures in this, the penultimate month of the season. Beginning with the first of two games to be played at the Vetch across four days: Barnsley came to west Wales and left empty-handed via a 3-1 defeat. Robbie and his team mates were able to pick themselves up after the recent Welsh Cup disappointments and he scored his third goal within a game that had seen them go 0-1 behind. It was their seventh match across three weeks and it showed in a weary performance. The manager demanded that his team continue to play their open football and he was rewarded by seeing a diving header from Bray, his fourteenth of the campaign, coming from a Robbie cross. Thomas added another and Robbie struck the third. The Swans had now scored forty-eight times, equalling their 1974/75 total and there was still fourteen games remaining. They would advance to a total of sixty-six (including three O.Gs).

With thirteen games remaining, a tough match against soon-to-be-Champions Lincoln City followed and finished a commendable 2-2 in front of a 4,000 crowd. The Swans had advanced to 2-1 up thanks to Thomas and Curt, but a set piece goal once more did for them. A superb goal from Curtis, now enjoying his new striker role, came in a well fought match proving an exceptional advertisement for the standard of football that some teams could produce in the Fourth Division.

Defeat at Huddersfield Town was put behind the Swans by successive home victories against Doncaster Rovers and Stockport County, with the team playing every three days to meet their fixtures schedule. Harry Griffiths was again incensed at the tactics employed by Huddersfield, viewing the game as a bruising affair for his players. Town was also aided by their keeper enjoying a good game, blocking shots from Smith and a dipping effort from Robbie James.

Elsewhere in Welsh football, Jimmy Scoular, who had brought a young Robbie to Cardiff City a few years previously, was revealed as the new Newport manager this month.

Stockport's loss of form eventually led them having to seek re-election and it wasn't hard to see why when they were beaten 5-0 at the Vetch on 19 March. A guileless County found Robbie and others enjoying ample freedom against hopeless opposition. 3-0 up by half time, the Swans players were queuing up for strikes on goal across a match that they dominated. Robbie and the visiting trainer both managed to get themselves cautioned whilst the former also produced some good stuff on the pitch: namely setting up two goals, both from corners. The game, the fifth this month for a busy Swansea City team, came after a 2-1 win against Doncaster at home. Rovers again featured young Irish striker Brendan O'Callaghan, as well as Les Chappell. Les would soon be signed by the Swans before advancing to a youth team coaching role under John Toshack, as well as fulfilling caretaker manager duties on three separate occasions. Swansea made amends for an earlier 2-1 defeat and beat their under-performing visitors in an evening game at the Vetch. Griffiths had tipped them as early promotion candidates but they failed to enhance their impressive away form against a determined Swans unit. Smith and a resurgent Curt played well with midfield man Robbie contributing to both goals. The first coming from the hard working captain resulted in a characteristic, hard and low shot on goal by Robbie. It comically evaded the attention of the keeper thanks to a sliced clearance.

A rock solid Hartlepool pitch at their Victoria ground failed to prevent Robbie from featuring heavily in the 1-0 away defeat for his club in the final week of March. He set up a number of chances and was also involved in his own attempts but none produced a goal. Played on a windy afternoon, it seems that most of the players failed in innumerable attempts to put the ball in the back of the net that day.

Neither Messrs James nor Curtis succeeded in scoring against a skilful Tranmere Rovers side in a 3-0 defeat from a team that had opened Swansea's season back in August with a share of the points. However, in the return, Robbie had a couple of efforts: one was struck wide and the other went in to the side netting. The match proved a busy encounter for stopper Stephen Potter, whose agility kept the score down. Both Robbie and ex-Brighton player Conway missed the draw with Scunthorpe, the former due to a nasty poisoned leg! A disappointed Griffiths selected a fit again Robbie in a Welsh League match with Caerleon, played the day after the Scunthorpe defeat. "Robbie goes gay with four" was the sniggering match report headline, documenting the four goals put in by Robbie in a resounding 7-2 clattering at the Vetch.

Three days later saw Swansea playing a rare Saturday afternoon game, instead of their usual Friday evenings, against a Southport team possessing a diabolical present League record. No doubt some supporters took a can of Coke to the match, costing less than 10p at the local supermarket. Whilst elsewhere in the town, the Odeon had a revival of The Sound of Music playing. Swansea rightly dominated proceedings, despite a gap of close to an hour between their goals against visitors that barely offered anything other than to defend. The Swans failed to latch onto numerous scoring opportunities in a team selection which incorporated teenagers Stephen Morris and Nigel Stephenson. The twosome had been paired previously in the Reserves and Griffiths saw the game as an opportunity for his younger players to gain some first team experience. Whilst Robbie buzzed about and created options for his side, Lally and a returning Conway combined efficiently, with the latter providing a cross in to Robbie who met the ball with a brilliant diving header which squeezed into the goal via the keeper and post. It was his eighth goal of the season against an opposition that would finish bottom-but-one in the final table. His was the second goal in a 2-0 win watched by a respectable 2,147. Conway and Robbie were paired up-front alongside Alan Curtis, in the news after being selected for Wales in their European Championship match at Cardiff with Yugoslavia. That match saw the appearance of future Vetch team mate Dzemal 'Jimmy' Hadziabdic literally battling with John Toshack.

With only a half-dozen games left, a number of Swansea City players were close to reaching the twenty point threshold which would automatically trigger a suspension. Robbie had been booked and suspended this season. Bans occurring at the end of a season could now be carried over in to the start of the next, possibly impacting on the fortunes of a team come the close of that subsequent campaign.

Defeats at Brentford, a 1-0, and Watford, a 2-1, saw the Swans accumulate three points from a possible ten. Brentford sunk them with a late winner after a draw was looking the likeliest outcome. Robbie showed tremendous industry in the middle of the park, battling away to create openings for the forwards. His Swansea team proved unable to complete the League double over the Hornets, after an exciting 4-1 Boxing Day victory at the Vetch. Going a goal down, and against the run of play, Curt and Robbie gelled effectively in their attacks on the Watford goal, manned by a debutant keeper. Also making his debut was future England star Luther Blissett. It was the latter that put the home side 2-0 up before a well-taken consolation goal came from Robbie, following a pass from Curt. The game proved another fine example of creative football involving two teams that would soon advance up the divisions. It was Robbie's final goal this season, his ninth.

Four games across a frantic eight days saw four draws, three at the Vetch and a final, rearranged fixture away at lowly-Darlington. Commencing with AFC Bournemouth visiting Vetch Field; they had beaten the Swans back in December and only a late goal gave them a share of the points in a heavily-contested battle that garnered many bookings, including ones for Robbie and team mate Bruton.

Rochdale was the club's forty-fourth game across eight months but it was to be the final home game played on a Monday evening against Brentford, which recorded the lowest attendance at the Vetch of the whole season: 1,311. In a promising start, within a game that created four goals, it was not a classic. The Swans fell 2-0 down before a Bray brace got them back level and he almost collected a hat trick; only to see a late lob hit the post. And that was the closing match seen at the Vetch in the 1975/76 season. Robbie had contributed nine goals to the team as thier overall tally peaked at fifty-one against twenty-one.

There was one more game to fulfil, a rearranged trip to Darlington on 28 April. The result was of little significance to the Swans but to their hosts, it meant a lot as they were close to the re-election zone. A late equaliser from the head of Wyndham Evans came in a tetchy affair encompassing a number of individual scraps between opposing players. Adding to the rumpus was a certain Robbie James, back in the number nine shirt, who shortly into the second half, laid out Darlington player David Crosson in an off the ball incident. The game finished 1-1 in front of a largely relieved crowd totalling 4,295.

In total, Swansea scored sixty-six League goals, with a further eleven in the various Cup competitions. They finished eleventh out of twenty-four with their away form proving atrocious: letting in thirty-six against fifteen scored. Coincidentally, they lost as many times as they had won at the Vetch: fourteen. But one positive was the Reserves winning the Western League South Division Championship with some advancing into the first team. The 1976/77 close season saw lots of changes for Robbie and his fellow professionals at the Vetch during the long hot summer. Pitches were so hard and dried-out that the players were unable to wear their studded boots during training. Recent F.A Cup winners Southampton had brought a team to play a friendly on Tuesday 11 May and saw the likes of Peter Osgood and Mick Channon in their side. The match had been organised by Swans boss Harry Griffiths, who knew his Saints equivalent, Lawrie McMenemy. A few seasons later, the two clubs would meet in a match sponsored by Patrick sports.

Above: The new Swans squad for the 1976/ 77 campaign.
Robbie is pictured standing, top row, second left.

Lots of players were released by the club during this time, including the unlucky Jan Bekker, Glen Davies and Paul Abbott. Incredibly, at the close of the 1975/ 76 season, the club only had eleven first team players on its books!

New arrivals were a who's who of seasoned-pros: former Wrexham captain Eddie May, Gil Reece, Les Chappell and a 6'2" striker called Gary Moore. Manager Harry Griffiths realised that relying upon very young players was not going to get Swansea City out of Division Four and therefore older heads were drafted in to bring some experience into the team. Doing so raised the level of professionalism at the club whilst also stimulating competition for places.

Robbie, Alan Curtis and teenager Jeremy Charles would prove to be the nucleus of an exciting attack formation this season. Both Curt and Robbie were selected for all forty-six League fixtures, including a handful of substitutions, whilst 'Charlo' would be a great success across thirty-six games.

Astonishingly, this dynamic trio would contribute fifty-three of the ninety-two League goals scored this season by the Swans: the highest in the whole Football League. Conversely, the club conceded eighty-four. Individually, Robbie would score eighteen goals, including Cup strikes, across a campaign which would see the team wearing a new Bukta-manufactured kit. Although, in some fixtures the team ran out in badge-less shirts, still a common sight in 1970s football. Supporters or local business concerns could help the club by sponsoring a player's kit and B.Gibbs of Parc Sports paid £25 for Robbie's.

Griffiths had pleaded in the final match day programme of the recent season for continued support, "Be back with us, please…because then I am certain we will have even more to put on show," requested the manager, in his second season in charge, "This is a club on its way up." The bookies agreed and presented Swansea City as 5/2 to gain promotion and offered 16/1 for them to go up as Champions.

With the impetus on attacking, open football still adhered to, the manager freely conceded that his team lost games last season, particularly away, when they should not have done so. Reading the record for the 1975 / 76 season, you will see what an understatement this was.

Friendlies with Briton Ferry, Cardiff and Merthyr Tydfil, the latter two being clubs that Robbie would subsequently play for, were arranged to allow the manager to experiment with team formations prior to the season start of 21 August.

Robbie had a new confidence which meant that he was happy to try his luck in games and not worry if the move failed to succeed, as there would be other opportunities. But like all players, he suffered the odd off-game. His early form in the League Cup was poor and across a long season, he would be substituted in three League games. Often one player's ropey form leads to an opportunity for another. That was exactly what happened following Robbie being taken off during the opening game of the season on 14 August, at home to Newport in the League Cup. A tasty Welsh derby set the season in motion, as a Vetch Field crowd of close to 3,300 enjoyed a 4-1 victory. An under-par showing by Robbie saw him lose the ball to County player John Emmanuel which then led to Newport going in at half-time at 1-1. John's brother, Gary, was at Swansea when Robbie returned to his home town club for a second spell some years later. But back to the match, the visitors, wearing their bright orange Adidas kit, were in heavy debt this season and had seen eight players leave during the close period. The clubs would face each other on four occasions this year, with the Swans winning three of the games. The introduction of sixteen-year-old substitute Jeremy Charles proved an instant success by scoring twice, before a fourth was added by Geoff Bray. Swans supporters were shocked at seeing Robbie come off in what Mr Griffiths termed a "gamble". But the move worked during a game when a draw looked likely.

Four days later, looking resplendent in their new club suits, the Swansea playing squad travelled to Somerton Park for the return tie. They lost 1-0 but still qualified via a 4-2 aggregate score after employing a cautious, safety-first approach. It was a major achievement, as the Swans had not advanced to the second round of the competition in their previous four attempts. Jeremy's father Mel, a former player at the Vetch and Uncle John, recently youth team coach there, both attended the match which saw Jeremy selected in the starting line-up but subsequently pick up an injury. Robbie dropped down to the bench but returned in the next match partly due to Jeremy's injury. The club had ten youngsters on their ground staff, a number in keeping with the leading clubs across the country at the time. Developing teenaged footballers in the region now wanted to play for the Swans as it clearly was possible to step up into first team reckoning: if you were good enough. This was a better option than going with the larger clubs and ending up lost in their many reserve sides and it was also a marvellous incentive.

The 1976/ 77 season was going to be a long and arduous experience, forty-six League fixtures plus an additional nine Cup games. Apart from being selected as sub in an early League match, Robbie would play in every single game. By the coming March/ April, the team would be obliged to play across sixteen matches.

An increase in season ticket sales, especially for family ones in the West stand, boosted the gate tally for the visit of Darlington to the Vetch on 21 August for the inaugural League fixture of the new season. Attendances would peak at a majestic 11,000 for the final home game of the campaign against Watford but for the opening game, 3,830 turned up.

Robbie would score against the visitors in the away meeting but here, he was selected at number nine whilst Charles occupied the subs bench.

Below: The Swans squad in their new Bukta kit.
Robbie can be found fourth right, standing row.

Darlington had only avoided having to seek re-election at the end of the previous season by virtue of a slightly better goal aggregate than Newport. The Swans extended their splendid home record and won the game 2-1. Indeed, in the League, they would not be beaten at the Vetch until March 1977. The game proved to be a strenuous encounter that saw Robbie flattened by an off-the-ball tackle. He was involved in much of the action whilst Charlo was regularly playing in the Welsh League team in which Swansea City subsequently finished eighth out of a roster of eighteen.

Robbie had enjoyed favourable form away at Valley Parade previously but he saw his side clipped 4-1 by Bradford, four days after the Darlington game. The Bantams would complete the League double over them this season and finish a place above them in the final table positions. Whilst Swansea City was losing in Yorkshire, rivals Cardiff City faced Bristol Rovers. Both Welsh sides lost and Eddie May, in the Swansea defence, had what is known as a 'mare'. Years later, Big Eddie would manage the Bluebirds and enjoy success there, winning promotion and teh Welsh Cup in the same season. He would bring Robbie in from his then present club, namely Bradford City.

The Swans had lost twice and conceded eight goals in their first three League games and so established blocker Stephen Potter was dropped for their third game against Stockport and replaced by Dutchman Nico Schroeder for what transpired as being his only appearance. He made football history by becoming the first foreign player to sign for a Football League club following a new E.E.C employment initiative. Not given much of a chance, he let in three goals. Perhaps the next away trip to Chester, in the second round of the League Cup, was regarded as a necessary distraction. Torquay United, a fellow Division Four side, had put Swansea out of the competition last season but Chester failed to repeat this: losing 2-3 with an injury-time winner coming from Charles. The victory meant a mid-September tie in the next round, away to a familiar foe: Torquay!

September proved to be a fruitful month for Robbie as he struck four goals, the first of which was the winner at the Vetch against Barnsley. The Swans won 2-1, in a striking example of lower League football: full of hearty endeavour from both teams. Simply laid on by opening scorer Gary Moore, Robbie's goal sealed two points for his side. Moore would suffer from injuries this season but still manage to contribute six goals. An established pro, with former clubs including Sunderland and Chester, his arrival usurped the Curtis-Bray partnership introduced mid-way through the 1975/76 season because Harry Griffiths felt that Moore could provide a positive influence on the younger players. Meanwhile, whilst Robbie featured in the first team, cousin Anthony was in the Reserves playing against Pembrokeshire on the same day. He would advance to the first team in the coming season.

New team mate Gil Reece had joined the club as a part-timer, living and training in Cardiff. A former Wales international, he struggled by not making it into Griffiths' team selection and proved unable to hide his displeasure at playing for the Reserves, as to many in the game, the standard there was low.

This season saw the Swans draw eight matches, the first of which was the 2-2 away at Huddersfield on 11 September. It would be the start of a three game run of draws; 1-1 with Doncaster and a 2-2 with Aldershot, with Robbie scoring in the first and last of them. Huddersfield got a lucky, late equaliser after the referee awarded them a corner rather than a Swansea goal kick. This sent Griffiths in to a fury and captain George Smith got sent off as a result of his response to the goal that followed. Robbie would suffer with an ankle injury this campaign and after the game, he was looking doubtful for the oncoming Doncaster fixture. Returning to the Huddersfield match, Smith put in a penalty, awarded to the team after a foul on Robbie. The industrious Jamo added a second shortly before half time, after chasing down a ball, pinching it off the player and striking a thirty yard shot! Aided by the wind, hit low and hard, it flew into the net after the keeper proved too slow in his response. In another engaging encounter, the teams might have shared the points but the Swans proved the more dominant. Robbie shot wide of the post and generated a great deal in midfield, whilst also combining well with Curtis. The Swans defence settled down well after some jittery first half moments, with Robbie putting in another workmanlike performance.

A third round League Cup trip to Torquay came with the incentive of a possible big-money draw in the next round for the winners, in the last sixteen. The rivals knew each other well and had met twice in the competition last season, where United sank the Swans. But they would not fair so well in the League encounters. However, Cup games are often very different to domestic encounters and so Mr Griffiths told his team to continue playing their attacking brand of football and keep it positive. "There will not be a defensive outlook," he told the Evening Post. Cardiff manager and ex-player, Jimmy Andrews shared the same view, stating that the paying fans should be entertained. His team was away in Russia playing in the European Cup Winners' Cup against Dynamo Tiblisi (they lost 3-0). In a tension-filled encounter, the Swans presented a dazzling team presentation, with Lally, Curtis, Smith and Robbie all contributing greatly in a fast-paced drama with Torquay, won by a late goal from Curt. Robbie, playing up front in his familial number eight shirt, saw his shot hit the post as his team went in a goal down at half time. A truly individual moment came when Robbie passed a defender, avoided a sliding tackle and beat the keeper with a glorious left foot shot. "A quality goal from a quality player," was how Post Reporter John Burgum fittingly described it. Robbie's future Stoke City team mate Mickey Thomas was in blistering form for Welsh cousins Wrexham, who pulled off a surprise away win at Spurs, to join the Swans in the next round. Coincidentally, they would famously lose future Cup battles against both Cardiff City and Swansea City.

Self discipline was a concern for Robbie James this season, as in the Torquay game he was booked for dissent, something which had happened in the previous round, also. The club was clamping down on such things and so fined him.

Tom Baker as Dr Who was in his Tardis on television this month whilst the Swansea team bus only needed to transported to Hampshire, to the Recreation ground, home of Aldershot F.C. The long trip resulted in a share of the points after a combative encounter. Charles scored the first goal before Robbie contributed the second, in an entertaining 2-2 watched by 5,120. His goal came on forty-nine minutes, following a couple of punches by the 'Shots keeper had failed to clear the ball and enabled Robbie to tap into an empty net. He also had a part in the first goal; working hard before Moore set in a ground level cross that was gratefully put in by Charlo at close range. Come March 1977, the clubs would meet at the Vetch and both Swansea players would once more see themselves on the score sheet. Londoner Lally, back with the Swans after a loan spell, put in a spirited display against Aldershot and commented that team morale was excellent. He added that he felt the Swans had a strong chance of promotion: how right he proved to be.

October showed itself to be an exciting month, with six fixtures including a late visit from Division Two's Bolton in the League Cup. Robbie was in rich form, collecting five goals.

Beginning with the visit to the Vetch Field for lowly Southport, the attendance was a little shy of topping the opening day figure.

Robbie and his team mates had each been inoculated against flu but poor Jeremy Charles was already suffering and so missed the game against a team that had yet to record a win this season. He watched a great afternoon for Man-of-the-Match Robbie, in amidst an encounter that saw the Swans fail to capitalise on innumerable scoring opportunities. Les Chappell made his home debut on a smashing sunny afternoon. Robbie produced a number of his trade mark rocket shots and competed aggressively; getting himself another booking but also being the victim of fouls, too. With their combined height, May and Charles caused fear amongst the Southport defence and this led to a penalty being awarded after the hosts had fallen 0-1 behind. It was confidently put away by Robbie and brought the score level. Many openings were created including a close range effort from RJ and he also chose the wrong option by not passing to an unmarked Moore in another instance. But with only minutes remaining, a low shot from Robbie cannoned between the throng of players to provide the winner against an opposition that failed to win away all season. Some late time wasting endeavours by the visitors irked Harry Griffiths, a man fully aware that everybody expected his team to beat such lowly opponents. But as we know, football doesn't always follow the script and this game saw Swansea concede a goal on fourteen minutes, again from a set piece.

After beating them 2-1 in the League Cup, Swansea City managed to lose by the same score in a League fixture away at Torquay next. Ironically, Griffiths regarded the team's performance as the best of the season, despite the outcome. Played on a Saturday night, Robbie was substituted at half-time after complaining of stomach problems. He could only watch as his team lost the game thanks to a goal three minutes in to injury time (again from a free kick). He and Curt had played excellently in the previous League Cup meeting with United at their ground in the previous month, scoring a goal a piece. Charles came on as his replacement and was again selected in the absence of the injured Moore. Mid-October saw a presentation to mark Robbie's landmark hundred League appearances by the Vice Presidents of Swansea City F.C. Taking place at a Swansea nightclub, his manager had been watching the club's next League Cup opponents but had dashed back to be present. Griffiths proved very complimentary about his young player upon addressing those invited. Robbie's performance in the subsequent game against west London club Brentford would no doubt have pleased him, too. He grabbed a brace to add to the six previous goals collected this season as the Swans smashed their visitors 5-3. Meanwhile team mate Charles developed a habit of scoring against Newport County and grabbed a couple in a wet and windy 0-2 win at Somerton Park. Eddie May marshalled his defence and worked admirably with Dave Bruton in a fixture some four days before the big Cup meeting with Bolton at the Vetch on 26 October. Swans fans wanting to see that, had to collect a voucher given out at recent home games and some 5,000 did exactly that.

A rousing 13,600 filled the Vetch in anticipation of seeing the team face a club two divisions higher than their own and enjoyed seeing their team go 1-0 thanks to the midfield players feeding the forwards. A Robbie corner was flicked on by Wyndham Evans, who seemed to have lost his goal touch this season, for Curtis to then head the ball into the net. Wanderers boss Ian Greaves was complimentary about the Swans and offered that they deserved to be in a higher division. The game concluded at 1-1 following lots of creative use of the ball by both teams and a replay on 2 November was scheduled with the club's coffers boosted to the sum of £9,300 afterwards. Greaves had completed his National Service with Swansea boss Harry Griffiths and would return to the Vetch in March, observing the progress of Alan Curtis as a possible transfer target.

Defeat at Crewe was not the best preparation for the Swans as the fourth round replay on a slippery Burnden Park arrived. Three goals had been leaked in the former, and a further five came in this encounter attended by a stunning 14,955. Robbie got what transpired as a consolation goal, his only strike of the month, as the Swans took a surprise lead on four minutes thanks to a poacher's goal from the youngster. Well-beaten by a 5-1 score line, the eventual trophy was won by Aston Villa.

A goal-less draw with Exeter and a 1-0 away defeat to Halifax Town would be capped by an embarrassing first round departure from the F.A Cup by Minehead. After recent mistakes in the last two games, Potter was rested and thirty-year-old keeper Graham Brown came in on loan. Rain continued to hamper conditions away at Halifax, where a freaky goal saw the Swans lose. The hosts were able to marshal Curt, Charlo and Robbie effectively in a game that saw May break his nose during open play but carry on playing! That was an injury familiar to Robbie, as he broke his own on more than one occasion. Town were in good form, recently smashing Doncaster 6-0.

Swansea had conceded eight goals in two games by the time of facing Exeter on a muddy Vetch Field. The game was looking likely to be postponed due to heavy rain which left much of the playing surface waterlogged. Robbie and others proved unable to beat talented visiting keeper Richard Key, including a move set up by Curtis and Batley that saw a Robbie header produce a stunning save from a man that kept his team in the game thanks to a confident showing. With the Swans mounting wave after wave of attacks, Robbie came closest to scoring in the second half; only for his curling shot to fly wide of the post.

A build-up of fixtures occurred due to their progress in the League Cup and coming F.A Cup obligations with Isthmian League side Minehead. The tie came with the Swans in the bottom three of Division Four and it saw a return to the Vetch for ex-player Andy Leitch in the visitor's line-up. He had made nineteen appearances for them and had scored nine goals alongside Robbie before being released from his contract in October 1975. A crowd totalling 3,435 attend the game to witness a bruising affair settled by a last minute winner by the visitors. Robbie was in amongst things, squaring up to the keeper early into the second half, when the visitors had been holding their hosts at 0-0. He had earlier seen his header pushed over the bar and also watched as his thirty-yard rocket grazed the crossbar. Following a number of bookings, including one as a result of a foul on Robbie, a free kick led to the decider with Leitch quickest to respond when the Swans keeper failed to hold onto a ball. Elsewhere in the Cup, Wrexham won 6-0 and Newport drew at Bournemouth. Manager Griffiths warned that unless he saw a greater effort from many of his players, they could leave the club. In this penultimate month of 1976, Swansea had sixteen professionals on their books.

And so the manager switched the playing system and now attempted to utilize Robbie as an outside right in a team consisting of five changes to face Workington. The threat worked, as it galvanised the team, who recorded a healthy 4-0 win at the end of the month. Highlighted by a Curt wonder goal, it delighted his boss but overall, the team performance was not great. The victory put an end to a five game run without a win across which they had conceded ten goals. The pressure was on for the team to win promotion, this being recognised as being the primary objective by the club.

December revealed that Cardiff City F.C produced an operational loss of £125,000 and Newport County F.C was close to bankruptcy. On the field, Watford beat the Swans 2-0 at Vicarage road. The talented Hornets would complete the League double over them this season but ultimately fail to gain promotion. The score proved to be a fair result after an ineffective team performance from the visitors. Robbie had a few shots on goal but he and Curt failed to break through a rigid defence. Swansea never looked like scoring whilst Watford missed plenty of chances in a one-sided match favouring the men in yellow shirts. A distinct lack of confidence saw the Swans down to seventeenth in the table as Watford extended their unbeaten home status. After the match, the team spent two long hours with their manager discussing their present problems: finding themselves eight points behind the leaders at the time.

Robbie, Curt and team mate Danny Bartley were all selected for a South Wales XI to play against Manchester United at Ninian Park on Wednesday 7 December, in a fund raiser for the ailing Newport County. A telling cross from Jamo was met by the head of local hero Phil Dwyer in the only goal of the match. Known as 'Joe' due to his likeness to Everton and England player Joe Royle, Phil made his debut for City aged eighteen-years and when the Swans met the Bluebirds more often, he loved playing against them. So much so that when Leighton James joined the Swans, he moaned at the big man to ease off a little as they were Wales team mates at the time! He and Robbie played together for Wales on two occasions (Germany and Scotland).

Robbie and Curt enjoyed a busy month, travelling to Wolverhampton to play for Wales Under-21 against England straight after the League fixture with Scunthorpe at the Vetch on 11 December. The visitors brought Llanelli-born goal keeper Glan Letheren in their team, a player that would sign for the Swans in the 1979/ 80 season and was also in the squad to face England. He later worked as chief scout/ keeper coach with the club. Coming after defeat at Watford, the Swans took a well-earned two points thanks to a 2-0 victory in the first game of the month at the Vetch Field. Potter returned to keep goal and remained for the rest of the season. Team mate Robbie James continued to harass Division Four defenders and would often be fouled, with the offender usually receiving a booking.

A visit from table-toppers Cambridge United followed a week later and saw an unexpected home win for the Swans by 3-1. Another Man-of-the-Match performance from Robbie was chalked up as his creativity saw him selflessly working to create opportunities for his team mates. He also produced his own chances on goal but it was a Curtis-James-Charles combination that put the Swans 1-0 up shortly before half time. Robbie was again involved in the second; his corner flying across to meet the head of veteran Chappell. Prior to the game, a crowd of 2,392, a thousand less than the subsequent Cambridge match, watched the 2-0 win against Scunthorpe. Eddie May scored six times for the Swans across the 1976/ 77 campaign and his confidence in playing alongside Pat Lally allowed him to come up for free kicks and corners. This was something that he loved to do and a goal to the good, Robbie sent in a corner which was put into the net by the marvellous May. United would again be beaten, in April, with one of the three Swans goals scored by Robbie.

On to the Cambridge game, it was the best result of the season so far and was applauded by visiting boss Ron Atkinson, who admired the "pressure football." He commented, "They never stopped coming at us, knocked the ball about intelligently and looked a very good side." This was quite a compliment from the manager of a club that would advance to being Division Four Champions in May. Robbie, Curt, Charles, Chappell and Lally were all marked out for their exceptional performances in the game which resulted in United toppled from top of the table.

Scheduled a day after Boxing Day, Robbie collected a fine goal for his visiting side at Bournemouth in a 1-1 watched by a holiday crowd totalling 6,329. It arrived some seven minutes before half time and he had to work amazingly hard to finish it: with a ball played out of defence, Robbie ran down the right of the pitch and cut inside to shoot from twenty-five yards. The ball bounced under the keeper and in. Putting them 1-0 up, they were unlucky not to win the match. The club's last away victory came back in October but they would chalk up a few subsequent wins this season. It was his tenth goal of the season and marked a tremendous improvement in form for the team, in this their nineteenth League fixture. In the remaining twenty-six games, they would lose only seven times. Consecutive home wins before that saw five goals scored against one conceded and included that tremendous 3-1 victory over Cambridge, as detailed.

Strong vocal support for the Robbie and his team came in a win over Colchester in the final game of 1976. The Swans saw out the year with a 2-1 win watched by the highest attendance at the Vetch so far this season: 5,666.

Advancing in to 1977, there was no rest for Robbie and his fellow pros, as they had a New Year's Day trip to rivals Exeter City to fulfil. They lost 2-0 before a mere three days later found them back at home and beating Crewe 3-0. Robbie collected the opening goal before Charles and Chappell added. It was the twenty-second League game of the campaign and the team had scored twenty-three times at home (plus another five times in the Cup). Gregg showed no mercy for his former club, some two years since leaving, with a succession of Swansea players picking up injuries in the game, including bruised ribs for Robbie. The win saw the Swans go up in to sixth place in Division Four and boosted the player's wage packets. As they were in the top eight, this meant that a bonus kicked in and would be doubled if they advanced into the top four. Welsh soccer legend John Charles was at the match and was convinced that the club would go up after watching the 3-0 win. Young Charlo and Conway combined to set up a cross for Robbie, who in turn, pushed the ball under soon-to-be Swans keeper Geoff Crudgington. That super win came after the team had lost on a muddy pitch away at Rochdale, thanks to the arrival of a first-half goal when a draw had been looking likely.

A break from League endeavours arrived with a fifth round Welsh Cup tie at home to Newport, whom they had previously beaten 2-0 back in October. A ten minute hat-trick from Alan Curtis and a goal from Eddie May saw off their rivals 4-1 and were rewarded by a quarter final tie away at Wrexham. Curt's first, a rare header, came from a perfect cross from Robbie, in what was to be the final game in charge for County boss Jimmy Scoular before he took up a chief scouting post with the Swans. He had held the job for almost eleven months and had seen the club struggle with a six figure debt before things proved too much for him. His appointment was a wise one, utilising the experience of this former Portsmouth and Scotland international who had managed Cardiff City from 1964 - 1973. Robbie had a handful of scoring chances during the game which came after a recent League game with Bradford at the Vetch was abandoned due to torrential rain rendering the pitch markings unclear. Smith had put them ahead, with a goal made by Robbie but otherwise, the youngster was not enjoying a good game. Rearranged for 1 March, that would see a different outcome: the Bantams winning 2-3 and completing a double.

Another four goals came at Darlington next, with the fourth coming from Robbie in a great game which could have finished at twice the final 0-4 score line. The win completed the double for the Swans, one of seven this campaign, and further enhanced their reputation as one of the better football playing sides in the lower divisions. In an exceptional and pleasing team display favouring the skilful cross field passing of a certain Robbie James, Darlington could offer little on a quagmire-like pitch. Three second half goals added to an earlier Charles strike, with Robbie slotting in a well deserved fourth. In later years, some fans would make disparaging comments about his lack of pace but in his prime with Swansea, Robbie could and would, out-sprint opponents. This match was a perfect example; with his goal seeing him race away from a defender's before poking a low shot past the advancing keeper.

With their last two home games attracting over 5,000 supporters in each, this upsurge increased and was enhanced with another four goals being attained by the free-scoring Swans when Hartlepool United came to Wales at the end of January. Initially producing an anxious start, the Swans fell behind on eight minutes against their visitors from the north east, who twice took the lead in the game. The Robbie-Curt attacking axis shone brightest in the second half; especially 65 upon the latter. A Robbie header was flicked on to Curtis, who still had a lot to do before the ball eventually hit the back of the net. With Swansea 4-2 up on seventy-two minutes, skipper Smith unleashed a thirty yard shot, ala Robbie, which dipped over the cross bar and was followed by a Robbie volley that just missed the post. The final score came against an opposition that had been the early form side in the division. It showed how things could change: they would finish third from bottom come May. The recent goal frenzy, which the fans would have loved, was also useful because goal ratios were a new consideration introduced by the Football League then.

The early months of 1977 proved problematic to Swansea City, as postponements due to flooded pitches meant a fixtures pile-up. Although when they did get to play, across February, the team lost all three games. Commencing with a long hike up to Barnsley, Robbie narrowly missed poaching an early goal, working effectively with Conway and Curtis in a match where the hosts took the initiative. The Swans proved unable to add to their recent away win at Darlington, sunk by a late headed goal against a club that closed their campaign three points below them. The Swans were unfortunate to lose a match that they deserved at least a point from; complimented by their host's manager that they were the best team that they had faced this season. A 2-1 loss at Doncaster's

Belle Vue ground closed a disappointing February for Robbie and his Swansea team mates who conceded seven goals against three scored, without a single win. Robbie missed two simple chances and the only positive was seeing young Jeremy Charles reaching a lucky for him, thirteen goals this season. On the same afternoon, Cardiff exited the F.A Cup by an Everton team that had future team mate Bob Latchford in its line-up. Bryan Hamilton, later manager at Leicester when Robbie joined them, also played.

Another waterlogged pitch at the Racecourse ground, Wrexham, meant their sixth round Welsh Cup meeting was called off. Bad news to the Swansea squad as their team bus had already completed its 360 mile trip to north Wales before hearing of the postponement. Robbie remained, linking up with the Wales Under-21 camp. The Reds had an exceptional home record this season and when the game was rescheduled, for the end of the third week of February, it saw the Swans beaten 4-1.

Away defeats at Barnsley and Doncaster Rovers continued into March with a 2-3 loss in the rearranged home fixture with Bradford where Robbie, playing in the number seven shirt, was substituted. The month produced a congested, seven games fixture list for the Swans, beginning with the Bradford game. Results soon improved, with the Swans advancing to picking up eight points from a possible eight in their next four games (remembering that two points for a win was still the norm). Four days later saw the visit of Aldershot to the Vetch Field, with Robbie scoring the third of the four goals for the Swans in a 4-2 victory, their sixth game in which they scored four or more times this season. There were five more games left this month, with the next, an away win watched by 972 spectators at Southport. Swansea completed the double over them with this 1-2 win, adding to a 2-1 at the Vetch back in October when Robbie got both goals. A successive away win at Southend surfaced next, thanks to a 1-2 score line. Torquay came to Wales and Robbie scored the Swans' second after an opening O.G in a 4-1 whipping. The most dramatic match of the season arrived five days later with an eight goal thriller at the Vetch with Stockport. Originally scheduled for 5 February, that fixture had been called-off only fifteen minutes before kick-off due to a water-strewn pitch but the rescheduled meeting was worth the wait. Astonishingly, the Swans came back from a 0-4 deficit to gain a point in an extraordinary game of football. Errors included an O.G and two suicidal back passes. Watched by 6,383, the game was played on Robbie's twentieth birthday.

Three days later the Swans ventured to Brentford and got hammered 4-0. The teams had previously met in October, where eight goals were scored; with Robbie contributing two of the five notched up by the Swans in a 5-3 victory.

In an equally-congested April, a ridiculous nine League games were played. Newport County made their third visit of the 1976/77 season to the Vetch Field. Attended by a 3,577 crowd, a drop on the last two home games, the Swans won 3-1 and saw them put County out of both the League Cup and Welsh Cup, as well as completing a League double over them! Managed by the newly-appointed Colin Addison, his name would be linked with the vacant Swansea post later but he did not take up the position despite the board wanting him to do so. (However, in September 2001 he did become Swans boss).

Then a 1-1 with Colchester United away was followed before the Vetch faithful saw Robbie score the third goal in a shining 3-0 success against seaside club Bournemouth, unusually played on a Monday evening. Ridiculously superseded the next day with the visit of Southend, whom the Swans beat 2-0. Four days later and they were away to Scunthorpe United and Robbie scored the third goal after Smith had struck twice in a 3-0 win. There then came, two days after, a share of the points away at Hartlepool followed by a 2-1 win against Halifax Town at the Vetch when there was no room for dropping points. Robbie put in both goals before a large 7,344 gate against the visitors who had not won away all season long. Terrific form saw the team only dropping five points from the last possible twenty-four. Rain before kick-off failed to deter Robbie scoring his first goal on twenty-two minutes after missing two earlier chances. It came thanks to a superbly constructed piece of skill by Danny Bartley, who beat three players and crossed to a composed Robbie who then placed the ball with a perfectly-weighted header. James caused problems for the Town defenders, sending in a cross for May to head on to another player only for the keeper to smother. Robbie and a defender confronted each other amidst the pressure exerted from the home side. His second was to be his final goal of a terrific season, seeing him collect sixteen League goals plus two Cup strikes. The result pleased Harry Griffiths enormously, terming his team "football purists". Three days later and another home game produced a 2-1 victory against strugglers Huddersfield Town. They employed a defensive game when they came to the Vetch on a Tuesday evening game attended by 9,613. Ultimately that failed thanks to headed goals from experts May and Charles. Not a stunning spectacle as a game, it was the result that proved terrific. Oddly, a seventy-year-old gentleman died as the start of the match, repeating the same occurrence by another man at the recent Halifax fixture. With four games remaining, the final one in April was an away visit to soon-to-be-relegated Workington. Taking both points, thanks to a 1-3 score, the Swans completed another League double, this time against opposition that exited the Football League at the season close. Admirably, Swansea came back from being behind in both games, fully aware that they needed to keep winning and hope for others around them to drop points. Robbie contributed to the equaliser by crossing to striker Gary Moore, recently struggling with injuries, who managed to score.

May saw three games left: home to Rochdale and Watford and finally, away to eventual champions Cambridge. Rochdale came to Wales and lost 2-3; two from Alan Curtis and immensely enjoyed by the 10,689 crowd, keen to see if Robbie and his Swans could attain promotion. Perched in fourth position in the table, it was looking good. Again our Mr James was instrumental in contributing much to the game, setting up one of the three goals. Four days later on 7 May, Watford provided the final opposition to be seen at the Vetch Field, where 11,000 watched them destroy Swansea 1-4 after advancing to a 0-4 lead before a consolation goal arrived via Jeremy Charles. Robbie worked hard, hitting the side netting at one point but defensive bloopers caused the damage. Watford completed their own double over them after beating the Welsh side 2-0 in December at their place. Finally, a week later, Swansea travelled to Cambridge and came away with a commendable 2-3 victory. Another brace from Curt, making it fourteen League goals for him this season supplemented by another six in Cup games including a hat-trick against Newport County in the Welsh Cup. Charles scored the other goal, concluding his total for the campaign at twenty-three plus another three Cup goals capping a remarkable first full season as a professional.

Swansea City finished in fifth position in Division Four, behind Bradford City, Colchester United and Cambridge United. Cruelly robbed of promotion by a single point, they won eighteen matches, drew eight and lost the remaining twenty: although the manager felt that the pressure got to some of his playing staff. With the Robbie-Curtis-Charles goal machine accounting for fifty-three League strikes, at ninety-two, they were top scorers in the division (champions Cambridge collected five less). Although it meant another campaign in the bottom division, the club topped the Football League goal scoring chart, continuing the good form pre-dated by their manager back in the 1950s, when a player and the then-current Swans side scored ninety in the 1956/ 57 campaign.

With the disappointment of missing out on promotion still fresh in the minds of everyone at Swansea City, the club commenced another season of toil in Division Four. The lower divisions were notoriously difficult to get out of but the fortunes of those that did manage it usually saw success in the higher divisions.

Attendances at the Vetch for the 1977/ 78 season would rise by some 36% on the previous campaign. August saw an IRA terrorist campaign on mainland Britain in the same month that Elvis died. Whilst the King favoured jump suits in his later years, the Swans squad looked sharp in their snazzy Bukta branded kit, with its collar and v-neck in black, the club badge was now positioned in the centre of the chest. Particularly of note, was its new, circular design with a flat, black Swan at its centre. The strip proved to be popular with the fans and is still fondly remembered by many today. Supporters could wear a Swansea scarf purchased form the club shop at £1.15 whilst local business concerns could sponsor a home game for £300. A more economical alternative was to sponsor the match ball; at a cheaper £15 fee. Commercial ventures were now proving invaluable and those at the club concerned with such were proving astute enough to recognise this, it being a boom time and financial necessity to develop such areas. Other endeavours included the introduction of the Cascade Club Lottery, whereby the purchase of a ticket offered the chance of scooping a regular £1,000 prize. The Swans players, including Robbie, would regularly be seen stiffly presenting the winning cheque to supporters in photos included in the match day programme.

The season opened with great controversy on Saturday 13 August with a League Cup visit from Swindon Town (followed three days later by the return leg at the County Ground). Admission cost from £1.50 / 80p, with an extra reduction for senior citizens but regrettably, it would be the events off the field that would capture the attention of most. Football grounds back in the 1970s could be hazardous places, with virtually no fan segregation. The Vetch and its surrounds, had suffered incidents of hooliganism before, during and after the

3pm kick-off that day. There was much violence, including Swindon youngsters seen scrambling over fencing to get at home supporters on the North Bank. Many believed that the events were premeditated, with some youths attending simply looking for a scrap. Astonishingly, the fighting on the terraces continued as Robbie and the other players ran-out on to the pitch, following on all afternoon whilst the game was being played. Stone throwing and the introduction of police dogs caused concern to club Secretary Gordon Daniels and the bombastic Malcolm Struel, the latter keenly advocating the rein-troduction of corporal punishment! Returning to the football, Robbie played in the number seven shirt in a disappointing 1-3 loss against their Third Division visitors. It didn't get any better in the return tie, which the Swans lost 2-1. The violence witnessed at the Vetch was not an isolated occurrence, as clubs across the country, in all divisions, would record similar skirmishes during the season.

A pre-season friendly with Salisbury found manager Harry Griffiths underplaying any promotion proclamations but he did

concede that he was "reasonably optimistic" about the coming campaign. Now the only manager in the Football League in charge of his home town club, Mr Griffiths introduced three new signings for the new season. One of them was Gary Moore, who picked up an injury in the friendly but went on to score against Swindon. He had experienced First Division football and along with his namesake, Kevin, would subsequently come under much criticism from fans during the season. Swansea had fallen 0-3 behind by half time before a Robbie cross was met by the head of the former Sunderland player.

Steve Potter made the first of his five appearances at number one this season in the League Cup defeat at the Vetch before Londoner Keith Barber replaced him for the return tie. Brought in from Luton Town, he became first choice after a poorly disciplined defence saw the end for his predecessor. Potter retuned in November but played no further part thereafter. The team performance at Swindon proved disastrous: awkward and hesitant in defence, tepid in midfield and blunt in attack it was capped by Robbie being dismissed along with an opposition player. This resulted in an automatic suspension meaning that he would miss the opening League game: away to Huddersfield Town on 20 August. Still only twenty, Robbie's ill-discipline stretched further the selection woes for Griffiths, in an already injury-ravaged squad. Jeremy Charles struggled with injuries but his goal against the Terriers proved a positive for his manager but young Charlo was not going to be the goal machine of the previous season. It was to be Alan Curtis, whose contribution here would prove invaluable, contributing a mammoth thirty-three goals alongside Robbie, who would collect seventeen, including a number from the penalty spot. Griffiths gave Robbie a severe reprimand and club fine, stressing that poor self-discipline would not be tolerated under his guardianship. The player's importance to the team was clear.

A score-less encounter at Town's place was a point lost for a Swansea contribution that deserved both points. Employing a 4-4-2 to incorporate a revised team selection, the manager termed his team's performance as "thoroughly professional".

After the well-earned draw with Huddersfield, Robbie was selected as substitute for the first League fixture at the Vetch, a Tuesday night meeting with Doncaster Rovers on 23 August. Producing a hearty 3-0 win, the game was attended by an impressive 6,284. This superseded the 5,878 that had seen the disappointing Cup encounter a week previously.

The super-efficient team performance against Donny saw the Swans a goal up on two minutes and Curt looking sharp in a game within which he scored via a terrific twenty-five yard shot ala Robbie James. A plethora of Division One scouts attended the match to monitor Curt as the Swans attacked well in the first half before a reverse in the second. For those foolhardy enough not to be at the Vetch that night, the New Seekers provided alternate entertainment at the Grand theatre. Rovers were fortunate not to concede more than three during a game where Robbie's future Stoke team mate Brendan O'Callaghan proved unable to penetrate a defence dominated by a battling Eddie May. Robbie entered proceedings as a second-half replacement for Dave Bruton, a versatile individual able to play either in defence or midfield.

With a gate slightly up on the recent Doncaster game, the Swans were offered as promotion favourites alongside Brentford, Watford and next visitors, Barnsley. In a much anticipated early season affair, the clubs had finished their respective previous campaigns closely and the Swans manager was keen for a continuation of his team's recent good form. It did, thanks to a 2-1 victory against a team that featured future managers Neil Warnock and Mick McCarthy. Robbie was chosen in preference to Charles.

Without any added Cup commitments until November, September saw a half-dozen fixtures for the Swans, commencing with a 1-1 at Darlington watched by a lowly 1,778. A hard-fought draw found Robbie back in his erstwhile number eight shirt and enjoying seeing his side score first. Dominating possession for most of the first half, the second proved very different for Darlington, yet to see a victory this season. Arguments in the Swansea rearguard led to tempers boiling over and resulted in Curt and Robbie being dispatched in attack, whilst the back-four sought to keep the opposition out. A win at the Vetch, against Rochdale saw Curtis in buzzing form whilst a Monday evening defeat at Roots Hall, home of Southend United, now found the Swans playing Saturdays, Mondays and Friday evenings. The Rochdale game proved an aggressive encounter, complete with bookings, whilst it was a cross from Robbie that was met by the head of May in the first minute to put the Swans 1-0 up. Ed had been advised by Griffiths to conserve his energy rather than keep dashing up for crosses, as was his wont. It proved to be the first of his two goals this season, and by the close of the campaign he would retire from playing in favour of a coaching position at Leicester City. May's opening strike was followed more than an hour later by goals from Charles and Curtis, before the Swans attack was stifled and long-range efforts followed. Robbie was involved in a move with Charles which put the Swans 2-0 up.

Robbie sustained a groin injury during this period but both he and Pat Lally were used in a 2-0 victory over Grimsby Town despite neither player being fully fit. The former had picked up his niggle in the Southend game and his chance of playing against Town had looked unlikely. The game produced the biggest crowd of the season so far and saw a penalty by Robbie beat the keeper purely by its sheer force. He also had a 1-on-1 with him but was beaten to the final ball. Grimsby, relegated from Division Three back in June, would see Robbie score against them in the corresponding away fixture in April.

Illness within the ranks saw the Swans clipped 1-0 away at Newport in the first of their four battles with their Welsh cousins this season. On paper it was a surprising defeat for Swansea City against a dogged opponent that included Ernie Woods, a Vetch transfer target previously. He kept the visitor's defence busy throughout a game which found the Swans unable to make their chances count against Colin Addison's boys. Groin and knee injuries for the battered Robbie saw him limping within the first five minutes and contributing little until being substituted in the second half by new pro Nigel Dalling. The Newport game saw the poorest performance of the new campaign from the Swans, with a rear guard run ragged, whilst the midfield succeeded in proffering opportunities only to be wasted by misfiring forwards.

October was an important time for the club, as Griffiths was coming under heavy pressure to get his team up the table. He acknowledged that the standard of play that he demanded was not being attained at present but he remained convinced that an improvement would be forthcoming. But the question being, was would he still be in the job by this unspecified time? The month saw the continued progression of Anthony James and Nigel Stevenson as exciting, young first-team talent, with the seventeen-year-old Anthony joining his cousin in the first team across a number of games this season. After coming off in the Newport game, Robbie subsequently struggled in the away trip to Scunthorpe three days later, being replaced by Anthony! Losing the match 1-0, the Swans manager was pleased by the display put in by his team and enjoyed the compliment awarded by an attending First Division scout, there to report on Curtis.

Following the loss of recent leads against Darlington and Southend, players and coaching staff met to discuss their concerns soon after, in an attempt to address concerns. The Swans were well beaten by a strong United side that would gain promotion by the season finale, in a hugely competitive game between two of the more cultured football sides in Division Four. Amongst the crowd was future Swansea boss John Bond, here manager of a promising Norwich team.

A fit-again Robbie missed the first of two consecutive home games, beginning with Aldershot but he would play in the next game, against Southport. The 1-0 win in the former came from a rare Curt penalty, after a foul on big Eddie resulted in a defeat for an opposition that had previously enjoyed a 100% away record. Robbie had scored against them in last season, a 4-2 home win.

James would make it into the history books as the youngest footballer to play across 100, 200 and 300 League games whilst his Swansea team mate May reached 500 appearances in this, his final season.

Southport would finish towards the bottom of the division by the end of the season but managed to hold the Swans to a 1-1 draw, due in part to the bluntness of their host's attack. October saw the announcement that Swansea City Football Club had made an operational profit last season amounting to £12,221; the first time they had been out of the 'red' in thirteen years. Interestingly, the total was not influenced by transfer fees, something that John Toshack would be held accountable for during his reign as manager from 1978 onwards. Still a Liverpool player, Tosh was in the Wales squad to play Scotland, with Curt in reserve, this month.

Results were proving erratic for the Swans and an away trip to eventual champions Watford offered little; they were beaten 2-1 by the division pace setters, watched by an impressive 10,252 gate. Despite the loss, they must have been doing something right, as the home fans booed their own team during this challenging encounter which saw solid defending stifling many attacks. The Hornets had been somewhat of a hoodoo side for Swansea after ending their previous promotion hopes via a 1-4 thrashing at the Vetch. By the time of their return visit to West Wales, in March 1978, things would be different in a six goals extravaganza. York City, the next visitors to the Vetch Field, had recently been relegated from Division Three and had collected eight points against the fifteen gathered by the Swans when they played out a 1-1.

Five wins from their initial thirteen fixtures saw the pressure mounting on the manager, who dropped Robbie in exchange for a new outfield formation away at Stockport County. It didn't work as they lost 2-0, with Griffiths describing his team's performance as "dreadful". Meanwhile Robbie found himself selected for the reserves, where he joined his cousin in a 3-0 win over Pembroke at the Vetch, with the former nabbing one of the goals. Both Robbie and Jeremy Charles were experiencing an inevitable purple patch of poor form coupled with niggling injuries and so far, Robbie had scored one goal and Charlo, three.

For Griffiths, flexibility in the type of playing style that he sought his team to incorporate sometimes produced mixed results. Showing concern, he needed his misfiring players to realize their potential and that was what they did in the final game of the month, a 2-1 at home against Reading. One of the goals came from Harry's namesake, Jeff, a Swansea-born youngster who had signed professional terms this season. A recalled Robbie was back in at number eight.

The Swansea board decided to make a managerial change in October and so Harry Griffiths was asked to step down along with coach, Roy Saunders. In charge since January 1975, many fans were furious at his dismissal but this was not quite the end of the story for 'Mr Swansea'. It would be made public that Colin Addison had decided to remain at Somerton Park rather than become the next Swans manager and so Griffiths was reinstated as caretaker manager. Now aided by new player-coach and club captain, Eddie May, this Epping-born player was coming to the end of his career and was devoting so much of his time to coaching that his own fitness was affected.

Their first game together was a Bonfire night trip to meet League newcomers Wimbledon, with the clubs sharing the points after a 1-1. The Swans should have sealed a win by half time but missed ample opportunities.

A morale-boosting thrashing of Crewe on a cold and rainy afternoon in Swansea was highlighted by a hat-trick from Alan Curtis. Kick-off had been brought forward to avoid the power cut that would directly affect the ground later that day in a month that also saw a national firefighters strike. Bookings were received by both May and Robbie in an agitated encounter between the clubs.

Robbie remained in his customary number eight shirt in all but one of the next twenty-eight League games and he put in a splendid display in the 0-2 away win at Brentford. The Swans would enjoy a domestic double over the Londoners, beating them at the Vetch in March. A thirty-yard attempted goal hit by Robbie was disallowed for offside whilst his future manager Mr May did well in defence. Remarkably, it was the first away win of the season for Swansea in a nasty Griffin Park affair saved by sharp strikes by Curt and a speedy Micky Conway.

A welcome respite from the League presented itself on 27 November with a visit to Isthmian League part-timers Leatherhead. Part of a busy F.A Cup first round afternoon where some forty games produced ninety goals, this match was not one of them: it ended 0-0. The Surrey-based Tanners put their visitors under much pressure and Robbie's own defensive capabilities were ably demonstrated by his perfectly-timed tackle on the stroke of half time. His interception prevented a certain goal for Leatherhead striker Baker playing for a club with a pedigree for beating League opposition. Progress in the competition had eluded Swansea in recent seasons; the last occasion that they had enjoyed a win being back in January 1972. Griffiths was sure that his team could beat them and Robbie put in a great performance at Fetcham, watched by a crowd totaling 3,000. The draw necessitated a Tuesday night replay back at the Vetch where goals from Charlo and Curt resulted in a 2-1 victory watched by a healthy if chilly, 7,235 spectators. Robbie, Lally and Charles saw much of the ball in the heart of a midfield struggling on a difficult surface recently overcoming a frost.

Attacking midfielder Anthony James joined Robbie on the Vetch pitch as a second half sub in a stinging, 4-2 reverse against Northampton. Poor defending combined with a problematic playing surface, conspired to lose them the game. Robbie had a starring role in the match, despite the result, seeing a header go close and a thirty-five yard speculative strike fly wide. One of those dedicated professionals unafraid to put his body on the line, Robbie unfortunately collided with the goal post during the game. He would later experience a similar moment in a game against Cambridge United. Wales team mate Ian Rush recounts this in his autobiography, cheekily adding that the upright came off worse! Returning to the Northampton match, Robbie was playing in midfield alongside another teenager, Jeremy Charles, and the two would enjoy a long association as team mates and future opponents. Later at Q.P.R, he faced Robbie in the Milk (League) Cup final, when the former was an Oxford United player. The two James boys might have made it as professionals but not for other youngsters at Swansea, namely Nigel Dalling and Mark Grey, who both left the club in 1978.

The Halifax away game was the first of six matches played by the Swans across a twenty-three day period. Town was a team nestled at the bottom of Division Four, whilst their visitors were eleventh but Swansea fell 3-0 behind. Rob was heavily involved in creating chances for his team, hitting the crossbar twice and forcing a save and a subsequent corner kick. Working hard, he scored in injury time thanks to a powerful shot from outside of the area which managed to penetrate a congested goalmouth. A revitalized Robbie James was back to his scintillating best after a couple of Welsh League games.

Defeating Cardiff City in the 2008 F.A Cup final might have delighted partisan Swans fans but back in 1977, Portsmouth were a soon-to-be-relegated Division Three side preparing for the visit of Swansea City in a second round tie at Fratton Park. Anthony joined Robbie in midfield and after taking the lead thanks to a returning Alan Curtis, he and Curt almost succeeded in combining for a late winner with the score at 2-2. Only a brave save from the Pompey keeper foiled the advancing Curt, chasing a perfectly-pitched ball from Robbie's boot.

A leaky Swans defence had conceded nine goals in the last three fixtures and would add to this tally in the Tuesday night Vetch Field replay. The James boys were again selected for this match, which was won 2-1 by the Swans. Another tantalising showing from Robbie saw him tanking toward the opposition goal and causing all manner of problems for Portsmouth. He almost scored with one of his trade mark booming shots, this time smashing off the post only for team mate Gary Moore to follow-up with the goal that put them into the third round. A crowd of 8,844 was the biggest of the season so far.

Robbie, married this year to first wife, Yvonne, would have had to inform his new spouse that the Swansea playing staff would be required to make their way to a Gower retreat on the evening of Christmas day, to prepare for two oncoming matches: a Boxing Day visit from Torquay United and a day later, a trip to meet AFC Bournemouth. Already the team had fulfilled twenty-six various Cup and League fixtures.

So whilst Dad's Army star Clive Dunn was smashing box office records in Cinderella at the Grand Theatre, Robbie and his team mates faced high-flyers Torquay. He collected his second penalty success of the campaign, his third goal of the 1977/ 78 seasons in the 1-1 holiday draw. He also hit the crossbar late on. The next day saw the team bus make the journey to the seaside worthwhile, thanks to a goal by Moore. Coincidentally, namesake Kevin, would score the winner at the Vetch in the corresponding meeting; also a 1-0.

Jubilee year was not quite finished as the Swans had a New Year's Eve visit to Hartlepool and departed with a resounding 0-4 away win collected. Five goals scored against nil conceded in their closing two games made December's departure somewhat worthwhile.

Harry Griffiths had been in the game long enough to know how cruel it could be but he was happy to return as caretaker boss, decreeing that he had no personal ambition to take charge but originally took the post because he cared about the future of his beloved Swans. And so the forty-six-year-old returned. Finding the job demanding, Harry would offer that the club needed a young, track-suited manager to fill the role but until such time, he continued, assisted by Eddie May.

The partnership ploughed on with a Monday evening visit of Wimbledon, making their first appearance at the Vetch for an aggressive encounter watched by 9,700 on the second day of 1978. "Please come early to avoid congestion" suggested the advert in the local paper, and for those that did, they saw a typical attempt on goal from Robbie early on, a long-range shot. After drawing back in November, the Swans made no mistake this time. Future 'Crazy Gang' manager Dave Bassett endured a nightmare of a game and was solely responsible for two of the three goals conceded by his team in a 3-0 defeat. Robbie scored via the penalty spot, after an infringement upon hard working striker, Kevin Moore. It was the first of three goals that he would score in the opening weeks of 1978. January was another fixture-packed month and it saw the Swans play seven games, including F.A Cup, Welsh Cup ties and in the League.

A week later saw Swansea City F.C roundly beaten by mid-table, Division Three side Walsall on a third round F.A Cup weekend that also saw Division Two strugglers Cardiff City exit the competition. Having slipped 4-0 down, the industrious Robbie scored a late consolation goal after Moore and Chappell had combined well to set him up. The Welsh side had been held as underdogs against the Saddlers, a club that had beaten them on three previous occasions in the Cup. In spite of his midfield exploits, the Swans were 2-0 down by half time in a pulsating match seeing ample chances go begging.

Robbie had yet to enjoy winning the Welsh Cup but he would soon advance to grasping the beautiful trophy both as a Swan and Bluebird player. This season saw elimination by Newport County in a fifth round replay at Somerton Park, from which Robbie was suspended. The previous day had seen him obliged to attend an F.A.W disciplinary commission in Cardiff, having reached twenty penalty points this season. He did play in the goal-less affair at the Vetch, previously. Both clubs were prospering in Division Four but the need to bolster the squad with a new striker/ midfielder was clear. The Swans played nine Cup games and won only two times this season.

He saw a great deal of the ball, something that he always wanted, in the enjoyable 1-0 home triumph over Huddersfield Town. It was he who instigated a goal mouth scramble within the first five minutes of kick-off, involving a number of players but not resulting in a goal. It all stemmed from an initial shot from the midfielder which the keeper was unable to hold. A point was added in a subsequent away draw at a cold Doncaster; in a game that should have been won. After beginning the month with a goal, Robbie closed it with another, a late penalty, in a 2-1 defeat by Darlington on a heavily-sanded Vetch Field: it was his sixth of the season. An underperforming team showing emphasised the absence of top scorer Alan Curtis whilst the fans berated the players. Robbie was back in a midfield role with Chappell and Bartley and did have efforts on goal, including a move where he beat three players only to see his shot turned away by the keeper. Another opportunity presented itself in the second half but was again thwarted by the keeper.

Having endured a laborious gap between games due to adverse weather conditions, the frustrated Swans had suffered three postponements before a 17 February match was played at the Vetch. Coming after the disappointments of Darlington, they faced the same team for the fourth time: Newport. Strikes from Conway and Evans were concluded by a Robbie brace watched by a 6,056 crowd, the win somewhat making amends for their recent Welsh Cup exit.

With Swansea City in the market for new players to strengthen a squad lacking in fire power, an underwhelming bid of £165,000 from Sunderland for Alan Curtis was rejected. However, it would not be long before the ambitious Curt left.

A 2-2 away at Aldershot and a 2-1 defeat at Rochdale concluded a mixed four weeks for the Swans. After thirty League fixtures played and a further sixteen remaining, the team had won thirteen, drawn eight and lost the remainder. However, in amongst the lowly 1,057 spectators at Rochdale for a Monday night game, was a twenty-eight-year-old who would soon have a major impact on the club. His name was John Toshack.

Harry Griffiths had felt that the club needed a young manager able to balance the multi-tasking position such that he had found himself working in. Coming in the early months of 1978, Griffiths, in his third season in charge, was to resign twice but advocated that the new man would need to possess the zeal and energy needed to motivate the staff at the club. Malcolm Struel stated Swansea was seeking a managerial candidate, "of the highest caliber." And by mid-February, Colin Addison was announced as their primary target. Chelsea manager Eddie McCreadie and Newcastle's manager had by this time already turned down the vacancy. McCreadie had been at the Vetch during this month to see the Swans crush Addison's Newport side 4-0 but chose to remain at Stamford Bridge.

Towards the end of the month in a snow-struck Wales, the name of John Toshack is first motioned for the Swans vacancy. The 7p Swansea Evening Post incorrectly reported his decision to see out his playing contract with Liverpool, only a month after he failed a medical with Belgian side Anderlecht and with it an £80k transfer fee. In fact, John had received offers from a number of clubs keen to take on a man who had alongside Kevin Keegan, made up the top scoring duo in Division One. Writing in his autobiography, he professed that he wanted to return to Cardiff City as a player or in a player/coach mode although City boss Jimmy Andrews decreed that Tosh was too expensive for the Second Division Bluebirds. Andrews also pondered his lack of formal coaching qualifications but tellingly, Toshack felt that his prospective involvement was viewed as a threat to those already there. He famously quipped that the City boss, in charge at Cardiff since 1974, should view his First Division Championship medals, F.A Cup, U.E.F.A Cup and Charity Shield trinkets as advocates of his relevant vocational suitability. Tosh had left the Bluebirds in 1971 for a record transfer fee of £100,000 but in the present day, Cardiff was in a poor financial state, losing £5,000 a week and rooted to the bottom of Division Two. They resorted to a "Save City" fund, similar to the Swansea scheme some years later and continued the struggle for all Welsh clubs this decade. Curt states that Tosh was interviewed at Cardiff in early-1978 but claims that John assumed it was for the manager post, not assistant. Whatever the actual truth and despite his rejection of playing there on loan some months earlier, John Toshack was not to return to Cardiff City F.C. He also rejected a player-manager role with Hereford United (where John Charles had enjoyed a similar role in the mid-1960s) after hearing that fellow Anfield team-mate and future Swan Tommy Smith had already declined the post. Norwich, Leicester and Newcastle were also said to be after the Welsh international.

A sponsorship commitment with sports goods company Gola, at a hotel in Swansea took John's attention away from the Cardiff debacle. Looking at some team photos featuring Robbie at Swansea, the company had established links to the club as one of their branded sports bags can clearly be seen. The idea of working with the Swans would first be formulated by Struel, after the latter had heard about the event on his local radio station. After making only four appearances in the first part of the 1977/78 season for Liverpool, alongside Messrs Griffiths, Daniels and Struel, the appointment was sealed after Toshack had seen the away defeat at bottom-of-the-table Rochdale. Alan Curtis states that along with Jeremy Charles and Robbie, he had bumped in to Tosh in Swansea town centre but that the Wales star denied the speculation that he was to become the new Swans manager. But a couple of days later he was revealed as being just that! Rochdale collected their first win since Boxing Day, via a 2-1 final score, with victory coming partly due to the visitors missing a multitude of goal scoring opportunities. Emlyn Hughes had accompanied Tosh to the game and justifiably questioned the decision by his room-mate to take on the player-manager role on offer. Tosh was convinced that the time was right for him to be at the club and soon set about bringing in ex-Swansea player Terry Medwin, as his assistant. The two had known each other professionally since the 1960s when Tosh was a rising star at Cardiff City. Terry, who had played alongside Harry Griffiths as a Swan, had recently been working as a coach with Cardiff City and his arrival was well-received with much respect shown by the players. The new player-manager made it public that he would not have taken the job if Griffiths was not retained. Harry switched to youth development, where he was soon said to be enjoying his new role. Harry had nurtured the young Alan Curtis, and at one point even had him lodging with them at the family home. Nigel Stevenson, a player who would make his name under Toshack, worked with the two Harry's: Gregg and Griffiths, and reflects on his then-new boss, "Tosh was way ahead of most managers in his game plans and training methods."

By March 1978, the club had fifteen games of the season remaining and found itself in fifth position in the division, on thirty-four points. Some way behind leaders Watford, five behind second place Southend, with Barnsley and Stockport immediately above them. A lucky seven games were pencilled-in for the club across the month commencing with the visit of Graham Taylor's Watford. Despite seeing the recent woeful defeat at Rochdale, Tosh was keen to learn his trade as a manager by taking his first step with Swansea. He kept his opening team selection private until before the kick-off on the Friday evening, in the same week as the Rochdale game played on Monday. Watford, leading scorers in the League with sixty-one goals scored at home and twenty-seven away, should have made it obvious that the match might produce goals. It did, ending 3-3 after the Swans had sped to a 2-0 lead before slipping to a 2-3 deficit. With a mere seven minutes remaining Curt scored a priceless equaliser in a match that had seen Robbie affected by an early injury. Things had changed from their previous meeting at the Vetch, where Watford put in four goals across fifteen minutes and won 1-4.

Toshack was amazed by the strength of home support exhibited during the game, "With that kind of backing, there is nothing that cannot be achieved here."Beset by injury, worsened on his debut, the Wales international still had a great deal to offer after seven years at Anfield.

Continuing the high attendance, this time 11,316 filled the Vetch to see a goal-less Tuesday evening affair with Southend four days after the Watford game. Although ending in a draw, the Swans did not look like a side that would lose the game. It found Robbie trying various times to break the deadlock in a game which the injured Tosh made him captain. The new manager felt that his team should have won both games and although he may have proved a divisive character, he was keen to make the Swans a collective. Upon arrival, he was amazed to see that the players brought in their own training kit. "Before he arrived," remembers Stevenson again, "we used to have one bar of soap between twenty pro's cut up into one cm strips and shared out. We had to take our own kit home to wash and darn until Tosh took over and had washing machines plumbed in and new training kits. This made you feel a part of something big was about to happen under him." Other improvements introduced included transport for the players to travel to training.

Two second half penalties conceded after they had gone 1-0 up against a York City side languishing at the bottom of the table saw the Swans lose 2-1 with both James cousins in the starting XI. With Swansea in eighth position in the division, and their visitors, Stockport, in sixth, Tosh finally enjoyed his first win, a 3-1 at home with goals from himself, Curt and a penalty from Robbie in a game which saw a sterling performance from the player-manager. Meanwhile Reading were defeated by a brace of penalties scored by Robbie with another two from team mates Curtis and nineteen-year-old Stephen Morris combining to record the double over the Royals. Away at Elm Park, Swansea fell 1-0 behind before a Robbie penalty came a little before half time. It was the first of two almost identical strikes. Future Swansea City favourite Leighton James, then a Q.P.R player, as Robbie would later be, was at the game and was impressed with Wales team mate Tosh and his new club.

Robbie missed only his fourth League game of the season, through injury, in another 1-0 and double extracted in terrible conditions at Bournemouth at the close of March. Whilst the Swans hit a rich run of form with a 2-4 win at Torquay achieved despite being handicapped with a long injury list.

A mammoth nine games would be played in April, the final month of the season, seeing the club win five of them and with Robbie contributing six goals. A half-dozen victories were attained; twenty-three goals scored and in only eight games out of fifty-four League / Cup fixtures did the Swans fail to score.

Recent Swans skipper George Smith had left the club in the previous November, to take up a player-coach role with fellow Division Four side Hartlepool. Bringing his new team to a virtually grassless Vetch for an April Fool's day fixture, little did he realise what the next ninety minutes had in store. Perhaps the 4-0 defeat at Victoria Park back in December might have been an indicator that more was to follow. Two goals from Curtis and Kevin Moore had done the damage that day but the return was going to see something quite unique: a double hat-trick.

Watching televised matches nowadays, you will often see a player clutching the match ball after scoring three goals although in this fixture, Swansea would produce an 8-0 win with both Robbie and Curt scoring a hat-trick! Alan was magnanimous enough to offer the souvenir to his team mate, seeing that he had previously collected one against Crewe, back in November. Between them, the duo would contribute fifty-one of the ninety-six goals scored by the team across the season. It was the biggest win for the Swans in more than forty years and produced a Man-of-the-Match showing from Robbie James. He scored twice in the first half, including one from the penalty spot and his third came in the second half: on nineteen minutes, thirty minutes and eighty-one minutes. Not only that, he set up goals for Curtis and Lally during a game which delighted the 6,961 spectators. Smith, whose club would finish the season third from bottom, was seen castigating his team mates as the goals flew in. Afterwards Robbie and his club mates were taken to watch the latest Merseyside derby, as guests of Everton. Of course, Toshack would go on to bring many players and backroom staff from both these clubs to join in his Vetch revolution. In the dressing room, the new man got his players believing in their abilities.

Remaining in the area, the Swans next met Southport on 4 April, coming away with a 0-3 win with Anthony James opening the scoring with an important goal, helping to settle the team after a battling first half. With seven games remaining, following six games without defeat, Crewe beat the Swans 2-1 and poor Toshack suffered a concussion. Changes at the club proved decisive for a number of players already at the Vetch, one suffering being Eddie May. Selected by Toshack after his arrival, the latter informed Ed that he would be taking over the captaincy to which the pragmatic May agreed. It seems that Tosh was concerned with the amount of influence that Eddie exerted amongst the other players but for Ed, relieved of his coaching duties, he carried on playing and was happy to be selected by the new boss.

Two goals from Robbie at Barnsley saw the Swans take away both points in a 0-2 away win and with it, add another League double. Robbie's first goal came thanks to a poor clearance punch from the keeper which fell straight to him and he made no mistake with a right foot volley from all of twelve yards out. His second was as a result of Alan Curtis succeeding in splitting the defence on seventy-six minutes. The team effort pleased their new manager immensely during an important week for the club with three games across a week (11 April onwards). Watched by Barnsley's biggest gate of the season, the Swans moved on to play a Brentford team doing well in the division. Robbie's team was fourth in the division, a point ahead of rivals Barnsley and saw them win 2-1 at the Vetch and another League double enjoyed by the Swansea supporters. It was the two hundredth League appearance for Robbie and was watched by the highest attended match of the season, a gate of 16,140. A case of whisky was presented to hat trick stars Robbie and Curt before the match, in recognition of their endeavours against Hartlepool. Against Brentford, Robbie had chances to score but didn't manage to do so but contributed much to the team.

Now with four games remaining, Grimsby beat the Swans 2-1 with a Robbie goal not proving enough to prevent a defeat against opposition that they had beaten 2-1 in August. The lads suffered with a delayed journey home after the match due to a flat tyre experienced by the team coach. Another away defeat arrived at Northampton where the Cobblers won 3-1 after a 4-2 defeat for the Swans earlier in the season. A goal down on two minutes, a growing injury list proved debhillitating for the Swans. Despite probing from Robbie during the game, it was the second defeat in four days for the club at a stage of the season when they had been doing so well. With two games left, they needed three points to attain promotion in games with Scunthorpe and Halifax (remembering that this was when two points were awarded for a win).

Football was put in perspective with the death of Harry Griffiths at the Vetch on the morning of the Tuesday match with Scunthorpe. The players decided to go ahead with playing the game, in tribute to him, and they did him proud thanks to a 3-1 win seen by 12,288. Before the kick-off, the players gathered around the centre circle and heads lowered, fell silent. Wearing black armbands as a mark of respect, the returning Curtis, a Griffiths protégée, helped his team to two goals in the first four minutes of the game. Harry collapsed whilst treating Les Chappell in the treatment room in his role of club physio.

Tosh was known to be very tactically aware and his teams incorporated an attacking style but at this point he was struggling to contend with a mass of injuries to key personnel, including Robbie suffering from a knee injury acquired in the Northampton defeat. By the following season, he would sign a number of players to boost the small playing squad. Halifax would follow four days later at the Vetch in the corresponding fixture that had seen Robbie score the consolation goal in a 3-1 defeat back in December. However, here saw his team come away with a 2-0 victory in this the final game of the season. Lastly promoted back in the 1969/70 season, prior to the match, the Swans were positioned fourth in the table, two points behind Brentford, five behind Southend United and eighteen behind Watford before the kick-off. Town were known as draw experts but the Swans succeeded in breaking them down after more than an hour of play, when Toshack got a deflected goal and Curt tap-in sealed the win against the yellow and green-shirted visitors. It saw them pip Brentford to third place on goal difference in front of a Vetch crowd totalling 16,130. Robbie was given much time to move on the ball and did so with a number of attacks on the defence. He combined well with Tosh and Curt against opponents that would just avoid needing to seek re-election. As the whistle for full-time was blown, the Swans fans flooded onto the field to celebrate promotion and remained there until the players came out and acknowledged them from the Director's box. Swansea finished third on fifty-six points, behind Southend and Watford.

Robbie scored seventeen times this season, including one in a Cup match and a number by way of penalties: an impressive total but still a fair way behind the magnificent Curtis on thirty-three. Across the season, the Swans scored ninety-five goals whilst conceding sixty-two (only Liverpool scored more League goals). Cup progress proved mediocre this season with a third round exit in the F.A Cup and fifth round departure in the Welsh Cup. In a peculiar season, results were varied, including that astonishing 8-0 win against Hartlepool thanks to a Robbie inspired hat-trick. Swansea scored three or more goals in a match on thirteen occasions and their worst defeat was a 4-1 against Watford. Full international recognition with Wales was soon to follow for Robbie.

"Take me to the Vetch Field, way down by
the sea, where I will follow Swansea,
Swansea City."

The Ballad of Swansea Jack - Roger Evans.

The late-1970s didn't seem to be a glamorous time for football players like Robbie, making a living in the lower divisions. This period would see him and his wife Yvonne, whom he had married in 1977, zooming about north Gower in their Vauxhall Viva, whilst living in a bungalow in the little village of Dunvant. Familiar faces as neighbours included team mates Curtis, Waddle and Bartley. On into 1979, a special year for the young James couple as it saw the birth of their daughter.

For the 1978/79 pre-season warm-up games for Robbie and his Swansea team mates included playing a Liverpool Select XI up in Merseyside, at their Melwood training ground. A young Sammy Lee was in the Reds team and would join Robbie later at Q.P.R. The Swans had drawn 4-4 with Everton and beat the Liverpool 1-2. They were then off to Scotland, where they ran-out against Dunfermline in a testimonial match, coming away with a 2-0 win. Robbie was combining well with Curt and Charlo in the game and things were looking good for the approaching Division Three season.

This was to be a momentous campaign for Robbie as it introduced his famous moustache to the world! Now resembling a P.E teacher or equally as fitting, a rugby player, he would forever be known for it. Although, whilst at Bradford, in the latter stages of his playing career, he could be seen both with and without it during the two seasons spent with the Bantams. Now wearing a new Bukta-manufactured kit, with a round neck, the away design was striking but more of that shortly. Fellow Division Three opponents Chesterfield and Southend each wore Bukta kits but both were very basic and uninspiring when compared to the elegant Swansea offerings.

Having gone up a division, there were many changes at the Vetch in anticipation of the new 1978/79 campaign. Somewhat lazily to be tagged Liverpool Reserves, Swansea City would soon have a number of Everton players in their ranks: Dai Davies, Gary Stanley, Neil Robinson and Bob Latchford against soon-arriving Liverpool names including Ian Callaghan, Tommy Smith, Phil Boersma and Alan Waddle. The squad needed both a central defender and midfielder and Smith and "Cally" were perfect fits. Both veterans were coming to the end of their careers but would contribute much to the progress being made at the Vetch Field. Each had enjoyed a summer spent playing in the U.S Soccer League and the prestigious netting of these experienced pros was highly valued by the Swans manager, not only for their on-field aptitude but also because their arrival presented the club with a shot in the arm. Their presence made training sessions a much anticipated event for the youngsters at the club. "I got Smith and Callaghan and they brought good habits into the dressing room..." commented the boss. Tosh believed that the signings proved that his quest for success was sincere since attaining his first goal of promotion out of Division Four. Both players were M.B.E. holders, something that their new manager would also be the recipient of soon enough. The Merseyside influx was not exclusive to Swansea City, as Newport County had a new manager, former player Len Ashurst, and had signed the prolific Tommy Tynan, who both hailed from the area. Tynan had previously played alongside Robbie during a loan spell at the Vetch a few seasons previously whilst Ashurst would manage Robbie at Weston-super-Mare F.C, some years later.

Allocated a transfer kitty Tosh brought in Alan Waddle and new keeper Geoff Crudgington, for £25,000 from Leicester City and £30,000 from Crewe, respectively. It would not be the last money spent during this season. The Swans still had a major investment on developing local talent, with a number breaking through this year, namely Chris Marustik, Nigel Stevenson, Dudley Lewis, Jimmy Loveridge, Chris Sander, Mark Baker and others. Still a teenager, Chris demonstrated his promise in the Harry Griffiths benefit match staged pre-season against an Everton Select. It proved particularly pertinent to Chris as 'H' had signed him originally and then Tosh took him on as a full-time pro. Robbie was in the Swansea squad for the game played on 26 July, with a certain Bob Latchford in opposition.

Ex-Spurs player Terry Medwin was assisting Tosh and had been since the close of the previous season, whilst Les Chappell took charge of the Reserves. Robbie found himself with the exciting prospect of playing against First Division big boys Tottenham Hotspur with its stars Glenn Hoddle and World Cup winners Osvaldo Ardiles and Ricky Villa. This early-season fixture was to record the highest home attendance of the season, as 24,375 packed into the ground for a stupendous League Cup tie on Tuesday 29 August. This second round meeting is mainly remembered for a crunching tackle by hard nut Smith on the slight South American debutant, Ardiles. Tommy, an elementary hard-man defender, left little Ossie squirming and his boss Keith Berkinshaw furious. "This is not a kid's game!" exhorted the old-school stopper in response to the furor generated after his first-minute lunge. Tommy's former manager at Liverpool, Bill Shankly, once said that Smithy could cause an argument in an empty room! Ardiles limped off early in to the second half. Swansea, then a Third Division team, went 2-0 up with goals by Robbie and Charlo while their visitors looked nothing like victors. Robbie's strike, an excellent volley, came from an Alan Curtis cross from the left to his centrally-positioned team mate. It was his eighth goal in five matches. Both men played exceptionally well. Tosh, wearing his managerial hat, had thrust local teenagers Morris and Stevenson in the heart of the defense, due to squad injuries, where they were both to perform admirably. Wearing their unusual, yellow away kit made by Admiral, a sparkling Hoddle penalty and further strike by Irish international Gerry Armstrong (who would also play for Watford at the Vetch in December 1980) leveled things. This, despite Swans goal keeper Crudgington putting in an excellent showing between the sticks for his new club. Gate receipts totalled £28,300 and were demonstrative of the interest in the tie. More excitement was to come in the replay at White Hart Lane, only a week later.

Stepping back to the opening game of the season at the Vetch, a 5-0 win against Division Four side Newport County, it saw a Robbie hat-trick and Charles brace overturn an earlier 2-1 away defeat in this first round League Cup meeting. Before the return leg in London, with Spurs, Swansea opened their domestic season with a trip to Colchester United which concluded at 2-2. Watched by a lowly 2,918 crowd, Robbie's season was off to a flyer, as he scored a brace in the game. Funnily enough, he would also score against them in the coming March fixture at the Vetch, too. The fans flocked to watch the team, beginning with 16,750 present for the opening League game, a 3-0 defeat of the Red Imps aka Lincoln City, a week before Spurs visited. How fortunes change, as in the previous season, they had beaten the Swans 4-0 and drawn at the Vetch. The attendance total would increase by more than a thousand for another home match, a 2-2 with Walsall in April. Re-arranged games late in the season, with Watford, Shrewsbury and Chesterfield topped this.

Robbie struck twice in the final League game of August, away at Oxford's Manor Ground, and he had now scored a terrific eight times across six games. From the 4,947 that attended that game, some 30,700 (or more, depending on your source) saw the "Glamour boys crushed by Welsh braves," as the Daily Express headline of 7 September, 1978 reported. The last time that the Welsh visitors had scalped a First Division club had been back in 1964 when Swansea Town astonished the football world by winning at Liverpool. Tottenham, recently murdered 7-0 by them, had last faced the Swans in1970. Now in charge for his first full season, Toshack selected a team that would exploit the Londoners' vulnerability in the air, made apparent in the previous game. Utilising the height of young Stevenson in midfield, Swansea City outplayed their hosts and ran out 3-1 winners. Collectively, goals by centre-half Tosh, Charles and Curt sank the mighty Spurs. With the Swans wearing their unusual yellow shirts, complete with two-coloured sash crossing the shoulder down to the side of the waist, the first goal, scored from the head of their player-manager, came on nineteen minutes and was thanks to a Robbie corner kick. The reason behind the design was said to relate to some kind of sponsorship with a local business (relating to the colours) but this cannot be confirmed. Whatever the reason for the design, it remains a classic shirt. They would occasionally wear it, one time being an F.A Cup replay with Woking. Back to the match, Robbie also had a part to play in the third goal. Maddeningly, they were then knocked out in the next round, in October, by a future club that Robbie would play for from mid-1984 onwards: Q.P.R. Watching from the stands was former Liverpool stalwart Ian Callaghan, who had been convinced to sign for the Swans after seeing the Spurs match.

After five League games played, including an impressive 0-2 away win at eventual runners-up Watford, the Swans had won three times. Tosh was keen to stress the importance of taking points against sides like Bury, defeated visitors at the Vetch in September thanks to goals from Robbie and Curt. The manager articulated the need to focus upon what he termed the "bread and butter business of League football". His goal against Lancashire side Bury was Robbie's ninth of the season and would be added to by in a 2-1, late-September win at home in which Toshack would be named Manager of the Month. Recent home games against Rotherham United and Tranmere Rovers must have been exciting to watch, as collectively, they produced fifteen goals! David Gwyther, a former Swan, now wearing the number eight shirt for Rotherham, scored a hat trick against his old club in an eventual 4-4. The visitors, who had recently defeated Arsenal in the League Cup, advanced to being 1-4 up before Swansea fought their way back and collected what the match summariser deemed, "a point where none seemed possible." Dai scored seventy-three times for the Swans across 1964-73 and afterwards said that he believed that the club would gain promotion, come May. The Swans continued with the goal frenzy by scoring four times again in a subsequent 4-3 victory against Tranmere. Attendances for those games had peaked at 16,000+ and Tosh and his players were especially appreciative of the inspirational level of away support. So far, the team had collected ten points from a possible twelve.

Then in the space of three days, the team lost twice, at Chester and then Carlisle; both via a 2-0 score line. Injuries to key personnel saw a direct affect upon team selection, with Robbie missing the Tranmere game. However, he was back to face the red and white stripes of Brentford at the end of the month. He stuck in one of the two goals scored in a pleasing 2-1 win. It was his final goal for the month and in the following one, he would only add one more to his total. Some thirty-two goals had been seen at the Vetch in this early part of the 1978/ 79 campaign, a half-dozen provided by Robbie.

October was an enjoyable month if you watched Swansea at home, as they won all three of their games. Robbie scored one of the goals in a 3-2 against the 'Stags' of Mansfield Town but it was the 4-1 success over Peterborough that provided the best team performance so far. All the games saw attendance figures reach five figures but away from home, the Swans faired less favourably. Q.P.R put them out of the League Cup, as previously mentioned, and Chesterfield also beat them, making it four defeats on the trot. The month ended with a 2-2 against Hull City. In amidst all these games, Robbie received his first full cap for Wales against Malta, in a mid-week international at Wrexham. Also in this month, Tosh took a Swansea squad including Robbie, to play against a Liverpool Select in the testimonial match for Chris Lawler. Tosh, Emlyn Hughes and Kevin Keegan guested.

The cultured Leighton Phillips, formerly of Cardiff City and Aston Villa, became the ninth player to make his League debut for the Swans this season after joining the club for £70,000 from Villa. He and Toshack had known each other since their Cardiff days, as well as being involved in the present Wales set-up. Neath-born Leighton played in the Welsh side that met Malta this season. He had collected fifty-eight caps and would add to this total whilst with Swansea.

After scoring home and away against Colchester, Robbie repeated this against Bury in November, providing the winner in a 0-1 victory. After a 1-1 with Oxford at the Vetch, the F.A Cup second round necessitated a visit from Southern League Premier Division side Hillingdon Borough. It was their first visit to the ground and one that they would remember, thanks to a 4-1 defeat. Robbie got the first goal, with Waddle adding, whilst young Jeremy Charles hit a brace before a crowd totaling 7,824. Waddle was a past squad and sometime Reserves player with Tosh at Liverpool, and he would contribute much to the team this season. Robbie's wife, Yvonne, would be joined by the wives of both Alan Curtis and Alan Waddle, with the birth of their babies in 1979.

December saw seven games for the Swans and it started off well with wins against Sheffield Wednesday and Southend United. Isthmian League side Woking came to Wales and held out to a 2-2 draw necessitating a replay. Swansea had scored thirty-nine times at home and sixteen away, by the time of this Cup match. Robbie got one of the five goals in the return, against a Woking team that had already played seven games to reach this stage. They lost 3-5 a.e.t, with late goals from Robbie and Alan Curtis (who collected a hat trick) and managed to cram in 4,800 into their ground to see the Swans in opposition. The Christmas holiday period wouldn't be the same without festive football and it was Bobby Smith's Swindon Town who would return to Wiltshire content with their 1-2 Boxing Day win. Attended by a 16,700 gate, Town would finish fifth in the division come May and Smith later worked with Swansea. A long trip up to Blackpool rounded off the year nicely with a 0-1 win for the Swans against the recently-relegated Seasiders.

A cold January 1979 saw many postponements for the Swans, with only a single match played at home and away. Bristol Rovers came to the Vetch and succeeded in putting the Swans out of the F.A Cup via a 0-1 win. Robbie and his team mates simply could not score in a Monday evening encounter within which visiting Welsh keeper Martin Thomas played well. The youngster would line-up alongside Robbie in his only full Wales cap, a 1-1 with Finland in September 1986. It was the first occasion this season that the club had not scored at home. Seventeen previous games had produced forty-two goals, six of those seeing more than four scored during the match. In the Rovers team that day was Gary Emmanuel, a latter team mate of Robbie's during his second spell with the

Swans. At the end of the month, Kidderminster got smashed 6-1 at the Vetch, with a hat trick from Robbie, a brace from Curt and one from Charles. Sadly, only 4,100 turned out to see the game. It brought his goal tally to seventeen; Charlo was on seventeen and Curt was on sixteen. Two draws at home and two defeats and an away draw, saw the Swans collect three points from a possible ten and concede more goals than they managed to score. The 2-2 at the Vetch with Chester provided familiar opposition for Robbie, as future Swans coach Doug Livermore and Wales international Ian Edwards were in their team. The latter had been selected to play alongside Robbie in the Malta international.

March produced the need to complete a ridiculous nine League and Cup fixtures, mainly re-arrangements of previously postponed games. In a season where a match day programme at the Vetch Field cost 15p, Toshack struck a stunning header in the 5-3 defeat of Hull City; a club that he had enjoyed scoring a hat trick against whilst a Cardiff City player in the decade before. John had scored one of the two Swansea goals against Chester, in the preceding League fixture. Alan Curtis, now a proven goal scorer, coupled with Waddle, both proved effective in the Swansea attack. Waddle closed the season as chief marksman. Phil Boersma, brought in from Luton Town, a team much admired by his new boss, had made his debut for Swansea back in December but had a wretched time with injury forcing his retirement from playing by the following April. Across four away games the Swans did not record a single win but Robbie scored in two of them (a Welsh Cup exit at Wrexham and a 2-1 loss at bottom-of-the-table Lincoln). After the win against Hull, Gillingham came to west Wales and got beat 3-1 at the Vetch. Watched by a gate of 10,832, the Gills would miss out on promotion this season, finishing a point behind the Swans. However, at the time of this meeting, they were a point ahead of them. The biggest game of the season came with the Elton John-backed Watford coming to play a re-arranged, Tuesday evening match on 20 March. The visitors were top of the table, four points the better of their hosts but saw the Swans complete an impressive League double over them, via a 3-2 win. Not surprisingly, the meeting produced the highest League attendance at the Vetch of the whole season: 19,867. A goal from Robbie proved to be the decider, after Curt had struck twice. An enthralling encounter, at one stage in the second half a stray dog somehow managed to get on to the pitch! Another Tuesday night fixture found Colchester United play at the Vetch after the Gillingham win. The Swans had already traveled to Layer Road back in August, when Robbie scored twice in a 2-2 and he extended his scoring ratio by contributing another goal in a 4-1 win. It was his twenty-first of the season and more would follow as the campaign reached its critical stage. Plymouth had not yet met Swansea during this long season but they did on the final day of March, the recipients of a 2-1 away defeat before taking the Swans to their ground in the final away fixture for them.

April marked the penultimate month of the season and with it home games with Shrewsbury, Walsall and Southend. Away matches would take the Swans to Tranmere, Sheffield Wednesday, Swindon Town, Blackpool and Mansfield. Robbie would contribute four goals to the cause: three away from home. Tranmere would suffer relegation this year, with a 1-2 loss against Robbie and the boys watched by the second lowest away attendance of the season. A goal-less encounter at Wednesday was superseded by a 1-1 at the Vetch with the eventual champions, Shrewsbury. Robbie snatched a goal in the game attended by 19,566. It came after they had lost the away meeting 3-0 back in December. A valuable 0-1 away at Swindon was seen by the third largest gate involving Swansea this season: the winning goal being scored by Robbie. Only the Cup games with Tottenham Hotspur and Q.P.R proved higher. Lowly Walsall, slipping out of Division Three by the season close, secured a point in a 2-2 at the Vetch, with two more home games remaining. Blackpool and Mansfield Town came next, both away, and Robbie scored in the latter, a 2-2. The 1-3 win against Blackpool recorded another 'double' for the Swans.

The Anfield Iron, Tommy Smith, had made 650 appearances for Liverpool across seventeen years but was now coming to the end of his career. He was to miss the last five games of the season due to injury and in one of them, at home to Southend, an Alan Waddle hat trick sealed a 3-2 victory; with the winner arriving in the dying moments. The win came five days after Mansfield where new dads Robbie and Waddle had scored.

A trip to Plymouth Argyle and additional home game with Chesterfield would provide the final two games in May. Supporters could buy a ticket for the special train laid on to take them on the lengthy journey at a cost of £5.50. The away fans boosted the attendance to 13,406. The players were most appreciative of the support and the match with the Pilgrims closed at 2-2, with goals from Curtis and the player-manager.

The game marked the first occasion that the Swans were featured on Match of the Day. The point saw Watford leapfrog Swansea to take the top slot in the division.

For the crucial fixture with Chesterfield, a team that had beaten Swansea City back in October, found the promotion race being pushed to the limit. Toshack recognized the amazing transformation within the club as they marched nearer towards Division Two after an absence of fourteen years. Former England school boy international and present Swans number 1 Geoff Crudgington completed his forty-sixth League appearance this season whilst the Chesterfield stopper Glan Letheren was to take over half-way into the following season. He subsequently worked at the Vetch as coach. The latter had played for Wales Youth alongside Robbie, previously. 'Crudge' had further developed his trade under the guidance of former Manchester United player and Swansea boss Harry Gregg at Crewe. Staged on a Friday night, this most memorable game found the Swans requiring a win to finish in the top three. After twelve minutes had passed, the visitors went 1-0 up until a Waddle equalizer came with ten

minutes remaining via an all-important headed goal. Advancing on into the second half and substitute Toshack replaced Attley and managed to connect his head with a Bartley free kick, to put the Swans into a 2-1 lead in the eighty-second minute. The home team was always in charge of the match but had been susceptible to a Chesterfield attack throughout. They held on to win and succeeded but needed to await the result of the corresponding Sheffield Wednesday v Swindon match which would have a direct bearing on who gained promotion. Rivals Swindon lost 2-1 and even missed a late penalty. Toshack was ecstatic and held his winning header as one of the most significant of his career. As the jubilant fans invaded the Vetch pitch at full-time, in the Swansea dressing room there was big praise for their player-manager, "Only Tosh could do that!" beamed assistant boss Terry Medwin in a timely, post-match interview. The Swans overcame their opponents in spite of facing a five-man Chesterfield defense that night and were strengthened by the introduction of their secret weapon as Alan Curtis deemed Toshack, from the bench. "The scenes after the match were tremendous,"reflected Wyndham Evans in his testimonial programme later, "The fans, magnificent on the night as they had been all season, gave us a marvelous ovation. The champagne flowed freely and most of us (players) were still in our kit long after 10pm, making the moments last as long as possible...The one regret I had was that the man who would have cherished those moments, Harry Griffiths, wasn't alive to see Swansea back in Division Two, somewhere he always felt they deserved to be..."

Total season attendance for the Vetch Field at 316,152 proved to be the highest in Division Three, the significance of which was expressed in a readers letter in the Post (16 May): "The quantity and quality of the support which was thundered out, was unquestionably to my mind the reason why Swansea won (against Chesterfield). The crowd lifted the team by its bootlaces and refused to believe it could lose."

The game was recorded for television and saw Robbie being interviewed post-match, "We started to sweat a bit after the last two results against Swindon and Shrewsbury; tonight was really great. Everybody in the town wanted us to get promotion and we're there, and I just hope that we can hold our own next year." The Swansea team against Chesterfield was Crudgington, Evans, Bartley, Stevenson, Phillips, Attley, Curtis, Waddle, Charles, Robbie, Callaghan. Super sub: Tosh.

A total of eighty-three Swansea goals were scored against sixty-one conceded in a campaign that found Shrewsbury win the championship followed by Watford, one point behind and the Swans in third position. The season was a propitious one for Toshack, as he netted fifteen times across all competitions; three of them coming in the last few League games. Many more goals are struck by the Swans throughout the ten month campaign with five players making it into double figures. The Toshack/ Curtis/ Robbie James trio hit sixty-one goals between them but it was a ratio not to be repeated in the oncoming season as Curtis left to join Leeds for a record £350,000 fee. The close of every season found Alan rumoured to be leaving and this one was no different. After pulling on the white shirt some 248 times and striking seventy-two goals, he finally did make the break away. His club manager and international room-mate was complimentary and did not wish to see him leave. Also in the news at the Vetch was the emergence of young Martin James, another cousin to Robbie, doing well in the Swansea schools team. He would later play at Llanelli when Robbie was associated with the club. As for Anthony, he could be seen sitting alongside his famous cousin in the team photo but would only be involved in a couple of first team matches and the remainder in the Reserves.

The players were able to enjoy a dinner at the Mansion house in Swansea given by the mayor to mark their achievement on Wednesday 16 May. Some five days after the success in gaining promotion found Toshack in cautionary mood, "We are all eager to progress even further," he informed the Evening Post, "but we must realize that the hard work is only just beginning." Of the forty-six League games played across the season Swansea won twenty-four, drew twelve and lost ten. Robbie had played in fifty-four of the fifty-seven fixtures this season, recorded two hat tricks and also became a full international with Wales.

"Be Proud to be a Swan."

New season arrivals joining Robbie on the playing staff at the Vetch for the 1979/ 80 campaign included Dave Rushbury, Tommy Craig and second cousin to the Swansea manager, John 'Josh' Mahoney. All three would make major contributions to the club in the coming Division Two campaign and were all purchased using the funds generated by the transfer of Alan Curtis to Leeds.

Tosh set about introducing changes to the team formation: seeing Jeremy Charles switching to a centre half role whilst the attack was realigned. By Christmas 1979 the manager had signed twelve players, including a trio of free transfers, since taking charge of the club back in March 1978. Although loathed to accept a season of consolidation, with a half-dozen new faces slotting into the team, this is what was to transpire.

Pre-season friendlies produced three wins but life in the Second Division was to be a lot tougher than anything previously experienced by Robbie and many of his team mates used to playing in the lower divisions. The club would now be playing against the likes of Q.P.R, West Ham United, Newcastle United, Leicester City and Fulham, not forgetting Welsh derbies with Wrexham and Cardiff City, both residents in the division. They had beaten a Liverpool Select by 1-0 as part of their ten day, pre-season tour which also included fixtures with Scottish clubs Raith Rovers and Dunfermline. The Swans had scored four times in these games before returning to the Vetch for training at the start of the second week of August. Unfortunately for Robbie, he had picked-up a knee injury during the second half against Raith which necessitated his exit. The knock impacted on his season, as would a groin and thigh strain.

It was to be a Robbie strike which provided the first goal in the new division for the Swans, in a 2-0 win against Shrewsbury Town at the Vetch on 18 August. Always proficient in heading the ball, it was an early opportunity that came Robbie's way which was well-saved by the keeper in a goal-free first half before his magical goal late in the game. Latching on to a Rushbury throw-in, Robbie advanced between two defenders before striking the ball within the narrowest of space and seeing it bend in between the posts. It was another superb piece of individual skill and combined with the veteran Craig playing behind him, the duo had their manager excited at the future, "People will come just to see what these two can do." He commented in his early programme notes, after signing a new, five-year contract with the club this same month. Watched by a pleasing gate totalling 17,400 the home supporters proved vocal, especially during the second half when the team was struggling. The slightly-built Craig had previously played at the Vetch for Scotland against Wales back in February 1975. Promoted as champions, Shrewsbury would subsequently knock the Swans out of the Welsh Cup at the semi-final stage early into 1980. The Shrews pitted themselves against Swansea on four occasions this season, losing the aforementioned 2-0 and drawing 2-2 at theirs in the League, as well as a further brace of 2-2 draws in the Cup.

Expectations were high for the newly-promoted Swans, as Leighton Phillips took on the captaincy from the now-retired Tommy Smith. Rushbury, a defender but also strong in attack, would prove to be a bargain buy since signing from Sheffield Wednesday for £60,000.

Back to the stylish Craig, he was known to have an exceptional left-foot shot and was a penalty-taker to rival Robbie whilst Mahoney was the regarded as the consummate professional. The traditional team photograph often included Swansea youngsters alongside the established pros and this year continued the tradition. Robbie was found in the second row, with his cousin Anthony looming over in the top set. Prior to the opening League fixture, the Swans commenced their season with two games against AFC Bournemouth in the League Cup, a week before. Supporters could pick up a match ticket from between £2.50 - £1.10, in anticipation of seeing the visit of a team with an awful away form: they had managed only three wins across the whole of last season. Their luck did not improve as they were beaten 4-1 with Robbie wearing the number nine shirt and Waddle hitting a hat-trick. The return tie at Dean Court ended goal-less, watched by 5,824; considerably less than the 13,500 that had seen the first.

Admission prices to the Vetch for the new campaign had been increased, with the team now wearing an Adidas-branded kit showing off a plain Swan without the 'Swansea City F.C' lettering or circle around it, as with the previous badge. A new club crest was revealed, featuring a large Swan swooping down on to the club name from above a castle. It had been created via a competition open to supporters: if only the foreign owners of neighbours Cardiff City had done similar in recent years!

Robbie played in the first four games of the new season before missing the next six due to injury, against opposition that included future clubs Stoke City and Q.P.R. Soon-to-be team mate Leighton James was then a Burnley player whose team didn't fair too well against the Swans this season.

Defeats against Luton and the other clubs named above came before Robbie was available for selection in a 0-0 away fixture with Notts County. As well as seeing the much-needed return of their talisman, the game also saw a debut in goal for Llanelli-born Glan Letheren following the transfer of Crudgington to Plymouth. Unfortunately, Robbie had to leave the field at County but he would prove fit enough to play in the next thirty-four matches in another season overflowing with fixtures.

A 2-0 defeat at the Vetch to Leicester City saw Robbie wearing the number eight shirt and after the game incidents of hooliganism were reported. Wins against Cambridge United and Watford arrived before a resounding 4-1 win against Fulham came at home. The clubs had a tradition of scoring lots of goals against each other and all the Swans strikes came from different players: including one from Robbie. Now free from injury, Robbie enjoyed a terrific performance; menacing the defense and being involved with three of the Swansea goals. In a game played at a frenetic pace, he had a number of scoring opportunities and provided the third goal on twenty-eight minutes. Advancing to 4-1 up after half-time, it was a Robbie header to lanky team mate Nigel Stephenson that had opened the scoring and a cross from Mr James was headed in to the Fulham net by one of their own players to send the Swans 2-0 ahead, previously. When his goal came, it was a surprise to the Cottagers keeper as Robbie reacted most swiftly to a Leighton Phillips free-kick by advancing to push the ball past the goalie. The visitors had now conceded twenty-two times away from home this season and would finish their campaign third from bottom.

Still struggling to find their feet in Division Two, the team had a week's break for international games before their next game, away at Birmingham City. Robbie, Tosh, Phillips and Mahoney flew to Germany on the Sunday after the Fulham game as part of the Wales squad to face West Germany in Cologne. Once there, they were heavily beaten, with a consolation goal from Alan Curtis not making the 5-1 score line any less palatable.

A disappointing 2-0 defeat at St Andrews came after the Swans had been on top for a good hour of the game before a poor last twenty minutes saw the goals leaked. The Blues would complete the double over Swansea this season, as well as gain promotion.

The 1979/80 season again produced some peculiar results, with Robbie providing both goals in a 2-0 win at the Vetch against Oldham Athletic contrasted with a 4-1 away loss in the coming March. He had now scored four times across ten appearances. A crowd totaling 12,654 saw his powerful headed goal, the first of two such strikes this season, in a match that found the Swans in complete control and one that only time would tell when they would score in (it took over an hour of play). "The James master class" was how the Evening Post deemed his commanding performance within which he managed to get a booking!

November saw a tough set of games commence with Shrewsbury, then Sunderland, West Ham and Newcastle. Robbie needed a complete rest from playing to help his thigh injury but with an away game at the Hammers coming up, he soldiered on. Another draw was produced with the Shrews before Robbie struck one of the three goals against Sunderland at the Vetch. After a manic first half, Robbie's goal was a perfect example of a striker's prowess: seizing the ball from a weak clearance and with no support around him, he was left to work the move alone and did so with aplomb: speeding past a defender and whacking a right foot shot which left the keeper powerless to stop. Enjoyed by a 15,826 attendance, the large crowd saw Robbie smash a rocket of a shot that almost disabled the opposition's young goalie Chris Turner. The keeper had faced the Swans in the previous season, as a Sheffield Wednesday player, when the Vetch crowd had enjoyed a pleasing 4-2 victory. Despite letting in a goal in the first minute, Swansea won the game 3-1 in a campaign that recorded average attendances of 14,000 but lesser for Welsh Cup fixtures. Regrettably, the Sunderland game also saw town centre problems with more incidents of hooliganism recorded during their visit. It was a trend that had noticeably increased at clubs nationwide.

The Hammers continued their dominance via a 3-2 victory at the Boleyn Ground before Robbie contributed one of the goals in a 2-3 loss at home to Newcastle that was seen by 15,442. The sides had not met in the League in more than a decade and the Swans slipped two goals behind before Robbie scored the final goal on ninety minutes, a cracker that delighted his manager but regrettably, a good second half performance was not enough to defeat the second visitors from the North east. Robbie had characteristically managed to take the ball past two defenders only to be foiled by the keeper. However, his goal came when he locked on to a long ball out from defense, wherein he avoided a tackle before looping a shot wide of the goalie. The Magpies were managed by Bill McGarry, a candidate to replace Harry Griffiths prior to Toshack being appointed player-manager.

A 1 December away defeat at Wrexham was toppled by a 1-0 win at home against Charlton Athletic prior to a trio of consecutive defeats by Chelsea (3-0 at Stamford Bridge), 0-1 at home to Orient and a 4-1 loss at Eastville to Bristol Rovers, on Boxing Day. After the Wrexham game, the squad was off to Southport for a couple of days with another practice match with Liverpool penciled in. At the time of Charlton's visit, the Swans were twelfth place in the table, out of twenty-two teams, with eighteen points collected. Chelsea was on twenty-five points and managed by World Cup '66 hero Geoff Hurst, had the contrasting talents of Ron 'Chopper' Harris and future Robbie team mate Gary Chivers in their side that day. The Orient game was played on a Friday night and marked the 700th League appearance by Ian 'Cally' Callaghan, who had scored a classy winner against Charlton, previously. The final game of 1979 for Robbie and his Swansea team was a visit from another World Cup winner, namely Nobby Stiles, and his Preston North End team. They came to the Vetch and left with nothing thanks to a 1-0 defeat. After completing twenty-seven League and Cup games so far, the season was proving to be a taxing one for all the staff involved with the club, with more preparation required than ever before for Tosh and his backroom staff. In the meantime, fans could pay a visit the club shop, where they were encouraged to buy a branded jumper as endorsed by Robbie in an advertisement in the local paper (with Robbie giving the thumbs-up, something that he would do in many press photographs). In anticipation of purchasing Christmas presents, the jumper retailed £8, a scarf, £1.80 or flag for £1.00, amongst a growing number of lines availableto a blooming support base.

A dynamite start to 1980 came with the New Year's Day derby at the Vetch Field with Cardiff City. Played at 3pm on a Tuesday afternoon, the encounter was billed as an all-ticket affair, with entry on to the North Bank at £1.30, with children/OAPs at 70p for this long-awaited match which saw 21,400 crammed in to the ground. January also saw the worst winter in the UK for sixteen years but all credit to the ground staff for enabling the match to go ahead despite sub-zero temperatures. The clubs had not met in the League since the mid-1960s back when a certain John Toshack had scored two headers against the Swans in the 1968 Welsh Cup final. The present day Swansea team included former Bluebirds Leighton Phillips, Brian Attley, David Giles and the aforementioned Tosh. The contribution from two of Robbie's team mates proved decisive; Tosh scored first followed by a last minute winner from Gilo in a brilliant 2-1 win. However, City would have their revenge by beating a Robbie-free Swansea side 1-0 in the subsequent return fixture at Ninian Park. Giles, known in his playing days as 'Pixie', today works as a media pundit after a playing career which saw him play for all four Welsh clubs and should have reaped higher rewards. He and Waddle would finish joint top scorers.

Robbie played through to the second week of March, when Cambridge came to the Vetch and took away two points thanks to their 2-4 win. He left the pitch early into the game with a head injury which naturally caused some concern. Following a collision with an opposition player, it was later disclosed that he had incurred some damage to his inner ear and not a fracture, as thought. It would be serious enough to see the conclusion of his involvement with the first team but he was looking likely to be able to join the squad on its end of season holiday, as was Tommy Craig, who had broken his arm whilst playing. During a working life in football Robbie's body received quite a hammering and it is little wonder that footballers suffer the repercussions in later life. His former Swans team mate Eddie May would still feel the after affects of a painful ankle injury years after finishing playing.

But before seeing his season come to a premature end, Robbie had a major role in three epic Cup games against rising Division One stars Crystal Palace. They came to Wales for a third round F.A Cup fixture on 5 January 1980. Led by future England boss Terry Venables, his side was spearheaded by Robbie's Wales team mates Ian Walsh and Peter Nicholas. Termed the "Team of the Eighties", Palace wore a great shirt with red and blue stripes crossing the shoulder down to the waist, equally as theatrical as the recent yellow Swans away strip. Ask supporters of a certain age today, from either club, and they will likely recall both shirts fondly. The Swans played out a 2-2 draw, thanks to a late header from Tosh, which was followed by a 3-3 at Selhurst Park, where Robbie scored in this six-goal thriller. Charlo and Rushbury were linking well during the game before the latter sent in a cross which was met by the head of Robbie James for a rare headed goal. Big Alan Waddle also scored a header in the game and Robbie saw a shot strike the post as the tie moved in to extra-time. As a third match was required to be played at a neutral ground, bizarrely, the English F.A chose Ninian Park for the final fixture. A crowd of 20,012 attended and saw the Swans prove victorious via a 2-1 win thanks again to goals from Toshack and Giles. The latter had been signed from Wrexham in November 1978 and soon began to impress thanks to being given carte blanche by his new manager. Whilst with Swansea, this freedom proved endemic in the Keegan-like player winning further Wales recognition soon after. He and Robbie had previously played together in a young Wales team and for further information I would refer you to the Wales chapter. Surprisingly, Gilo would later leave the Swans in an exchange deal with Crystal Palace in 1982 that saw the midfield dynamo head to Selhurst Park whilst Ian Walsh joined Swansea. Between them, this talented twosome collected thirty full caps for Wales; many of which would come in a starting XI that included Robbie as a team mate.

Robbie had collected his seventh goal of the season in the first replay with Palace and his next goal came less than a week later, in a Welsh Cup fourth round tie with Pontllanfraith who played their football in the Welsh Premier Division. They would conclude their season in a respectable fourth place, one above Swansea Reserves. It does seem silly that the teams should meet here, rather than the Swans receiving appropriate seeding, as often these encounters would offer little to professional sides such as Swansea or Cardiff. With so many games in recent weeks, supporters stayed away as a low gate of 4,189 watched the match at the Vetch. Winning 4-0, Robbie contributed his eighth goal of the season and helped advance his club into a fifth round meeting with Kidderminster in mid-February. They would progress further after a 2-0 win in that game before being eliminated after a penalty shoot-out in the semi-final with Shrewsbury. Back then, the organizers set penalties rather than extra time, as a way of sorting games if they finished in a draw.

With the fixtures coming thick and fast, a massive 30,000+ watched the club exit the F.A Cup in the fifth round at the hands of West Ham after all their previous endeavours. The clubs faced each other three times this season with the Hammers winning twice to the Swans once. In between times, Swansea had seen off Reading 4-1 in the previous round and it saw Robbie's final goal of the campaign: totaling six in the League and three in Cup competitions. January proved to be a tremendously exciting month for both the Swansea City players and supporters and it also saw the return to the Vetch for former manager Roy Bentley. Then working for Third Division side Reading in an administrative capacity, his club came to Wales for a fourth round encounter at the end of the month. Mr Bentley, a hard nut when a player, had managed the Swans across 1969-1972 and had adopted a more physical playing style akin to subsequent boss Harry Gregg, another former professional player. Roy made a name for him self with Chelsea and also played for England, outrageously collecting a 1954 hat-trick against a Wales side that included John Charles and Ivor Allchurch! He had originally spotted Robbie as a schoolboy talent and also instigated the signing of Alan Curtis: both significant moments in the history and development of the club. Delighted with the progress made by the youngsters, Bentley's Reading came as underdogs and left empty-handed thanks to a commanding 4-1 thrashing. It was to be one of Swansea's best results of the season, with the 4-0 whitewash of lowly Pontllanfraith proving their highest across a campaign within which the Swans could only manage a string of three consecutive victories. Their heaviest defeat came at Luton via a 5-0 stomping, trailed by two 4-1 losses.

Prior to missing the final ten games of the season, Robbie had seen Dave Stewart selected as Toshack's fourth goal keeper option selected during the 1979/ 80 season, with the former Leeds stopper making his debut in a 1-1 away draw with eventual-Champions, Leicester, in February.

The introduction of the Safety of Sports Grounds Act (1979) necessitated a massive investment on improving facilities at the Vetch ground. All the while ambitious plans were unveiled for a new stand construction. Toshack had successfully introduced established names such as Craig and Mahoney into his team whilst utilising youngsters coming through the ranks just like Robbie had.

Teenagers Chris Marustik, Chris Sander and Jimmy Loveridge joined the already-progressed Nigel Stevenson into the first team but not everyone was enamoured with the Swansea youth policy. Writing in his autobiography, Dai Davies, soon to become a Swan but a Wrexham player this season, would later lambaste the Toshack methodology as being detrimental to the young players. But it was a policy that the player-manager never ceased to implement, regardless of the media response or criticism and one which had already been long established at the club. Coincidentally, Dai's team mate at the Racecourse, John Roberts, had played alongside Robbie in a Wales Under-21 game against England back in December 1976 but was in Wrexham colours when they beat Swansea in December 1979.

However, in the following April, they were dispatched by a goal from David Giles, in a 1-0 at the Vetch.

After remaining in mid-table throughout the season, the Swans concluded their 1979/ 80 campaign in twelfth spot in Division Two. Having collected forty-three points, they finished above Cardiff, Wrexham, Shrewsbury and Watford. Meanwhile at the top, Leicester went up as Champions, followed by Birmingham City and Chelsea.

The next season was to prove momentous for Robbie and everyone involved with the club and what an exciting chapter it proved to be.

"This is only the start!" was the bold proclamation from John Toshack for the 1980/ 81 season, as he addressed supporters during a civic ceremony held in honour of the achievement at the Guildhall after the club's promotion success of May 1981. Thousands of supporters and well-wishers thronged the building in celebration of the achievement. Tosh was convinced that his Swansea team was capable enough to sustain itself in Division One and could continue to develop.

The club was kitted out in an Adidas-made kit. But the badge had been changed, with the black circle outline introduced with the club name running around it. They would wear their usual white shirts with black shorts for away games but would often do so for home games also.

Robbie, now twenty-three, would play in forty League fixtures, two League Cup games and seven Welsh Cup ties. Across the previous campaign he scored nine times and by the close of this season, his overall total was seventy-eight, still some way behind 'Golden Boy' Ivor Allchurch on 174.

Above: A pensive Robbie pictured
second right, front row.

Joining the playing squad for a pre-season tour of Scotland, Robbie and his fellow Swansea players fulfilled their annual fixtures with Dunfermline and Raith Rovers in addition to Hibernian before returning to face a Spurs select at the Vetch at the start of the second week of August. The score lines of friendlies are insignificant but the Swans won the Spurs encounter 1-0 with a squad costing £400,000; in comparison to the £2.5m equivalent of their First Division visitors. A noteworthy arrival at the club was the acquisition of Wales star Leighton James back in May. Tosh brought him in along with keeper Dave Stewart, an ever-present this season, and declared that both had been rejected by their previous clubs. In another back-handed compliment, he added that when he signed 'Leight' no other club had wanted the talented winger! Tosh clearly had something to learn as a manager and the 1980/ 81 season would prove a deep learning curve for him. The signing of the other Mr James was significant as he would enjoy an explosive campaign. Combined with another new boy, Yugoslav international Dzemal Hadziabdic, they were an excellent coupling for the Swans this year. The latter was an attacking left back that had played against his new manager in the notorious Wales v Yugoslavia tie at Ninian Park back in 1976 where he had given Tosh quite a battering!

Robbie scored the first goal of the new season for Swansea City in a 2-1 away defeat at Graham Taylor's tricky Watford on 16 August. It came from the penalty spot on twenty-four minutes and would be his only such strike of the campaign (team mates Leighton James and the returning Alan Curtis taking the others). Involved in much of the game, Robbie harassed the defence and probed the keeper on a number of occasions in a game watched by 11,316. Wearing number eight, he featured in the initial eight games of the season, including two League Cup matches with Arsenal before missing games with Bolton and Sheff Wednesday.

The obvious club highlight saw Robbie and his team mates competing against First Division big boys Arsenal, the Gunners being a club which he could have permanently joined a few seasons back. Robbie was keen to face them, not only due to his past association but also because he relished the opportunity of competing with a top side. The first game ended 1-1 but the Swans lost the return, attended by 21,399 at Highbury and saw them exit the League Cup after a 3-1 (4-2 aggregate) score. Subsequent Bradford City cohort Frank Stapleton was in the present Gunners side, alongside future Swans manager John Hollins. The last time that the clubs had faced each other was when a record-breaking 32,786 filled the Vetch to see Bobby Gould provide the winner for the visitors back in 1968. 'Gouldy' now working as a media pundit with Talk Sport, had been on the Chelsea coaching staff in the previous season and would later experience a troublesome spell as Wales manager in the 1990s.

An early thigh strain saw a temporary loss of pace coupled with a dip in form for Robbie which led his manager to utilise him as a substitute across the next seven League games. Coming on in the draws with Wrexham, Luton Town and Blackburn Rovers and the wins against Derby County and Newcastle United, he then missed the defeat and draw with Orient and Shrewsbury, respectively. Toshack gave him an ultimatum to improve his form and it produced the required response. Robbie returned for a defeat at West Ham before scoring twice in a Welsh Cup game at the Vetch, which the Swans won 5-1 at the end of November. Robbie managed to pick up his performance level and he went on to play in all but two of the remaining thirty-one games.

Returning to the beginning of the 1980/ 81 campaign, Shrewsbury Town provided the opening home opponents for the Swans in this exciting period. A 12,750 gate was in attendance to observe a 2-1 win some three days after the Watford defeat, previously mentioned. Playing out a frustrating first half, two second half goals improved matters but unfortunately Jeremy

Charles picked up an early injury in the game. Draws against Q.P.R/ Cambridge gave way for Cup meetings.

September also found new Swan Leighton James scoring what turned out to be an excellent winning goal away at Ashton Gate, home of Bristol City. A draw at the Vetch with Notts County was added to by a strong 1-4 win at Bolton before closing the month with a disappointing loss to visitors Sheffield Wednesday in a dramatic 2-3. Leighton and Robbie both advanced to be full Welsh internationals and had faced each other at club level (in Swansea v Burnley fixtures). Incidentally, Leighton had been on the Vetch books as a teenager until signing for Burnley.

Football is nothing without its personalities and Swansea City had them in the form of the second Mr James, Leighton and Tosh. Both were suitable candidates for another "Mr Marmite" personality test, i.e. you either loved them or loathed them and that would include your own team mates! However, as a football player, the genius of the former was undeniable. Signed from Burnley for £100,000 in May 1980, he was arguably one of the best-ever wingers for the club.

But let's return to this current season, October saw a dubious Wrexham equaliser after David Giles had scored against his former club in a 1-1 at the Racecourse it was followed by a healthy 3-0 defeat of Oldham, the first of two consecutive games at the Vetch. The Swans took half an hour to break down a resilient Derby County defence before Leighton James put the Swans 1-0 up via a penalty. Swansea-born Leight offered a Man of the Match performance with a hat-trick against his former club after getting grief from the Rams fans. Wearing an all-white kit, the Swans followed the win with a fruitful away trip to Newcastle producing a 1-2 success. An away draw with Luton would be concluded with a 1-0 win at home Vetch in front of 12,928 diehards against Grimsby.

A heavy fixture across November commenced with an away trip for Robbie and the Swansea squad to Blackburn, then a 0-2 defeat against Orient at the Vetch before salvaging a point at Gay Meadow in a goal less encounter with Shrewsbury. Robbie would wear the number nine shirt for the first of two appearances before returning to his usual number eight, in a 2-0 defeat at West Ham United. In a much-changed side, the Swans welcomed Caerleon to the Vetch for a mid-week Welsh Cup tie at the Vetch in the following week. A Tosh header put them 1-0 up in a game which saw Robbie score twice. Now fully-fit, he got the third goal from a Waddle shot initially blocked by the keeper before being the quickest to respond. He added another following a powerful Tommy Craig shot, where he followed up the rebound. The small crowd enjoyed an easy 5-2 win. Visitors Preston North End got dealt with swiftly at Vetch Field with a commanding 3-0 arriving at the end of the twenty-first match of the season for the club. The teams would meet in the final game of the season in a hugely significant match for both: one seeking promotion and the other, avoid relegation.

At the time of travelling up to play Newcastle, the Swans had lost only four of their initial twenty-one games and sat in fourth place in the table and the win meant that they remained there. A typical Robbie attack seen during the game saw him again speed down the right flank and hit a low shot towards the left post which Charlo knocked in. Another episode saw him rush down the right and try a little chip over the keeper, who managed to block. His second chance was again thwarted before he put it in with his left foot: two attempts with his right foot then sealed with his left saw Robbie score on fourteen and sixty-four minutes in a brilliant win for the Swans watched by 11,672. The gate was down somewhat on the 20,067 that had seen Robbie and his team play out a 0-0 with Chelsea at the end of the first week of a testing December but this was a season where nationwide attendances dropped; rivals Cardiff City especially hit. Robbie scored the second Swans goal to put them 2-0 up. It was instigated by Rushbury who passed to Leighton James on the wing; he then hit it to Robbie on the left of the goal, facing him. Unmarked, Robbie struck the ball in to the net with his right foot whilst the ball was still in motion. He also hit the bar with another shot in front of The Match of the Day cameras, making their first visit to the Vetch to cover the game with Motty commentating! Although contributing much, Robbie felt disappointed not to have collected a hat-trick. Half time entertainment saw Santa parachuting down onto the pitch! But it was the return of, rather than arrival of, terrace hero Alan Curtis back after his disappointing sojourn at Leeds, that provided an added incentive to those playing. Goal-less against Watford at half-time, with the rain teeming down in to the second period, Curt came on as sub and scored the winning goal; a penalty on sixty-seven minutes which came as a result of a foul committed on Robbie.

It was Robbie who got the Swansea equaliser on twenty-five minutes away at Oldham, tricky opposition in recent times. It was added to by Curt but a late strike by the hosts saw the game conclude at 2-2. The former had tested the keeper early on and saw his goal created when John Mahoney latched on to a back pass before Robbie unleashed a shot from within the penalty area. This was initially saved by the keeper in advance of the Welshman battering in the return past a battling defence. The return to form was noted by his manager, who was "delighted to see Robbie...make a telling contribution after such a barren spell..." News was also revealed that Anthony James was being released by the club with Toshack again brutally honest in his summation as to why he was allowed to leave.

Back on the pitch, cousin Robbie scored one of the two goals at the next match staged at the Vetch, a 2-1 Boxing Day victory against Bristol Rovers. On TV that day, war epic Zulu Dawn was the highlight, whilst a holiday crowd totalling 15,135 came out to support the Swans. It was worth the effort, as Robbie produced another Man of the Match performance and netted the first goal. He would also score in the corresponding fixture at the Vetch in mid-April 1981 and here, set-up the other goal too. Funnily enough, his combining with Leighton James saw the latter facilitate the goal for Robbie; an exact replica of the one he scored at Oldham this same month. Future Swan Gary Emmanuel got the Pirates goal and started alongside young Welsh keeper Martin Thomas, who worked hard in stopping other Robbie strikes before the win took Swansea up in to second in the table. Then the next day, the Swans made the short journey to Ninian Park to meet a struggling Cardiff.

Players and fans alike all know the intensity of such derby matches today and back then it was just the same. The Swans brought a strong side that included Robbie and fellow Welsh internationals the two Leighton's; Phillips and James, Mahoney and Curtis. Of course, all of whom had or would go onto develop connections with both clubs. Whilst Robbie and his team mates would achieve promotion up into the First Division, Cardiff stayed in Division Two before succumbing to relegation down to the Third as Swansea City Football Club rose to become the top Welsh club of the era.

A massive 21,239 holiday crowd saw Cardiff take an early lead before Robinson equalised five minutes before the close of the first period in a half dominated by Swansea City. Then a speculative shot by Robbie from outside of the area was aimed directly at Bluebirds keeper Ron Healey in a crowd box. He could only push the ball away before Curt won the scramble to put in the rebound. Into the second half and Leighton James scored from a superbly-weighted header to put the Swans 3-1 up. The game saw a second Cardiff goal which really put the Swans under pressure. It was scored by

Peter Kitchen, another moustache-enthusiast, who was one of those players that always did well against them, no matter what club he was playing for. Wearing their smart red shirts, black shorts and socks, similar to the Q.P.R away design, the visitors from west Wales attracted the largest attendance seen at Ninian Park all season long. However, the drama was not quite over, as with two minutes of ordinary time remaining, Cardiff was awarded an indirect free kick some thirty-five yards away from Dave Stewart's goal. It was then that a moment of football magic occurred, Scotsman and Bob Bank favourite John Buchanan hit a thunderous shot which was still on the rise as it cannoned into the Swansea net to bring the final score to a breathtaking 3-3. Bluebirds stalwart Phil Dwyer remembers that Tosh, playing that day for the visitors, said to his team mates not to worry as 'Buchie' would not score due to the distance but what a strike, it was! Buchanan had joined the Bluebirds as part of an exchange deal with Northampton and it was whilst with them that he had played at the Vetch back in October 1973. Fans still talk about his goal and Toshack, Curt and most others involved that day publicly acknowledged it as the best goal that they had ever witnessed as professional footballers. What a fine accolade for a Scotsman that never received a testimonial for his services to Cardiff City F.C.

For the Swans players and staff, the result felt like a defeat and Tosh was none too pleased in the dressing room after the final whistle had been blown after this superbly fought out derby. They met once again in the following April again within which Leighton James missed a penalty (after a foul on Robbie). It was so well-saved by Healey that even the home crowd applauded!

Following the derby meeting, the Swans advanced to endure a woeful run of form: losing four League games and exiting the F.A. Cup via a 0-5 hammering at home to a rampant Middlesborough side. After a November loss at Upton Park, the Hammers came to Wales and won 1-2. Geoff Pike scored for them and he would later return as a Notts County player facing the Swans in 1989 when Robbie had just re-signed to the Vetch club. West Ham legend Trevor Brooking, who would go on to score the winning goal in the 1980 FA Cup final, tipped the Swans as promotional rivals as the season advanced. Cambridge United away saw the Swans lose 3-1, their third successive defeat. Coming straight after three consecutive losses, Robbie and his team mates made the short journey to face Merthyr Tydfil in the fourth round of the Welsh Cup. Martyrs manager Doug Rosser was a former Swansea player from the late-1960s and the referee for the game was the infamous Clive Thomas. Merthyr had won only five out of their last fifteen home games and this result wasn't going to improve matters as they lost 0-2 on a sandy Penydarren Park playing surface. The Swans had recently enjoyed a short Spanish break before returning for the game.

Toshack acknowledged that their recent form was ropey, with eleven goals conceded in their last three games before a difficult, end-of-January visit to Loftus Road, home of Queens Park Rangers, concluded in defeat. With fifteen games left, the Swans were wobbling. Both assistant manager Boersma and Tosh were unhappy and the former publicly stated that if any of their players could not take the pressure, then they should leave the club. Top of the table found West Ham on sixty-one points after playing thirty-nine games, Notts County then on forty-nine points after forty games, Blackburn forty-eight points after forty-one matches and Swansea on forty-seven points after forty games.

In February, Robbie was absent from team selection for two games: the 2-1 away loss at promotion-rivals Notts County and Welsh Cup success at the Vetch over Maesteg. However, he subsequently returned for the remaining seventeen fixtures and scored three goals for the club, all in April. Despite losing 2-0 away at Sheffield Wednesday, Wyndham Evans and Dudley Lewis, the Welsh cavalry, were drafted in to defence and proved effective there for the remainder of the season. Swansea went on to lose just one out of their last eighteen League fixtures in a timely run of form at the season climax. Lewis, then an eighteen-year-old, played in the last eighteen games and would spend nine seasons with Swansea whilst Evans was an established pro at the club who would be rewarded with an end-of-season testimonial match at the Vetch. That game featured Robbie and the current Swansea team against the Liverpool F.A Cup winning side of 1974, with star names including Tosh, Ian Callaghan, Emlyn Hughes, Tommy Smith and others. The Swans Select XI won on pens.

March saw a bad-tempered encounter with Wrexham at the Vetch, with Robbie collecting goal number eight of the season during a 3-1 win against their rivals from north Wales. Resulting from a mistake, Robbie's strike was the third in the game. Coincidentally, the draw for the semi-finals of the Welsh Cup saw the sides having to meet once again in the coming month. Bristol City shared the points at the Vetch after a 0-0 before the Swans lost by a single goal away at Grimsby prior to a 0-1 away win at the now-gone Baseball Ground, then the home of Derby County.

The penultimate month of the season found Robbie enjoying an eagle-eyed view of Nigel Stevenson's stunning goal in a 2-0 victory against promotion rivals Blackburn at the Vetch. Four draws followed; away at Wrexham for a Welsh Cup semi-final which closed at 2-2, a 1-1 at Orient, then the home return leg against Wrexham concludes at 1-1. Stragglers Cardiff City also paid a visit and played-out a 1-1 watched by a not insubstantial 19,038 crowd. They had John Lewis in there side, later at Weston-super-Mare F.C with Robbie.

The team also completed League doubles over Newcastle, Bolton, Derby and Preston this season. Conversely, West Ham and Sheffield Wednesday did likewise to them! Regrettably, Alan Waddle was transferred to Newport County in December after being unable to get in the first team and he would miss their rise to the First Division after having contributing much to the club.

Continuing his scoring penchant, Robbie struck his final League goal of the campaign against a somewhat uninspired Chelsea at the Vetch thanks to a 3-0 score line at the end of April. A troublesome, dipping shot from the talented Neil Robinson put the Swans 1-0 up before Hadziabdic scored his first goal in a Swansea shirt by beating fellow Yugoslav Borota, who struggled to prevent both strikes, from outside of the penalty area. Then on sixty-seven minutes, Leighton James began the move which saw the skilful Curt go on a weaving run past two defenders before passing to Robbie whose side-foot proved enough to see the ball trickle over the goal line and put his side 3-0 up on sixty-seven minutes, despite the efforts of a defender. Robbie immediately ran towards the North Bank before Curt jumped on him!

"Swansea can see the First Division beckoning…" heralded the telly summariser as Match of the Day cameras returned to record the match. They saw another great team performance, with Robbie proving dominant in the heart of the team and assisting in defence and the win being significant as it sealed seven games without defeat. It kept the Swans fourth in the table, behind West Ham, Notts County and Blackburn. As for Chelsea, they had sacked Geoff Hurst only a couple of days before the match and had Bobby Gould as Caretaker manager. "Robbie James is a player who has always impressed me," he told the local paper.

The Swans found themselves two points ahead of visitors Luton Town, who next visited the Vetch on 27 April. Advancing to being 2-0 up, with a Craig goal a clearly-rehearsed training ground move involving Evans, Curt and Robbie, the game closed at 2-2. The draw saw them step up a place and now requiring a win at Preston North End in the final fixture of the season to gain promotion. From a psychological perspective, Toshack felt that this was probably better as if his team played for a draw against Preston, then they may have take things a little easy.

The team traveled north the day before a Saturday showdown with Nobby Stiles' side. Under his guidance, the team was battling valiantly against relegation whilst the Swans were heading up and out of the division. The clubs had an interesting history as in 1964 Preston scored a freak goal which had prevented the Swans from reaching an F.A Cup final by winning the semi 2-1. Prior to the present match, the Swans squad was addressed by Bill Shankly, the recently-retired former Liverpool manager, at their hotel. The players realised what could be achieved as their coach pulled up to the ground. With "Johnny Toshack's Black & White Army!" all about them, it could have been mistaken for a home match if all reports were true. Wearing their eye-catching, two-tone blue, short-sleeve kit, Robbie and his fellow pros had prepared for the game under intense media coverage. Preston would later have an artificial pitch whilst its current surface looked devoid of grass after an arduous season. Robbie witnessed a peculiar goal that put Preston 1-0 up; a literal up-and-under that keeper Dave Stewart fumbled before the opposing player scored from during a match played on a sunny Saturday afternoon. A lackluster Swans performance into the second half saw the Preston players lining up to shoot, whilst Tosh and Boersma were seen urging their team on from the dug out.

With the Swansea supporters crowded in to the Town end of the ground, they were watching their team's twenty-first away match of the season with a results return of W5, D9, and L6. Leight scored first from a typical moment of magic, as defined by team mate Alan Curtis before the trusty Tommy Craig put the Swans 0-2 up by half-time with Robbie directly involved in the third and final goal. Attacking again and again, and with less than five minutes remaining, a long run down the right wing by Curt from within his own half saw a pass to Robbie, who controlled it with his left and with his right foot he sent the ball over to Jeremy Charles who scored a brilliant team goal to put them 1-3 ahead after North End had reduced the deficit to 1-2 after Stewart dropped a cross only to see seasoned poacher Bruce nail an easy goal. After the full-time whistle had blown, Tosh and his staff charged on to the pitch to embrace their players as the manager hugged Dudley Lewis for an age whilst jubilant fans and cameras swarmed around them. After sixty-one years, the Swans were back in the First Division, topping Cardiff as the last Welsh club to play in the top division some years before.

After the match Tosh was elated: "This is the greatest day of my life. I thought possibly that when I left Liverpool, I may have left things like this behind but I've never known anything quite like this. Three years ago we were in the Fourth Division and people have asked us the same question as we went to the Third, we coped alright, to the Second, we coped alright and now the First but I realise that there is a big gulf between the First Division and the other three. But what can we do? We can't go any more than go from the Fourth to the First in three seasons. We shall just have to see how we get on next year..." He added that he was excited about taking his Swansea side to Anfield to face his old club Liverpool. Shankly was in the dressing room after the match and singing Tosh's praises, proclaiming him to being possibly the manager of the decade. 'Shanks' also stated that the Swans players must believe that they can hold their own in the top division, re-enforcing the sentiments of Tommy Smith, who had said that the club and supporters should learn to accept success. Many of them were seen mainly drinking cans of Coke in the dressing room whilst Charlo held onto a bottle of champagne! On the bus home, he and Tommy Craig still had their kits on back in the days when football hadn't yet begun to carry shirt advertising. Footage of the team on the bus home showed Robbie wearing his Patrick tracksuit top and seen pouring out the champagne. All around children and families of the playing squad enjoyed the moment but many of the team could not quite believe what they had achieved. With promotion sealed, the team bus eventually arrived back in Swansea in the early hours of Sunday morning where the celebrations continued at The Bay View hotel on Oystermouth Road. Then later on an open top double-decker bus the players were greeted by fans around the town, with one banner reading "Super Swans. Division 1 here we come with Tosh."

The team finished in third place on fifty points collected, three behind Notts County and sixteen behind runaway Champions West Ham. As for the other three Welsh clubs, Newport County succeeded in consolidating their status in Division Three and stunningly reached the quarter finals of the European Cup Winners Cup with Tommy Tynan shining for them this season. (His cousin, Bobby, played many times against the Swans in the early-1970s). Cardiff managed to remain in the division, as did cousins Wrexham.

With promotion achieved in Lancashire, the season was not over yet as the Swans had the small matter of a two-leg, Welsh Cup Final with Hereford United to play. Unusually, they had the peculiar knowledge of being guaranteed entry into next season's European Cup Winners' Cup due to Hereford being ineligible. As a non-Welsh club, it would seem that English border clubs such as them were allowed entry into the competition for the financial benefits that it reaped. Whatever, the first leg was played at the Vetch on 4 May and the referee was again Clive Thomas, a true personality in the game back then. Tosh appreciated the value of a European place and so did the fans, as a gate of 13,182 attended the match in which Robbie produced the only goal of the game. Many of the supporters welcomed back a returning Danny Bartley in away colours. The team for the final was: Stewart, Evans, Hadziabdic, Robinson, Mahoney, Lewis, Curtis, Robbie, L James, Charles, Craig.

The return leg arrived a week later, with Robbie and the lads travelling to Edgar Street to play out a 1-1 in front of a crowd almost half that of the previous game. Robbie scored the Swansea goal, his twelfth of the campaign, in a team which had two changes from the first match: namely allowing starts for Attley and Giles. Winning the Welsh Cup this season was a major achievement, as the last time a Swansea side had held the lovely trophy was back in the 1965/66 season when they were known as Swansea Town F.C. It would not be the last time that Robbie would be on the winning side in a final, as he won it on five occasions: four whilst a Swan and once as a Bluebird. The Swans would successfully retain the trophy across the next three corresponding seasons.

The 1980/81 season finished nicely and set the Swans up nicely for their first season in Division One and it would provide arguably the best-ever campaign for Robbie. Swansea City Football Club had reached the pinnacle of British football: Division One. They also found themselves back in European contention after a gap of fifteen years.

There was a feverish anticipation during the summer of seeing the Swans face the likes of Liverpool, Arsenal and Manchester United but with a stadium capacity close to 27,000 (4,800 seated) season ticket prices were inevitably increased. It made little difference as the club took in £650,000 in pre-season sales for tickets that were priced at £90 for the West Stand and £100 for either the East or Centre.

Friendly fixtures included six matches and incorporated a short tour of Yugoslavia before a final Vetch warm-up against Luton Town where new boy Colin Irwin was unveiled to the crowd. Preseason training is usually dreaded by players and at Swansea it usually consisted of lots of running and a little ball work. However, from this season forth, it switched to both aspects being of equal importance. Practice matches arranged around the Vetch (often in the car park vicinity) were hugely contested affairs and not for the feint of heart!

Bob Latchford, Ian Walsh, Max Thompson and keeper Dai Davies were brought in for the new season whilst Leighton Phillips, David Giles and Dave Rushbury exited. Phillips was pretty dismissive of his former pal Tosh in a newspaper article that exposed the harsh methods adopted by his former Wales and Cardiff City team mate. It would not be the last time that such comments were made public, as Ray Kennedy, soon to sign for the Swans this season, would later share his own experience. Thommo and Irwin were past team-mates in the Liverpool Central League side and the former had played against Robbie

in a Blackpool side, previously. Backroom changes were also rife seeing Phil Boersma promoted to assistant manager in place of Terry Medwin. The latter's ill health saw him reduce his work load before bowing out of all involvement in April of the coming year. Welsh national coach and ex-Cardiff City captain Doug Livermore comes to the club as a coach. He had played against the Swans a number of times back in the mid-1970s and had known Robbie through the national side, as he was assistant to Mike England.

With a match day programme costing 50p, the first domestic test arrived on Saturday 29 August, 1981 with an opening day fixture with Leeds United at the Vetch. Irwin, then a twenty-four-year-old defender, was made club captain for the oncoming campaign and it was a game of special pertinence for returning local hero Alan Curtis. He had re-signed for the Swans after a disappointing eighteen months at Elland Road had been blighted by a lengthy injury absence. With six Welshmen in its team, nobody thought that Swansea City would fair well against the bigger name clubs in the First Division like Leeds, Manchester United, Liverpool, Spurs and Arsenal but some triumphant surprises were coming.

Future Swans boss and a Wales team mate of Robbie's, Brian Flynn was in the Leeds side on this glorious sunny afternoon match, where a hat-trick by fledgling Swan Bob Latchford sank United to the hypnotic terrace chant of "Super Swans! Super

Swans! Super Swans! Super Swans!" Collected across a rampant ten minutes, Bob's trio of strikes was overshadowed by a dazzling solo effort in the seventieth minute by Curt (and Jeremy Charles scoring the first Swans goal in Division One). Both Toshack and his Chairman acknowledged Latch's contribution and what a bargain he transpired to be at £125,000. The crowd of 23,500 reveled in the resulting 5-1 victory as did the club; thanks to the fulsome gate receipts gathered. Tosh stated, "I have put together five forwards, all internationals in their own right who have nearly 500 goals between them." Big Bob had the bulk of them, having netted 177 times across 396 League appearances after the United win. The celebrated Swansea side for that first game was: Davies, Robinson, Hadziabdic, Rajkovic, Irwin, Mahoney, Curtis, Robbie, Leighton James, Charles, Latchford. Leeds head honcho and former star player, Alan Clarke, declined to attend the post-match press conference saying only that "the result speaks for itself." It certainly did. "A First Division flyer as Super Swans sizzle" was the 10p Swansea Evening Post headline. Everyone at the Vetch was elated and amazed by the result and that included John Charles, a Leeds legend, who had come back to Wales to see the match. The Swans were kitted out in their shiny, round-necked Patrick kit and supporters could purchase their own replica strips for £11.64, for an adult shirt, £5.11 for the shorts and £1.70 for the socks.

The season saw a lengthy list of Swansea players being selected for Wales, at all levels, including established names such as Davies, Mahoney, Robbie and Leight and Curt complimented by Walsh, Charles, Marustik and Stevenson (the latter two winning their first caps). Robbie played in all forty-two League fixtures and twelve of the thirteen various Cup matches. Also, he played for Wales a further six times; making it a total of sixty-one appearances: a phenomenal achievement in a season that belonged to him.

A mixed bag of early League results saw the Swans defeat Brighton, Notts County, Spurs, Arsenal and Stoke City up until a scoreless encounter with Wolves at the end of October wiped out a 100 percent home record. There were early doors defeats away at West Brom, with the Swans wearing red but being sunk by a Regis hat-trick in a sound battering by the Baggies. Robbie was involved in a second half move created by Latchford, which saw him beat two defenders by hooking the ball over one of them and heading it on to Curtis in the penalty box. Another loss at Manchester United was ensured before the significant introduction of Gary Stanley in October. Signed from Everton, Gary scored on his debut, away at Stoke in a win that took his new club to the top of Division One. An early alarm call was sounded when the club failed in honouring repayments to his former club shortly after, which would see repercussions in the 1982/ 83 season for them.

Robbie and his team mates had faced a Man United side at Old Trafford before a humungous 47,309 crowd, only to be beaten by a single goal. Things would be different in the return fixture at the Vetch at the end of January, with Robbie scoring one of the Swansea goals in a 2-0 win.

Three days before making the long trip to Manchester, the Swans faced an early entry into the European Cup Winners' Cup with a two-game encounter with East German Cup winners Lokomotiv Leipzig. It would be Robbie's first taste of European club football. Having also won the Welsh Cup at the close of the previous season, they faced Loko at home on 16 September before the return some two weeks later. Indeed, Robbie, Curt and Wyndham Evans had come a long way since being in the Swansea side that needed to seek League re-election only a few years ago. They had also played alongside Robbie in his League debut as a Swansea player some seasons before.

Robbie had already played in the various levels of international football whilst with Wales but this was his first experience in a Swans shirt. Fans could attend the mid-week match for between £5.00 - £4.50 and 10,295 did so; seeing their team lose the 1st leg by a single strike but it was at the German's ground that Jeremy Charles scored exactly twenty-four years after his father, Mel, had done so for Wales in 1957. Charlo nicked an away goal in a fixture watched by a massive 22,500 crowd which produced a 2-1 defeat and saw the German side progress via a 3-1 aggregate. The defeats were the first experience of European football since 1966 for the Swans.

Current F.A Cup holders Tottenham Hotspur came to the Vetch Field next and went away 2-1 losers in a game which saw Robbie's first goal of the season in a highly vigorous match. His strike arrived on sixty-two minutes and it put the Swans 1-0 up and would be voted the best goal scored by a Swansea player this season by Daily Mail sports reporter Peter Jackson. This was particularly impressive as many of the Swansea players, including Robbie, carried injuries into the game. It was his miss in the first half that had been the only true chance for his team in front of a 22,206 gate. When his goal arrived, it was a volley from twelve yards out which flew past former Liverpool keeper Ray

Clemence following a cross from Latch. In a taxing encounter, Robbie and Mahoney battled constantly with Villa, Ardiles and Hoddle in the Spurs midfield. Wales team mate Paul Price also played for the visitors.

Injuries to key personal yet again proved a problem for the squad, with subsequent knocks affecting Charles, Curt, Kennedy and Walsh but more about them later. As for Charles, he was to eventually return to the side after being absent for some three months, in a February match with Midlesborough. Poor Charlo was to see his involvement in this prestigious campaign concluded by another injury, this time collected against Coventry, in a 0-0 draw at the Vetch in March, resulting in a minimal tally of appearances for the youngster.

Crowds at the Vetch for League matches in this marvellous, majestic and miraculous season averaged 20,000 except for a League Cup visit by Barnsley in October. Then managed by Norman 'Bite your legs' Hunter, goals from Leighton James, Irwin and Curtis failed to be sufficient in overturning an earlier away defeat and Barnsley went through 4-3 on aggregate. A Swansea manager some years later, John Hollins filled the number eleven shirt in the Arsenal side in an October defeat for the Gunners at the Vetch. A superb Max Thompson volleyed goal provided the highlight of the match which was won 2-0 by the super Swans. The sides had

previously competed in the League Cup during the 1979/80 season, when the result was very different. Wonderfully, Swansea completed the double over them this season, thanks to a 2-0 at Highbury, in February 1982 before the Gunners finished their season one place above the Swans.

Whilst away from home, Robbie and his fellow players enjoyed thrilling gates of 22,000+ in many games (including at Ipswich Town, Everton, Arsenal, West Ham and Spurs).

League runners-up in the 1979/ 80 season, Ipswich presented a tricky away fixture for Swansea in November, coming after a defeat and draw with Coventry and Wolves, respectively. Toshack's side pulled off a stunning 2-3 win all the more impressive in that Portman Road had not seen a home defeat all season. The media recognised their achievement and all the match reports proved glowing. Goals from Curt, Latch and Stanley sealed a marvelous result and we can only wonder if Town boss Bobby Robson regretted his comments in the Western Mail, back in May; "He (John Toshack) can consider he has done well if he keeps Swansea out of those bottom four or five places. He will even enjoy his season if he can do that and consolidate." Yugo Swan Ante Rajkovic, signed pre-season, performed well in this match and his presence in the team was singled out by Sunday Times reporter Mihir Bose as "the most effective of sweepers". The Daily Mirror's Jack Steggles elaborated, "John Toshack's superbly-organised side...went with a bold, imaginative approach and were good value for money." Toshack's impetus on team organisation was recognised elsewhere by the Mail's Jeff Powell, terming him, "Swansea's worker of miracles."

After the superb Leeds victory back in August, Latchford sought to have a visit to the Vetch by opponents viewed similarly to the trepidation shown by sides playing at Anfield during this period. Brighton manager Mike Bailey acquiesced after a 0-0 draw there in November, "Not many teams will come away from Swansea this season with a point, let alone a clean sheet." In the initial nine League and Cup fixtures played there thus far, the Swans had lost only once. This was further enhanced by a 1-0 victory against Latch's old club Birmingham City at the close of the month in which Robbie scored the winning goal, his second this season.

A busy December saw Vetch Field visits from European Cup winners Nottingham Forest and present-League champions, Aston Villa, culminating in a late 1-2 win for the former thanks to a dubious, last-minute penalty decision. Coincidentally, a header from Robbie contributed the only goal for the Swans. He would also score against the same opposition at the Vetch in the coming

May. Two further Robbie strikes arrived at the Vetch against Villa, who lost 2-1 some five days later on 15 December in a win that took Swansea to the top of Division One. Their stopper, Jimmy Rimmer, would later sign for the Swans, a decade after his original loan spell whilst a registered Manchester United player. The crowd showed their support for their team in a match that saw Swansea 2-1 up by half time. Both of Robbie's goals came from moves initiated via corners; the first a header from six yards out, whilst at 1-1, a shot from Rajkovic was blocked and the ball fortuitously ran to Robbie who intelligently placed it in to the corner of the net, from all of ten yards out. Booked in the second half for a foul on Villa's rising England star Gary Shaw, the match produced another thrilling encounter at the Vetch with Robbie heavily involved. Victory saw the Swans as table-toppers after nineteen games, with thirty-three points.

Already on five goals, Robbie added a further three to his tally in a mid-December, Welsh Cup tie with Worcester City at the Vetch. In a compelling 6-0 routing, he scored his side's first two goals and its final one, the sixth. Playing up front in the absence of Bob Latchford, Robbie again played well and had struck six times in the last three matches. He got his name on the scoreboard within ninety seconds, after connecting with a pass from local talent Marustik, holding off two players and still being able to hit a low shot past ex-Villa keeper Cumbes. His second arrived on twenty-two minutes, following on from some creative flair produced by Hadziabdic and Curtis before a Robbie flick, from his right foot, flew directly into the net. His hat-trick came on eighty-four minutes, with the Swans 5-0 up and saw Robbie as a poacher, latching on to a ball from a Worcester player before beating the keeper again.

Manager John Toshack's telepathic Liverpool team-mate from the 1970s, Kevin Keegan, saw them face each other at Southampton's compact ground the Dell on 28 December. The Saints won 3-1 but were to lose the return in front of a 23,771 Vetch crowd in April 1982 thanks to a great goal from Curt against his future employers. In the defense for the Saints was Ivan Golac, later to meet Robbie in the guise of assistant coach with the Yugos when playing Wales at the Vetch in 1988.

Ominously, the board at Swansea City revealed that the club was operating at a loss after its Division One promotion.

After a week or more of inactivity due to a particularly harsh winter, the Swans were obliged to fulfill a 16 January fixture away at Leeds. Since their early-season mauling at the Vetch,

United this time put in a winning, 2-0 performance despite Man-of-the-match Rajkovic's best efforts. It was their seventh loss in eleven away games, something that would worsen in their second subsequent season of Division One football.

Manchester United sauntered in for an away day at Swansea at the end of January probably expecting a win to add to their October 1-0 at Old Trafford. A humongous 47,000 crowd watched that game which was only the fifth Division One League match for the Swans. The return was a different affair altogether as Tosh unveiled his new signing: thirty-year-old former England player Ray Kennedy from Liverpool. Strikes from Curt and Robbie sealed a pulsating 2-0 victory watched by a gate of 24,115 whilst Reds boss Ron Atkinson, who had an established professional history with Robbie, watched on uncomfortably with his Chairman, from their grandstand directly above the dug outs. Afterwards, Kennedy, a class act as a player, professed his belief that his new side could win the title and advance to playing in Europe. Robbie had managed to avoid a wild challenge from Ray Wilkins, a player that had seen Swan Neil Robinson go off with a

gashed knee thanks to an earlier encounter with 'Butch'. However, Robbie was more nimble and he sent in a low cross that Bailey could only parry to Latch, whose shot was weakly cleared by big Gordon McQueen only for Robbie to finish off the move and make it Swansea City 2 Manchester United 0. By the end of the month, almost four years after a loss at Rochdale necessitated re-election back into the Football League; Swansea was in with a chance of winning the title.

Talking of Liverpool, Tosh's side had enjoyed a prodigious 2-2 October draw at Anfield in front of another bumper crowd; this time totalling 48,645. That fixture came soon after the death of his mentor, Bill Shankly. Tosh annoyed some Swans fans as when the camera panned along Swansea players such as Robbie, Davies and Hadziabdic; the player-manager unzipped his black tracksuit top to reveal a Liverpool shirt: which was his show of respect for the former Kop legend. Apart from the obligatory two League meetings, the Swans put in an impressive 2-0 February win at the Vetch, with a cracking goal scored by Leighton James and another by Curt. The sides had also been drawn together in the F.A Cup third round. Before that Toshack was selected to appear on the

This Is Your Life programme and one imagines that many of the playing staff made an appearance on the show. Returning to the Cup game with Liverpool, it was staged at the Vetch on 2 January, with the Merseysiders putting four past the home side in a dire result endured by a 24,179 crowd. Only in the Welsh Cup did Swansea prove consistent.

After collecting ten goals to no return in matches with Stafford Rangers and the aforementioned Worcester City, the Swans had to work a lot harder in the fifth round against a battling Colwyn Bay side. A 2-2 at the Vetch was erased thanks to a compelling 3-0, again at Swansea, with Robbie collecting two more goals on a rainy night. His first came via a side-foot from a Curt pass and was added to on fifty-eight minutes, with the Swans already 2-0 ahead, to take them on to a semi-final meeting with Bangor City, a club that Robbie would find himself playing against later in his career. They wore a kit resembling the Wales one from the mid-1970s.

Returning to the League, a 2-0 win against Liverpool on 16 February was one result in a nine match period that saw seven wins and two draws. It pleased the player-manager, awarded the M.B.E in the New Year Honours, immensely and saw several of his players selected for Wales immediately after (against England). That victory against Liverpool was added to by an away win at Arsenal, where Robbie scored another penalty in a 0-2 win which put the Swans second in the table with fifteen games remaining, nine of which were to be played away. A trio of injuries to key Swansea personnel didn't prevent Ray Kennedy from scoring against his former club followed by the Robbie penalty some twenty minutes into the second half. A foul on Curt meant that the visitor's were awarded a penalty and as Leighton James had already gone off, it was left to Robbie to take it. The win at Highbury came on the four year anniversary of Toshack joining the club.

Robbie continued with the goals in the next game, scoring twice at home to Stoke City in a 3-0 win attended by the lowest attendance for a League match at the Vetch this season. Although, there was a live international rugby match being screened on television that same night which had an effect on seeing 11,161 present. Goals from Robbie and Charlo succeeded in doing the double over a club that Mr James would subsequently join. They also repeated this against Notts County, Sunderland and Arsenal whilst Everton and Lokomotiv Leipzig did likewise to them. It was their sixth win in the last seven games despite being played on a terrible

Vetch pitch on an awful evening. Robbie's initial strike came from a volley and the second arrived two minutes before full time. He had now scored nine times in the League and was still to contribute a further five goals before the season close.

February and March saw much activity both on and off the field at Swansea City F.C: Welsh Number 1 'keeper Dai Davies, after a difficult early season start following his replacing of terrace favourite Dave Stewart, advanced to conceding only a single goal in seven matches. That came in a 1-2 reverse at the Vetch on 27 March against eventual League runners-up, the talented Ipswich. The game provided the thirteenth goal of the season for Robbie, including the Welsh Cup hat-trick. The performance produced by Swansea in this game was said to have been a vastly different one to the bold and adventurous one that took away a 2-3 win at Portman Road previously. Robbie netted via a penalty, following a hand ball incident, to level the score at 1-1. And with a draw looking likely, it took a wonderful strike by Eric Gates to take both points. Harry Gregg returned to the club as goalkeeping coach this month but soon left after financial cutbacks were

implemented. Out of sorts David Giles left the club in a player exchange that saw twenty-three-year-old striker Ian Walsh replace him at the Vetch. Both were Welsh international colleagues with Robbie and the latter had scored both goals for his country in a 2-0 win over Scotland played at the ground the previous May (Which did not feature Robbie). Davies guarded the Wales goal that day and featured in a line-up that had a strong Swansea linkage: the two Leighton, James and Phillips both selected. Walsh made only limited appearances for his new club, due to injury, yet still managed to score against Birmingham City and Wolves (a win which returned the Swans to top of the table). Regardless of losing at home to Ipswich at the close of March, the Swans could be found at the top of Division One having accumulated fifty-six points from thirty games played. Ipswich moved down into fifth spot but Swansea remained in the top six all season long. Across the space of two weeks, they faced West Ham, first in a 0-1 loss at the Vetch and then a 1-1 at Upton Park on 10 April where Robbie struck his eleventh League goal. It was a stunning effort from outside of the penalty area and from around twenty-five yards out, he hit the ball crisply and watched as it shot into the net.

An April encounter at the Vetch with Manchester City would see future Swansea boss John Bond's City side soundly beaten 2-0 with goals from Stanley and Latch, previously blitzed by a buzzing City 4-0 back in November.

The hectic activities of the season were to catch up with the team as the Swans lost six of their final seven League fixtures (against Birmingham City, Everton, Spurs, Middlesborough and Aston Villa). The only respite arriving thanks to a Robbie James brace in a 2-0 away win at Nottingham Forest's City Ground, in the fortieth match of a thrilling campaign in the top division. He had scored previously at the start of May in a 3-1 defeat at Everton before adding his final two goals of the season against Forest. His first came in the opening minute of the game with more chances coming in the second half, prior to sealing the win when he out ran a defender to beat England keeper Peter Shilton with another trademark low shot to put the Swans 2-0 up and into fifth in the table. In all, he scored nineteen League goals and five in the Welsh Cup.

Recognition from your favorite player as a young fan has always meant a lot and Robbie delighted a young boy traveling to see the Swans at Birmingham by returning his 'thumbs-up' from the back of the team bus. Perhaps only a small gesture, yet one of great significance to a teen-aged football fan.

Sandwiched in between the Forest victory and Everton defeat saw an away loss at F.A Cup finalists Tottenham Hotspur. During the game, a cross by Robbie was misjudged by the keeper only for Leighton James to follow-up with his twelfth goal of the season. Unfortunately, the Swans still lost 2-1 after beating them at the Vetch by the same score line back in September.

The significance of what the Swans had achieved across the 1981/82 season was noted across the soccer community, "Their success story can rarely have been surpassed in any footballing era," commented a scribe writing in the Arsenal programme, February 1982.

Robbie created a new appearance record for the club upon pulling on a Swansea shirt for the 348th time during the season. He would also be voted Player of the Year whilst Dai Davies was the Chairman's choice in what showed itself as an exhausting campaign for the players.

Finishing in sixth spot was better than any of the other sides that had come up with them from Division Two. Unfairly, the Swans were ineligible to take up a U.E.F.A Cup spot after closing their campaign in this position. Robbie team mate Robinson put in some stellar performances this season and a number of debuts are presented in the final match with Aston Villa. Robbie later commented that Villa Park was his favourite away ground to play at. Toshack rested seven established players and gave vital first team experience to nineteen-year olds Chris Sander, Dudley Lewis, Jimmy Loveridge and eighteen-year-old Darren Gale. Villa were awaiting their European Cup Final date a week later but still won the match 3-0 and closed their own season in eleventh spot. Loveridge was a Wales under-21 success that turned pro at the Vetch in late-1979 and who would play across forty-seven games for the Swans until leaving in 1985.

In all, the Swans scored fifty-eight times against forty-six conceded and collected a points total of sixty-nine; two behind Arsenal and Spurs, nine behind Manchester United, fourteen behind Ipswich and eighteen behind Champions Liverpool. In all, they won twenty games and lost fifteen, with a lesser return in away fixtures.

No sooner had League commitments been completed (with the exception of the away game at Villa) than a two-leg, Welsh Cup Final meeting with Cardiff City arrived for the present holders and a place in the European Cup Winners' Cup available for the victors. The Bluebirds had been relegated from Division Two after recently losing to Luton Town. In debt to the tune of £1.25m and losing £4,000 a week, their fortunes did not improve across these two games.

Robbie had been a fitness doubt for the first leg at Ninian Park but had played in the resulting 0-0, in a determined effort by a Cardiff side that was applauded by their former player John Toshack. A brace from Latchford saw them off in the return tie at the Vetch Field attended by 15,858, on 19 May, a week after the first game. Hooliganism concerns saw a heavy police presence for the Swansea-staged tie and some unpleasant incidents between factions of both clubs did occur. Swans captain Rajkovic got himself sent-off in the match during which his mistake allowed Bennett to put the blue City a goal up. The ever-reliable Latch then struck twice in eleven minutes to rescue the former's error and to allow Ante to return to the pitch at full time to raise the trophy after their 2-1 win. Swansea saw their name on the Cup for the seventh time and qualified for the U.E.F.A Cup but proved ineligible to take up a place, as mentioned.

The Swans played a massive fifty-eight games across the season and Robbie played in all of them bar the 2-0 League up defeat at Barnsley. He pulled on the number eight shirt except for an away tie in the European Cup Winners' Cup with Lokomotiv Leipzig, where he wore number ten.

Top scorers this campaign, in all competitions, presented Robbie out in front with nineteen, Latch was next, on fifteen and was followed by Curt and Leight. However, it was a season that belonged to the prodigious talent that was Robbie James.

Prior to the start of the 1982/ 83 season, Robbie's final, another pre-season tour of Scotland took in a testimonial match at Stark's Park with Raith Rovers and another at Dundee, supplemented by visits to Rotherham United and Wigan and at the Vetch against Leicester City, in readiness for this second and final season in the top flight for Robbie as a Swansea player (and for the club). A trading embargo on any new signings had been placed on the club by the Football League after they had fallen behind in repayments to Everton for Bob Latchford and Gary Stanley. A startling revelation would come this season with the news that the club was now £2m+ in debt. With its small pool of first team players; only seventeen professionals supplemented by a dozen juniors, the Swans were in for a testing campaign.

Robbie advanced to playing in all but two of the forty-two League games; away to Arsenal and home to Nottingham Forest and features in seventeen of the eighteen various Cup games this season. Optimistic odds of 28/1 had been offered for the Swans to land the First Division title at the start of a new campaign where Tosh made ex-team mate Ray Kennedy captain despite drawing to the attention of his manager the split between players and the poor team spirit. Ray would subsequently leave the club under a cloud after having been persuaded to sign for the Swans due to heir League position and obvious prospects. He later revealed that he felt out of things at the Vetch, recognising a divide between the Welsh-born players and the rest of the squad.

Be Proud to be a SWAN

Writing in his excellent autobiography, Ray of Hope, acknowledged, "Some of the Welsh boys like Curt, Jeremy Charles and Robbie were okay, but there was no real knitting together of the team as had occurred at Liverpool and no forward planning."

The new campaign saw Swans fans paying £3.50 or £3.00 for match day tickets with the first team playing a total of sixty games. Attendances would dip for this final season in the top flight, with season ticket sales reduced as a recession hit Wales. A season ticket for the West Stand cost £130; with match day admission in to the East stand was £5.60.

After retaining the Welsh Cup thanks to an aggregate victory over Cardiff City, the Swans commenced their season in the preliminary round of the European Cup Winners' Cup against Sporting Braga at the Vetch Field on 17 August. The Swans, who had been knocked-out of the competition in the first round last season, did a lot better this year commencing in the preliminary round stage. They won the game thanks to a marvelous 3-0 score line after advancing to a 1-0 lead by half time against their Portuguese opponents. A gate of 10,641 attended this season opener and saw a brace from Charles supplemented by an own goal. With Yugo Swans Hadziabdic and Rajkovic joining Robbie in the team, the return tie a week later at the Primeiro di Maio stadium ended in a 1-0 defeat thanks to an unfortunate own goal from young Chris Marustik, no doubt enjoyed by the 18,000 crowd. Despite the reverse, it meant that the Swans progressed to the next round where they would face Maltese minnows Sliema Wanderers in mid-September.

Before that, the domestic season started with a goal less draw with Notts County at Meadow Lane prior to the opening match at the Vetch, a Tuesday evening affair against Coventry City on 31 August. A somewhat underwhelming 11,712 came out to see Robbie score from the penalty spot before Latch added a second in a 2-0 win. The twosome repeated them selves in a successive win at home to Norwich City, with Latch scoring a hat-trick (the first of two, this season) in a 4-0 victory against the Division One new boys. The troublesome Watford beat the Swans 2-1 at their place whilst Stoke added another defeat thanks to a 4-1 win played out on a muddy pitch which glaringly revealed tactical errors employed by the visitors from west Wales. Worryingly for Kennedy, his debilitating illness was starting to show itself.

It was some while before Robbie next put his name on the score card as defeats at the Vetch to Liverpool and away at Aston Villa contrasted with an impressive 2-0 victory against F.A Cup holders Spurs on 2 October. Robbie had scored against them in a 2-1 win at the home in the previous season. The likes of Liverpool still produced marvellous attendances at the Vetch, with 20,232 and 16,381 there to see their visit and the Spurs game. Alas, there would be no return like last season as the Swans were well-beaten by a premium quality Reds side that contained Ian Rush. The 0-3 loss was watched by Wales boss Mike England. Kennedy was successfully switched to defence v Spurs.

Three days before the Liverpool visit, the Swans welcomed Maltese Cup winners Sliema to Wales. A lowly 5,130 crowd saw the record-breaking 12-0 obliteration of the visitors in what was City's eleventh European outing. Already 4-0 up by half-time thanks to Charlo, Loveridge, Irwin and Latchford, the second half saw another goal from Charles followed by strikes from Loveridge, Hadziabdic, Rajkovic, Stevenson and a hat-trick from Ian Walsh (introduced as a second half substitution). Just with his international debut in a 7-0 mauling of Malta, Robbie failed to get in on the act here after the Swans had the bizarre distinction of seeing eight different scorers! The Swansea City team line-up for this record victory, which still stands, was Davies, Marustik, Irwin, Stevenson, Hadziabdic; Robbie, Rajkovic, Kennedy; Loveridge, Latchford, Charles. The return leg, played two weeks later at the end of September at Ta Qali, Valletta, saw a much-changed Swansea side, minus Robbie, win 0-5 in front of a 2,000 gate. A brace from Curt and youngster Darren Gale was finished-off by a rare Toshack strike.

A draw at Brighton, where the visitors fell behind in the first minute before a Dudley Lewis equaliser curtailed a run of four away defeats then saw defeat at Goodison Park to Everton followed by Robbie collecting his third League goal of the season in an exciting 3-2 defeat of Southampton at the Vetch. That game saw the welcomed return of fan's favourite Rajkovic to the side after a five-week injury blip. The striking skills of a youthful Jimmy Loveridge saw him utilised on many occasions this season but it only saw a return of four goals. Fellow youngster Gale also made the high step-up to life in Division One.

October closed with a defeat at Manchester City, with the Swans having completed their first dozen League fixtures to a poor return: they had won four, lost six and drew two.

Ossie Ardiles returned to the Vetch in the white shirt of his new club, Paris St Germain, requiring the Swans to wear their dark blue kit, for a first round proper tie in the European Cup Winners' Cup on 20 October. He left with his club clutching a valuable 0-1 away lead in readiness for the return leg in Paris on 3 November. Ticket prices for the tie with the French Cup winners were cut as gates for the two previous home games against Sporting Braga and Sliema Wanderers had proven under-whelming. They continued, with less than 10k there to see the latest encounter against the "crack French side", as Tosh described them. Fortunately for the little Argentine, Tommy Smith had since retired and he managed to set-up the only goal of the game on seventy-one minutes. It was the first of three matches scheduled for the Vetch across a single week. The Swans put out a full-strength side that saw Robbie alongside players the likes of Mahoney, Kennedy, Stanley and Latch over at the Parc des Princes stadium, in which Tosh made three changes. It meant a return for young Nigel Stephenson, Rajkovic and Charlo to face an opposition in front of 49,700 spectators. It made no difference, as the Swans lost via a goal scored in each half, and went out of the competition 3-0 on aggregate.

November failed to see much of an improvement with only a decent 3-0 home defeat of Sunderland presented, followed by a 3-3 away at West Brom. Robbie scored a goal in each of those matches. But losses surfaced against Arsenal, whom Swansea had been twice in the previous season but had the opposite done to them this campaign and Ipswich before newly-promoted Luton, who ran the Swans so close in the 1980/81 promotion race, made their first Division One visit to the Vetch Field in December. The Hatters lost 2-0 on a muddy pitch noteworthy in that the fixture attracted the smallest crowd of the season: 9,556. Also of significance was John Mahoney reaching his hundredth appearance in a Swansea City shirt since signing from Middlesborough. Collecting fifty-one caps for Wales, a number of them found Robbie next to him in the line up.

With an out-of-form Curt and Leighton James soon to depart for Sunderland on a free transfer, December 1982 found the Swans seventeenth in the table after registering seven wins across twenty-one games. Robbie scored a consolation goal, his sixth of the season, in a 2-1 defeat at Forest only capped by an excellent performance from Dai Davies. Toshack was getting desperate and in his autobiography, Kennedy recounts his manager visiting the homes of the younger squad members in an attempt to motivate them. Old pro Ray would have none of it and his relationship with his former Liverpool colleague, where they would battle for a place in the starting XI, was souring as the club span out of control. The situation would degenerate so badly that Razor would miss the final five League matches and was harassed by the coaching staff before he was put on the transfer list and had his captaincy removed. Robbie was given the role thereafter but relegation was unavoidabe.

February found the team third from bottom in the division whilst an early visit from old adversaries Watford saw an encouraging 14,461 attend the Vetch. Thanks to the scheduling of the match on a Sunday, it was the first occasion that the day had been used in a number of years. They lost 1-3 but at least saw Ray Kennedy return to the fold. Spurs reversed their 2-0 away defeat recorded back in October with a 1-0 win in the return fixture a couple of days before St.Valentine's Day. Robbie scored again, against Everton in a 2-2 away draw which was seen by 17,112 and was a huge improvement on their loss at the Vetch the previous October Neville Southall kept Robbie and the Swans out in a 0-3 win.

Stopper Dai Davies had been an ever-present in goal, up until March when a trip to Southampton proved to be his final appearance between the sticks. He was replaced by twenty-year-old local lad Chris Sander, half the age of Dai, who would soon be allowed to leave the Vetch on a free transfer. Robbie, another certainty on the team sheet, had now played in all twenty-one League games up until he was hit by an injury which forced him to miss a trip to face Arsenal back on New Year's Day.

Further injury woes continued in March for Toshack, with Hadziabdic carried off in the last minute of the 2-1 defeat at Southampton. Decent victories that same month over Manchester City and West Bromwich Albion were countered by a 3-1 defeat at Luton's Kenilworth Road, in mid-March, which helped plonk the Swans at the bottom of the table. Another successful Robbie penalty, his second this season, was the final contribution in an impressive 4-1 defeat of Manchester City on 12 March, with the others coming from Latchford and Walsh. A subsequent 1-1 at Sunderland, with Leighton James now in their side, was followed by Robbie's final League strike, against the aforementioned West Brom before a gate totalling 11,222 at the Vetch.

Prior to the Luton match, the Swans failed to manage a win in four subsequent games; drawing 1-1 with Birmingham, losing 1-5 to West Ham and 3-0 at Liverpool before a 1-1 with Stoke.

A point salvaged a week after the defeat at Luton saw a 1-1 at the Vetch Field against visitors Ipswich failed to put a positive spin on the club's dire plight: with thirty-nine games played they had won only nine times against nineteen defeats

and eleven draws. They did beat European Cup holders Aston Villa before a 2-1 defeat at Old Trafford to a Manchester United side that would close the season in third place behind Watford and Champions Liverpool. "I felt very sorry for Swansea,"began their manager 'Big Ron' Atkinson in an interview with the Western Mail (9 May), "When they first came up they were a team of golden oldies. Now they have brought in younger men and have been caught." He also made further comments in his programme notes, "To be in the First Division in the first place is successful. So all right, relegation can hardly be called a trophy, but two years in the First Division after coming from nowhere is to be applauded."

That loss to United was the penultimate fixture of a disheartening domestic campaign and was concluded a week later with the visit of Nottingham Forest to the Vetch. The Swans had already been relegated by the time of this game and 9,226 watched them slip in to Division Two via a 0-3 score line. Tosh and his backroom staff ended up with a mere twelve players available for selection due to a culmination of injuries. The Old Trafford defeat, attended by 35,724, was understandable in that United had not lost at home across thirty-one games.

Above: Robbie often featured prominently in away
programmes, as these examples demonstrate.

Swansea suffered relegation sandwiched between Manchester City and Brighton and had the unwanted distinction of not winning a single away fixture all season; despite scoring sixty-one goals at home and thirty-one times away from the Vetch. In all, the team won eleven times across all competitions in comparison to the twenty-one victories of the previous season. However, they did manage good wins against the likes of Spurs, Manchester City and Aston Villa. "So many things seemed to go wrong…" lamented Tosh in his late match day programme notes in May 1983.

Relegation from Division One might have occurred but in the Welsh Cup Swansea stormed to retaining the trophy. Commencing with a 3-0 win at Newport County's Somerton Park against part-time amateurs Spencer Works, with Robbie grabbing the first two goals, it was followed by an impressive 2-1 win against rivals Shrewsbury Town. A fifth round home tie with Hereford United, a club against whom Robbie had scored against twice in the 1980/ 81 two-game final, found him again netting in a 3-1 success attended by 2,688. It was his third Cup goal of the season and helped to advance the Swans to a two-game semi-final meeting with Colwyn Bay which commenced with a single Latch goal proving enough in the first meeting. The return at the Vetch Field some two weeks later, in mid-March, finished in a win for the Swans. Again a low attendance, 2,932 proved disappointing but those that did come out to support their team saw a 3-0 victory and a final with old adversaries Wrexham scheduled for 10 May and 17 May. They beat them 1-2 at the Racecourse before 5,630 attended the Vetch in the closing game of the season: a 2-0 win, with top scorer Bob Latchford hitting both goals.

Robbie topped the appearances chart on forty League games in his final season as a Swansea player. He and his family packed-up their things and set-off on the 190 mile journey to Stoke-on-Trent, where he would next be playing his football at the Victoria Ground with Stoke City.

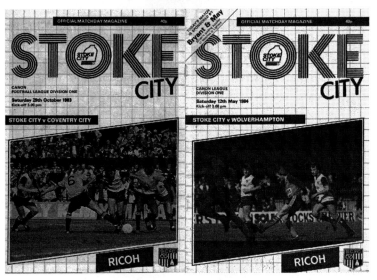

Stoke City

*"He would pick up the ball from just inside the opposition
half, set off down the middle and suddenly unleash a rocket
from about forty yards. In my memory, it seems like he did
that nearly every fortnight…"*

Stokecity-mad.co.uk

That was a quote from a Stokie aka a Stoke City supporter
upon remembering Robbie as a player with the club between
1983 and 1984. Presently aged twenty-six and an established
international, Robbie had chosen to leave Swansea City
during the summer of 1983, following their relegation from
the First Division after two eventful seasons. Stoke offered him
the opportunity to remain playing his football in the top flight
and so he signed for them on 10 July 1983, for an initial
£100,000 fee. He had rejected a new, three-year deal offered
by the Swans and with it, the promise of a lucrative testimonial
game at the Vetch. His former club wanted £250,000 for him,
whilst Stoke valued him at half that amount. The eventual fee
was decided via a tribunal, with the Potters required to fork
out that original £100,000, with an additional £60,000 to be
paid when Robbie advanced to making eighty appearances.

WALES
v
RUMANIA

STOKE CITY F.C.
CO. LTD.
VICTORIA GROUND
STOKE-ON-TRENT ST4 4EG

STOKE CITY F.C.
CO. LTD.
VICTORIA GROUND
STOKE-ON-TRENT ST4 4EG

The Racecourse, Wrexham

Wednesday 12th October 1983
Kick-off 7.30 pm

MICKEY THOMAS
Stoke City and Wales

ROBBIE JAMES
Stoke City and Wales

TICKETS FROM:

THE FOOTBALL ASSOCIATION OF WALES
3 FAIRY ROAD, WREXHAM, CLWYD, LL13 7PS

Stand Tickets: £6.00; £4.00; £3.00
(Family seat 2) £5.50

Admission to Ground: £2.00; Schoolchildren: £1.00
(by payment at the turnstile)

Mickey Thomas & Robbie James are both in the Welsh squad for this game.

The Swans would also be guaranteed fifty percent of any sell-on fee, thereafter. In actuality, he would play in fifty-five games for Stoke City before a subsequent transfer took him to Queens Park Rangers in mid-October 1984.

Leaving the Vetch allowed Robbie the opportunity to vent his frustration at his former club for allowing big name players to come in and take high wages. "There was an air of inevitability at what happened there," he told the Western Mail adding that the local youngsters were not being nurtured properly, dwarfed by the established names.

Robbie was one of four new signings made by manager Richie Barker joining the playing staff at the Victoria Ground in anticipation of the oncoming 1983/ 84 season. The club had finished their previous campaign in thirteenth place, with fifty-seven points collected in comparison to the Swans, relegated on forty-one. Robbie was brought in as replacement for Paul Bracewell, who had rejoined former City boss Alan Durban at Sunderland, where a certain Leighton James was filling the number eleven shirt. In a subsequent interview, Leight declared

that he felt that Robbie was the hardest footballer that ever lived! Robbie was also to be used to help flesh-out the talented midfield consisting of former Manchester United team mates Mickey Thomas and Sammy McIlroy. Mickey was a familiar face from various Wales squads whilst big George Berry was another player that had featured alongside Robbie in the national team. Indeed, Robbie and Thomas would continue to represent Wales whilst Stoke City players, as would McIlroy, only for Northern Ireland, in his case. Brendan O'Callaghan, known fondly as Big Bren, was a well-established international name at the club and he had competed against Robbie as a Doncaster Rovers youngster as far back as the 1974/ 75 season and in subsequent seasons. Known predominantly as a striker and a strong header of the ball, O'Callaghan had turned professional in 1973 and saw his career with Stoke span across eight years. Team captain McIlroy was another pedigree name now to become a friend and team mate. Sammy would play in a World Cup for his country, something that Robbie had always wanted to do with Wales. The two would later continue to cross paths as players and player/managers. Also in the team was rising England winger Mark Chamberlain and veteran keeper Peter Fox was another talent that played with Robbie this season. It would be a trying campaign which saw a managerial change by Christmas and a struggle to retain their First Division status extending to the final game, at home, to local rivals Wolverhampton Wanderers on 12

May. "We had a rag-tag bunch of players that made a good side that first season," remembers another City fan about their 1983/84 campaign in the newly-sponsored Canon Division One.

After another gruelling pre-season encompassing an extensive tour of Sweden, taking in a half-dozen games and resulting in fifty goals across eight matches, the future was looking good. Robbie managed to score in one of the encounters, a 4-0 win against Ljusdal before fixtures with Oswestry, Shrewsbury and Bournemouth were added once they returned, with the Welshman worrying his new employers by picking up a knock in the latter game.

His debut in a newly re-designed Stoke shirt, now minus the recognisable vertical red stripes, arrived away at Everton on Saturday, 27 August 1983 in a 1-2 defeat watched by 22,658. Wearing number four, his new team conceded a goal from a corner to lose the match, something that he had experienced as a Swansea player, previously. Ironically, in recent seasons Stoke had a reputation for scoring using this method.

Robbie would make forty appearances across the season and score seven times after initially struggling to adapt to a new playing style favoured by Barker. It would be something that led him to eventually lose his job as results plummeted despite the players being keen to adapt to the new structure. Thankfully for Robbie, he managed to blend in better once they changed to building attacks from midfield, thus allowing him to run at defenders and put in lots of shots, as he had done with the Swans. Back there, they used a sweeper system where all development stemmed from the rear of the team. Early opposition Everton had Neville Southall and Kevin Ratcliffe in their team, both Wales team mates alongside Robbie (and Rats later a club colleague, too).

As a pro, Robbie had played at the Victoria Ground as a Swans on a number of occasions. His new club had been an original founder of the Football League and would see the 'Vic' as their home for more than a century before moving to the Britannia Stadium in 1997. Funnily enough, the last Stoke player to score in a competitive match at the ground was Graham Kavanagh, later to play for a club familiar to Robbie; Cardiff City.

His home debut came against West Bromwich Albion, two days after the Everton defeat. Cyril Regis, who had scored a hat-trick against Robbie's Swansea side early in the 1981/82 season, was again in the opposition line-up. But there would be no repeat of that 4-0 demolition here, as Robbie's Stoke beat the Baggies 3-1 in front of a 16,156 crowd. A visit by Manchester United came next and their arrival pushed the gate up to 23,704, with the Reds taking away a 0-1 win. This result was to be repeated in the first of two away fixtures; at Birmingham City and then added to by a 5-0 thumping at Ipswich Town. A Robbie header against the former had flown just wide but in East Anglia, with future Leicester City team mate Paul Cooper in goal, Stoke suffered a heavy defeat. Despite this, Robbie, Thomas, O'Callaghan and Chamberlain would all be selected for international duties at the time of the next home game, a week later, against Watford. Barker's woes were expounded by a heavy 0-4 hammering from the recent Division One runners-up, extending a run of four defeats in what the manager termed a "shaky start". Halted thanks to a 2-2 at Leicester, where a definite two points had been lost due to the Potters advancing to 0-2 up within half hour.

On a personal note, now settled in the Trentham area, Robbie and his second wife Karen welcomed their new daughter Hannah into the world this September (as all pictured opposite). Robbie already had one other daughter, Samantha, born to first wife, Yvonne.

West Ham United had often proven difficult opponents whilst Robbie was a Swansea player but the hoodoo was broken with a  commendable 3-1 win at the "Vic" on 1 October. That game had seen Hammers boss John Lyall flabbergasted that his team had to wait until the end of the first half for a successful break through the heart of a resilient Stoke midfield. The lanky McAughtrie put Stoke 1-0 up and Robbie was the first to congratulate him as they advanced to defeat the-then League leaders. After the same player gave away a penalty for the score to be equalised, the team advanced to 2-1 on sixty-nine minutes with Robbie directly involved in the third and final goal scored by a jubilant Mickey Thomas. Collecting the ball from midfield, Robbie passed to Chamberlain on the right wing before motioning to him to play the ball back in front of him, as the winger's path was locked by two defenders. Robbie struck a shot which keeper Phil Parkes managed to get down low for and push to his right, only for an unmarked Thomas to put in an easy goal. Also this month, the BBC televised their very first live Division One fixture whilst being in attendance during this match, also.

Two weeks later and Sunderland's Roker Park saw two away goals from the Stoke number four; namely Robbie James. It was a special day as it saw him collect his hundredth League goal (more if you add his various Cup goals). His second strike, put in via a header, proved to be an outstanding one and the equaliser in an exciting 2-2 affair. Also memorable but for the wrong reason, was that during the match Robbie broke his nose (he would suffer this on four occasions during his long playing career). A tough cookie, he had it re-set in the following week and played in a specially arranged, private practice match soon after.

After a draw at Notts County, Robbie collected his third goal of the season, a thunderbolt shot, to record his side's second strike in a 2-1 League (Milk) Cup victory against Peterborough. The 0-0 at home, a few weeks earlier had troubled his manager, who was surprised at the lack of commitment shown by his team. Stoke had reached the quarter-finals back in 1979 but would fade in the fourth round of this season's competition.

A 3-1 defeat at home to Coventry City next was not welcomed and Barker was now under tremendous pressure but time was running low for him, despite having 18 months left on his contract still to run, he would not see it out. Not previously inexperienced, he had worked at Shrewsbury Town and Wolves but not in a full managerial capacity and had been a pro footballer earlier.

Three draws across a gruelling week saw the team obliged to play a total of eight times in November. The points came against Division One hot shots Spurs and Aston Villa and in a mid-week Milk Cup tie with Second Division side Huddersfield Town. The latter had held City to a goal-less encounter at the Victoria Ground and had already put out

Watford in the previous round; impressive in that they would complete a League 'double' over Stoke this season. The clubs had not played each other in more than a decade (with Stoke winning 1-0 at home). At the time of the match the Potters could be found fourth from bottom in Division One, after twelve games, winning only twice at home so far. The game finished 0-0, in front of a large 14,727 gate whilst the return, two weeks later, was won 0-2 by Stoke, after a recent draw with Villa and loss at Liverpool in the League. Prior to this, they had held Spurs to a 1-1 at White Hart Lane in an impressive team effort from the visitors. Robbie missed a 1-1 with Forest before returning for a fourth round League Cup tie with Sheffield Wednesday at the end of the month. Elimination from the Cup arrived courtesy of Wednesday, who beat them by a single goal. The match was attended by a handsome 18,653, the second largest of the campaign, which pleased the club, as it was not in a healthy financial footing. Utilised by all his clubs for off-field concerns, Robbie attended a Players Forum with supporters this month but staged in an area predominantly known as a Port Vale strong-hold(their rivals!)

Across the final month of 1983, Stoke looked to be extending their poor showings since dropping nine League points from a possible twelve in November and only managing a solitary win. It would prove a frustrating yet conversely, bountiful time for Robbie as the team fell to defeats by Southampton and Luton Town; both clubs which they would face in May, also. Robbie collected a consolation goal in the 3-1 loss to the Saints before a brace against Town proved inadequate to prevent a 4-2 defeat. Former Ipswich captain Mick Mills would advance to spend four years at Stoke during the autumn of his playing career and become club manager following his subsequent appointment in August 1985. Robbie had left by then but found the former England international to be very knowledgeable about the game and felt that he would be perfect to pursue a career as a coach or manager. Also in the Southampton team was former Swan Alan Curtis. In a period when it was proving hard for supporters to still "Be proud to be a Potter", most Stokies remembered the dramatic 4-4 with the Hatters at the Vic in the previous season and this one also produced the goods, including a Robbie penalty success. A goal-free away trip to regional rivals Wolves followed Richie Barker being sacked and former terrace favourite Bill Asprey fill the caretaker boss role as the club sat in twenty-first position in the table. He had been a valued servant of the club across 341 appearances as a versatile cog in the team since making his playing debut as a seventeen-year-old back in 1954. With Stoke in a coaching capacity for the past two years, he would progress to manage them until towards the end of the following campaign, where ill-health forced his departure as the team suffered relegation.

But back this season, Robbie recorded his lucky seventh goal of the season in a Boxing Day visit to the Vic by Norwich. Attended by a little over 12,000 supporters, they were rewarded with a late present, an absolute cracker from Robbie as the Canaries were flattened 2-0 with Maguire getting the other goal. New Year's Eve saw a not unexpected 1-0 defeat to eventual League runners-up Manchester United away, an exact same score line from the corresponding fixture in September. Nearly 24,000 had attended that game but at Old Trafford a splendid 40,164 came to watch.

Into the New Year and after completing twenty-five League and Cup games, Stoke welcomed Leicester City to the Victoria Ground on Monday 2 January. Hoping for at least a point, after sharing the spoils back in the end of September via a 2-2, the Stoke players had been obliged to attend training on New Year's Day in anticipation of the match. In the visitor's side was rising striker Gary Lineker, a recognised Robbie favourite and also in their line-up was Irish international Paul Ramsey. He and Robbie would eventually link-up at Leicester and later enjoy success as Cardiff City team mates. Returning to the present meeting, the Foxes spoilt the day by stealing a 0-1 win.

Below: A smiling Robbie pictured immediate left, top row. Also in the squad with him are fellow Wales team mates at some point, Mickey Thomas and George Berry.

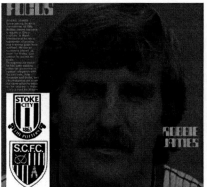

The F.A Cup was a necessary distraction next, with a testing, third round meeting with Everton. Pencilled in at home, scheduling decreed that the clubs would also meet for a second time, a week later, in the League. Robbie could only watch on as his team conceded twice to kiss goodbye to any further Cup advancement. The teams reconvened, again with Stoke as hosts, for a 1-1 League draw. Peculiarly but not so surprising, was the fact that the attendance for the first game was 16,462 proved to be twice the amount as those that attended the corresponding fixture. The inclement weather might have been a consideration as during one of the matches Robbie was pictured during a snow flurry!

It proved to be another hectic month, with six matches scheduled and despite the early results, Asprey still believed that his team possessed the drive to retain their First Division status. Coincidentally, with their lack of goals obvious, an attempt to bring in former Swan striker Bob Latchford, recently released by the Swans on a free, failed.

However, the worst result of the season was to arrive next in a 6-0 thrashing on the plastic pitch at Loftus Road, home of Queen's Park Rangers. Played on 17 January, the Stoke squad did have an opportunity to play on a similar surface the day before the match but most of them described the Rangers pitch as being the equivalent of playing on the M6 motorway! Installed at great financial cost, many in the game opposed its arrival but the trend was not exclusive to Rangers, as Preston, Luton and Oldham would also have them. The artificial surface of the time certainly proved harsh on the bodies of the older players and particularly on the knee joints. The Stoke fans are a passionate, loyal lot and they showed their vocal support to the players from behind one of the goals during the walloping. And Stoke still had the task of having to play them at home in mid-April, too.

The Q.P.R debacle was superseded by a fruitless jaunt to Vicarge Road and a 2-0 loss thanks to late strikes. With a strong Arsenal side coming to the Vic on 28 January, there had been hectic scenes at the ground as staff worked hard to remove a layer of surface snow in readiness for the game. Elsewhere in the team, Mickey Thomas proved elusive and missed training sessions whilst pre-empting a move to Chelsea. Meanwhile former old boy Alan Hudson returned to the club, on loan, after ten years away. Known as 'Huddy', he reveals that the spirit at the club is excellent and the best that he has known as a player. With Robbie establishing himself in the Swansea first team back in 1975, when Alan had made public his frustration with then-current England manager Don Revie for not proving consistent in selecting him. The Arsenal game saw a stunning Stoke victory, 1-0 with Huddy putting in a Man-of-the-Match showing. With seventeen games remaining, Stoke were far from finished.

February commenced badly with a visit to West Ham offering little in a 3-0 defeat watched by a healthy 18,775 gate before Ipswich are beaten by a very late winner at the Vic, to overturn that 5-0 hammering at Portman Road back in September. This is followed by a tricky trip to Coventry which saw a five goal thriller with the team twice coming from behind to take away a 2-3 win; their first of the season, in a game within which Robbie was substituted. A week later, at home, a 1-0 win and three valuable points are added after Notts County are sent packing in front of 11,725 supporters; bettering the recent visit by Ipswich. At a time when the Stoke manager stated that his team was going to play its way out of trouble, the players produced the goods and saw their third win of the month. their League position was unaffected but the club spirit is strong at this mid-season point.

Robbie is selected for Wales in an important match with Scotland while his club team mates fly out to Saudi Arabia on 27 February as late replacements for Nottingham Forest to play the national side. They win the encounter 1-4, whilst at Hampden Park, Robbie scores from twenty-five yards but still ends up on the losing side, as Wales fall to a 2-1 defeat.

Back in readiness for a 3 March fixture at Spurs, where they lose 1-0, City have by now played twenty-nine games, one less than next opponents, Aston Villa, whose visit sees a heightened 13,967 at the Vic for the first of three consecutive matches against Midlands clubs. Villa are nine places above them in the table but the afternoon sees Stoke produce another of their much-needed 1-0 wins. Birmingham City had been in decent recent form, with four wins on the trot taking them away from the relegation zone when they came to Stoke a week later. The Blues had beaten them at St.Andrews 1-0 in September, when The Potters had lost their last three of four matches. A Jekyll and Hide side, Stoke produce a 2-1, in front of 13,506. The game sees lots of bookings and a Birmingham player sent off in a fiery encounter that Hudson says is the best team performance he has seen since his return. He also said that the team should be proud to have won the match by playing a skillful, and well-crafted game. Keeper Peter Fox is quoted as being convinced that they would stay up. Robbie was an absentee for the trip to West Brom, only his second all season, this time concluding with a hefty 3-0 dismissal. On the last day of March, an important fixture for both Stoke and Sunderland is presented. Both in desperate need of points, Sunderland had former Newport boss Len Ashurst in charge, with Leighton James in their side after being he was brought to the club by previous manager Alan Durban on a free transfer from Swansea in January 1983. Stoke could be found one place below their opponents in the table but three points worse off. A 2-2 at Roker Park back in mid-October, with both goals from Robbie, was added to by a 2-1 victory enjoyed by 11,047.

The penultimate month of the season found the team in nineteenth place in Division One and presented with some strong challenges: namely Arsenal and Liverpool then Norwich, Q.P.R 144 and Nottingham Forest. The visit of Manchester United had so far proven to attract the largest crowd to the Vic but Arsenal saw 21,211 watch a game where the visitor's second goal, in a 1-3 win, was scored via a pinched throw-in. It would be Liverpool, soon to be crowned Champions, produce the highest gate of the 1983/ 84 season: 24,372. How the Stokies must have loved it as Robbie and his team mates soared to a 2-0 upset. It was a shock result against the top-of-the-table Reds and found Foxy playing well in goal. Robbie too had a good game, marshalling hard man midfielder Grahame Souness. The tough-tackling Scot was hugely complimentary about him afterwards. Momentum was sustained for a 2-2 at Norwich before Q.P.R beat City at the Vic, 1-2. The closing game of the month saw a point salvaged in a 0-0 away at the City Ground, to hosts Nottingham Forest but Robbie's team was firmly rooted to twentieth place in the table with only three games of the season remaining.

Southampton would record a commendable top five finish this year but they came to the Victoria Ground on 5 May after a recent 8-2 mauling by Coventry the previous week. Semi-finalists in this season's FA Cup, Saints talent Alan Curtis did not play in this meeting which saw a share of the points in a 1-1 draw. Two days later and three invaluable points came Stoke's way in a terrific 0-1 away win at Luton. With Wolves and Notts County beneath them, the latter having played a game less, City had beaten County 1-0 at home in February and drawn 1-1 back in October at Meadow

Lane. Against Wolves, a goal less draw had been played out at Molineux back in December and everything was set for the closing day of the season, at home, on 12 May.

The final match found City having collected forty-seven points, with County on forty and Wolves on twenty-nine. There were six teams above Stoke all within three points and so there was still a great deal left to play for. "Here we are," proclaimed manager Bill Asprey writing in his match programme notes, "and one that is on the knife edge like never before. Let us hope that fate can deal us the luck we need to keep our feet in the First Division." Wonderfully, his team put four goals past Wolves and rightfully avoided the drop by rising up to eighteenth, on the same points as Coventry but with a better goal difference. Birmingham, Notts County and Wolves finished as the bottom three clubs.

After the late drama experienced at the close of the 1983/84 season, Robbie must surely have been pleased to be starting his second campaign as a First Division player with Stoke City. An insipid 3-0, pre-season friendly defeat at Ninian Park with Cardiff City on Saturday 18 August 1984 took Robbie close to home, whilst the Bluebirds prepared for their oncoming season in Division Two.

Robbie had agreed to be the Supporters Club President at Stoke but little did anybody realise that his stay was to be an acutely short one this year. Mr Asprey had by now been rewarded with the managerial post as the team opened the season with a 2-1 defeat at Luton. Once more wearing number four, Robbie missed the second game, and the first at the Victoria Ground, a 1-3 defeat to Aston Villa attended by an opening day gate of 12,605. Not a bad figure but almost 4,000 down on the inaugural game of the previous season. A welcome first win of the new campaign arrived in a 2-1 home victory against Sheffield Wednesday less than a week later and boosted by an improved number of fans coming through the turnstiles. Soon after, a chronic bout of influenza swept through the playing squad, affecting Robbie and everyone else, with the peculiar exception of Brendan O'Callaghan! Despite this, a starting XI bravely held on to a lead despite a late goal by Wednesday and a player being dismissed for the Potters. The off-field ailments became so acute that in early September, no one was fit enough to even attend training.

Robbie recuperated well enough to be able to play for Wales in Iceland before returning in anticipation of a League game three days later, on 15 September. There had been an enforced, two-week break of fixtures until the third week of the month when Leicester came to the Victoria Ground and shared the points in a 2-2 draw. Still with his players unwell, Asprey had only two fully-fit men in his squad selected to travel to meet Norwich City. Pleading with the Football League for a postponement, this was denied and remarkably the team soldiered-on to take a point in a 0-0 at Carrow Road.

Highbury offered no solace as the Gunners mercilessly trounced their visitors 4-0 with Robbie being substituted during the game, the club's sixth of the season. Their luck did not improve with a visit from Rotherham in a second round, Milk Cup tie. United took away a 1-2 lead in readiness for the second leg on 9 October. Stoke would need to score at least twice in that return, if they were to progress in the competition. Advancing to that tie, Robbie had two attempts on goal excellently saved by the keeper, as he continued with his good recent form. "He must be wondering why his first goal of the season has been so long in coming," pondered team mate Ian Painter in an interview with sports reporter David Instone. Little could he know that Robbie would soon be leaving?

A fighting Stoke City performance saw them score two late goals in a 2-2 home draw with Sunderland, now minus Leighton James before the squad travelled to another club that Robbie had previously scored against: Notts Forest.

Facing a Forest team that would finish in fourth place in the table, the clubs had drawn 0-0 in the previous season and this time Robbie pursued a central midfield role and was involved in a lot of probing and pushing the ball forward during a strong first half for Stoke. In one highlight, his header was saved by their keeper after he had initially started the move out on the left before Chamberlain crossed for him to meet the ball a little outside of the area.

On eleven minutes, Robbie watched as forgotten man Berry scrambled in a goal from a corner kick. Wearing their stylish two-tone blue kit, Stoke provided good value before a second half saw them sustaining a lot of pressure from Clough's boys. A right foot volley from Robbie, struck from well outside of the box, almost proved successful as it narrowly whizzed past the right post and showed that Mr James still had a lot to offer. The club's fans recognised and appreciated this too, with one remembering, "...the hardest shot I have ever seen live at a game and although I don't think he scored many, the ones he did were screamers!" Berry's rare goal was the result of a recognisable Stoke set-piece utilised in recent seasons by the team. It arrived via an initial corner move, with the near post being hard to defend and compounded by tall players troubling the defence. Asprey had stated that his team needed a win against a quality side such as Forest to give them a confidence boost but it was definitely not helped by a sitter of a miss from O'Callaghan. But as we know in football the game is not over until the final whistle. Holding on to their slender lead, a late penalty from an unfortunate hand ball by Saunders, saw Forest equalise with minutes remaining.

A thoughtful club, the City board revealed that it would take a team to the Vetch for a testimonial scheduled for the early 1985 in aid of John Mahoney. An ankle injury had seen the conclusion of his playing career after serving both clubs well during his career.

A 1-2 loss at home to Rotherham in the League Cup, watched by 8,221 transpired to be Robbie's penultimate appearance for the club. Then on 13 October, at the Victoria Ground, Southampton paid a visit for what would be his last game in a Stoke City shirt. Starting for the visitors that afternoon was former England keeper Shilton, Mick Mills and Robbie's old Wales and Swansea City pal Alan Curtis. Stoke lost 1-3 and found themselves bottom of the table. By now, Robbie had completed forty-eight appearances across the two seasons, with an additional six various Cup games for them, scoring seven goals. In total, he played fifty-five times for the club.

All fans respect a player that tries his best and that was exactly how Robbie played. He might have lost his pace and never looked like he was starring in Chariots of Fire with his rigid running style but he was an experienced professional whose talent was appreciated by the supporters. "I can remember seeing him now, running around the Vic." Reflects one such fan on the excellent Oatcakes forum, "A mate that I used to go to the match with, now sadly passed away, used to call Robbie 'Casters' because of how he ran. Same as the underneath of an armchair..." Another was more succinct, "...a quality footballer...not too much pace...but hard as nails; good feet and ferocious shooting ability." Whilst a further Stokie adds, "Robbie was a good player. I always remember him for his shot. Not the most mobile player as he carried a bit of weight." Let's leave the final quote to a family relative whose sentiments have been echoed elsewhere. "Robbie was always a strong player, even when he was young and small; he would still go in hard for a tackle. Even though he was hard on the pitch, he was regarded as a real gentleman off it. Nothing was ever too much trouble for him, he would always be willing to help youngsters and do some presentations for schools or other football teams." Youngster Deborah Bomberg adds, in correspondence with the author, "We were fortunate to live next door to Robbie when he was with Stoke. We used to babysit his daughter Hannah and sometimes we were taken to matches to watch him play. He was an absolute gentleman. I remember being very sad when he suddenly passed away, we went to his funeral which was very sad."

Commendably, Stoke would send a team to Llanelli A.F.C, to play in a benefit match after Robbie's death.

Above: Robbie receiving yet another Man-of-the-Match award, this time for a cracking performance for Stoke against Norwich.

Queens Park Rangers
This is Loftus Road: We are Q.P.R

Joining Queens Park Rangers could definitely have been regarded as a career step-up for Robbie when he was signed by their new manager Alan Mullery in October 1984. Known as the "Super Hoops", "The R's" or simply "Rangers", the club had won the Division Two title in 1982/83 whilst Robbie and his Stoke City side avoided relegation on the final day of the following season's campaign and Rangers closed their campaign in the top flight in a highly-commendable third place. Therefore Robbie would have been optimistic after his £100,000 transfer took him to west London and Loftus Road, aka 'The Loft' and home of his new club. It had been whilst he had been away in Spain with Wales for a World Cup qualifier, that Rangers had shown an interest in signing him. And as Q.P.R. had qualified for the U.E.F.A Cup, the lure of European football proved decisive. Ironically, the club would be eliminated from the competition before he had a chance to get involved (but he would still see some European football with the Swans before his League career closed).

Founded in 1885 and taking the Queens Park Rangers mantle two years later, the club had installed Alan Mullery, a former Fulham and Spurs star, as its manager in June 1984 after the recent departure of former terrace favourite Terry Venables. However, despite enjoying earlier success with Brighton & Hove Albion, at Q.P.R, Mullery would not last the season. Coincidentally, 'Mullers' would be sacked after a 2-0 home defeat of Stoke at the beginning of December.

For Robbie, with absolutely no guarantee of automatic selection in the team possible, this did not seem to faze him. When he was selected, it was usually in midfield but he would often find himself back in defense. Robbie explained his methodology to Dennis Signy in a Rangers match day programme interview, "I play my best every time I am selected...if that's not good enough, I can't give more than my best." In his first season, he would wear the number seven, eight and nine shirts and advance to making twenty League appearances; four of them as a substitute and scoring twice.

Life at Loftus Road was going to prove somewhat different for Robbie as the club had recently installed a new Omniturf-branded artificial playing surface. It was billed as "The all weather pitch" by its manufacturer, but was regarded by many as being terrible to play on due to its erratic bounce. This caused much consternation to many away teams being obliged to play on it. But for those supporters that remember the Q.P.R pitch of the 1970s, the synthetic alternative could arguably be viewed as an improvement. Back in the 1980s, technological advancement was far inferior to what is available today, with modern day equivalents vastly superior. For many footballers plying their trade in the American Soccer League (the N.A.S.L) in the 1970s, the Astro turf pitches there were far worse. Some argued that the so-called 'plastic' pitches favoured by Q.P.R, Luton Town and Oldham offered unfair advantage to their hosts. They might have had a point, as by 1995 all such synthetic pitches would be banned from use in the Football League. Nonetheless, in recent seasons, Scottish football has embraced the trend once again; with four clubs making the switch to an artificial surface. In 2013, Cardiff Blues Rugby Club installed their own version as the viable alternative spread to the oval ball merchants, too. The Rangers pitch might have been acceptable for domestic games but entry into the U.E.F.A Cup this season, achieved and played before Robbie arrived, saw Arsenal's Highbury ground facilitating the match against Reykjavik F.C, due to the international body refusing to validate its credentials.

Most of the first team squad would be selected for the Reserves at some point and this was true for Robbie, too. He featured in their side visiting his old Vetch Field stomping ground on 19 October for a Football Combination fixture. He made many other appearances when not in contention for a first team spot and scored some goals also. Other clubs in the Combination included Millwall and Spurs.

The Rangers first-team squad included former Chelsea star Gary Chivers and ex-Brighton and Liverpool striker Michael Robinson. The former had been with the Swans for a brief loan period in the previous year when the Welsh club was situated in Division Two. He also played against Robbie as a Chelsea player, in the 1980/81 season and others.

Robbie had played against his new club on a number of occasions, as far back as his Swansea days but as a 'Super Hoop' player, he was introduced as a substitute in an away defeat at Arsenal on 17 November 1984. The 1-0 loss added to four matches without a win for his new team, then positioned in eighteenth place in the division. In the thirteen games of the domestic season completed before his arrival, Q.P.R. had won three, lost four and drawn six. In all, they had scored nineteen goals against twenty-four conceded. Across the 1984/85 season, the team would hit fifty goals against seventy-two leaked and with figures like that it was hardly surprising that they narrowly avoided relegation: beating the drop by a single point.

His home debut arrived in November with a stiff test against Aston Villa. The game provided Rangers with a 2-0 success which, by the following March, they would see a 5-2 reverse.

In the bread and butter dealings of League football, a trip to face a West Ham team that would finish their own campaign in a remarkable third, found Robbie listed as sub in the inaugural away game of the season; a 3-1 defeat. After being selected at number seven and being subbed against Ipswich Town in the season opener of 17 August, a 1-0 win, he advanced to wearing the number eight shirt across the next three games.

Stoke City, bottom of the table and doomed to exit the top division by the season close, traveled to Loftus Road in the first week of December and departed 2-0 losers. Oddly, the return at the Victoria Ground, at the end of the month, also concluded in a 2-0 win for Rangers, with Robbie scoring one of the

goals, his first of the campaign! Always having a good rapport with supporters, Robbie's return to the Vic was noted by the Stokies, "…every time he jogged over to take a corner for Q.P.R, the Stoke fans would all chant 'Boing! Boing! Boing' and he had a big smile on his face!" During his tenure in the Rangers camp, Robbie was unflatteringly termed "stiff legs" by the Loftus Road faithful but took it in good stead! In between City's visit, Q.P.R. also beat Villa 2-0 at home, as mentioned, but then lost away at Leicester City, a club that he would soon come to know.

When Robbie signed for Rangers they had twenty-eight League fixtures remaining and he advanced to featuring in all but eight of them. The Super Hoops managed eight more wins across the campaign, losing half-dozen others and achieving five draws. Noteworthy victories came against Arsenal and another, regarded as the best of the bunch; a 2-0 home win against Leicester in corresponding matches. Rangers managed a double over rivals West Ham but saw the same done to them by Luton and Manchester United. The win against Arsenal, after previously being defeated at their place, marked Robbie's second strike of the season in a Q.P.R. shirt, his goal proving to be an April 1985 winner at The Loft.

A mega 5-5 at home to Newcastle United back in September, prior to Robbie making his debut, is still talked of by fans today as it produced a stunning come back by Rangers. A respectable draw at Anfield against eventual League runners-up Liverpool also proved noteworthy but it was against Everton, a club that would win the title this year, which made the sporting headlines for the worst reasons. They traveled down to Shepherds Bush in the second week of December in a game which saw an extraordinary twenty-two man scuffle near the half-way line as a 0-0 draw was battled out.

No doubt Robbie and his team mates wished they hadn't bothered to make the away trip to Norwich this season, as it required the players changing in a nearby public house due to the aftereffects of a fire in City's main stand, earlier. A goal behind on fifteen minutes, Rangers lost 2-0 and even had to board their team coach still wearing their kit, to utilise the showering facilities at a local leisure centre afterwards. The teams played-out at a 2-2 at Loftus Road, in March, prior to being relegated.

Life as a professional footballer is a job like any other and poor Robbie had to play in a match on his twenty-eighth birthday on 23 March; a 2-0 loss away at Luton! Rangers, captained by former

Crystal Palace man Terry Fenwick, finished the 1984/ 85 season victims of a disappointing 1-3 home defeat by Manchester United. They would fill fourth place in the table whilst The R's collected fifty points, avoiding relegation by a single point, as mentioned. It meant that Norwich, Sunderland and Stoke headed out of the division as the bottom three.

So his first season as a Queens Park Rangers player could barely be considered a success for Robbie, necessitating another First Division struggle but what would the 1985/ 86 campaign have in store for him? Not having enjoyed his brief time in London with Arsenal whilst a teenager, Robbie later revealed that he was not happy living in the capital, feeling much more at home in Leicestershire subsequently and Stoke, previously. But for now, he would remain and play for Rangers across the next two seasons in the First Division.

The new 1985/ 86 season would show a slight improvement for Robbie and his team mates as Rangers appointed Jim 'Bald Eagle' Smith as their new manager on 11 June 1985. He replaced former Rangers player and manager, Frank Sibley who had acted as caretaker boss from December 1984 **153** through to the end of the previous season. Like Robbie, Sibley was still a teenager, aged fifteen, when he made his League debut and had looked after the team between 1977/ 78 previously. Meanwhile Smith had steered Oxford United up through the divisions, with the club enjoying huge success, just like the Swans had done when Robbie played for them (Watford and Wimbledon also achieved similar feats in recent years). The Q.P.R. job was his sixth managerial position and he had surprised everybody in the game by leaving Oxford after steering them to the Second Division championship: although his departure was not too much of a shock when we reveal that Robert Maxwell was the Chairman there. Smith would utilise Robbie on the left side of midfield across twenty-five League matches, three further as substitute and in a single F.A. Cup match.

Football always presents quirky coincidences and this season would be the same for Smith, as he would face his old club not only home and away in the League but also in the Milk (League) Cup Final in April which provided Robbie with the pleasure of an appearance at Wembley in April 1986. He had played two full international games there previously for visitors Wales but had yet to enjoy a win. Still selected by his country, Robbie started against Scotland in a September 1985 meeting at Ninian Park in Cardiff. By now, he had collected thirty-four caps in this his second season as a registered Q.P.R. player plying his trade in the highest division.

What a thrill it must have been for Robbie and his colleagues to make the walk out on to the lush Wembley pitch in front of a capacity crowd totaling more than 90,000. The team had worked hard to make it through to the final, playing eight times against five different opponents and taking in many chilly evening games played on wet pitches. The competition was now sponsored by The National Dairy Council and was then in its last year as the re-branded Milk Cup, when it hosted the Oxford v Q.P.R final on Sunday 20 April 1986.

Rangers had won the Cup back in 1967, the very first occasion that the final had been staged at Wembley, in a season that also saw the club crowned Third Division champions. And prior to Robbie joining them, they had pushed Spurs to a replay in the 1982 F.A Cup Final. Coincidentally, that same year saw the club celebrate its centenary whilst Robbie's Swansea side got beat by Liverpool in an early round.

Present League Cup holders Norwich City had seen Oxford put them out of contention in the fourth round whilst Rangers entered at the second round stage. They had already beaten Hull City and Watford before Robbie was selected for the side in a fourth round meeting with Nottingham Forest. That finished in a 3-0 success for the hosts meaning that rivals Chelsea would be played next.

Providing a sterner opposition, 27,000 crammed in to Loftus Road on 22 January, Rangers had annihilated Chelsea 6-0 on a mid-morning, Easter Monday after the sides had drawn their early League encounter. That was the case in this Cup game, a 1-1, with the replay offering the Super Hoops a 0-2 win on a muddy Stamford Bridge pitch, in front of a terrific 27,937 crowd on a cold evening. The reward was a semi-final meeting with Cup specialists Liverpool. Robbie played in the number eight shirt on the waterlogged Chelsea pitch, with manager Jim Smith still believing that his team could progress after an exciting previous meeting between the sides, a week before. Recently knocked-out of the F.A.Cup by Carlisle United and fifteenth in the First Division, Rangers had everything to play for whilst Chelsea was still marginally involved in the title race.

Robbie showed some deft little touches during the game, including a right foot, hooked pass to Bannister which tested the Blues and sometimes Wales keeper Eddie Neidzwiecki. Another moment saw Robbie speed off like a train from the half way line and race right through to the area before the move ultimately petered out.

The second half found the visitor's out early and saw Robbie smash a long-range power shot which required the keeper to dive down low to hold on to the ball. In a fast and furious second period, Robbie was still showing a sharp turn of pace in an enthralling battle between the London clubs. Hot headed Blues striker David Speedie was booked and cameras caught Robbie having a word with him shortly after! With the threat of extra time approaching it was not what any of the tired players wanted on this energy zapping pitch. But it was required and a Robbie header saw Neidzwiecki's handling tested by a Q.P.R. team mate. Robbie was the club corner taker and his repeat kick reached the head of Alan Macdonald, who got up the highest amongst five defenders, to score. With four minutes or so remaining in the second period of extra time, Robbie was still pumping away, legs and face full of mud. A super, last-gasp save from Rangers number one Paul Barron kept the score at 1-0 before an astonishing moment followed with his opposition number foolishly dribbling the ball out after a back pass (why is it all goalies want to play out-field?) Taking one touch too many after a challenge from Bannister, the ball spilled to Robinson, just inside the opposition half, who then took great delight in striking the ball all the way into an empty net. Confusion abounded with a slight delay immediately afterwards before Robbie and his team mates could enjoy the victory. Chelsea boss John Hollins was furious at the goal being allowed, feeling it was offside, whilst Smith felt the game was a battle well won by his Rangers side.

Liverpool had already been beaten by Q.P.R. in the League this season at Loftus Road, and Rangers beat them again 1-0, in the first leg semi-final which saw Robbie voted the Man-of-the-Match by club sponsors Guinness. His reward was a case of champagne from the sponsors (as featured on page 159).

The second leg, away at Anfield, ended 2-2 but Robbie and his team advanced to the final thanks to a 3-2 winning aggregate. Particularly admirable was the fact that Liverpool had won the League Cup in four of the last five seasons and they faced a Rangers team that had lost its last three games. But two own goals in the second game sealed their fate. Robbie played at number eight after returning from suspension during a game played out on a chilly evening.

Advancing to the day of the actual final, a 2.30pm kick off had been scheduled with the game coming before the close of the domestic season. In the League, Rangers had produced a 3-1 win against United at The Loft on New Year's Day when 16,348 supporters came out to watch the game. The subsequent return would see a 3-3 warm-up at the Manor Ground for the Milk Cup finalists with both sides still needing to concentrate on the League as they were each close to the relegation zone. Rangers found themselves in a slightly better position, eleven points better off.

The final would prove to be a huge disappoint to the Rangers players and their supporters, alas. Presented live on ITV with Brian Moore commentating and former Liverpool player Ian St John offering his expert analysis, the first half proved to be a dire affair until five minutes before the break when the opening goal arrived for Oxford. As a spectacle, the second half was quite something, with United putting in two further strikes, to no return. The second goal caught the Rangers players square and a bearded Jeremy Charles, a former Swansea and Wales team mate, finished things off in a 3-0 win. The mass of Q.P.R. fans were vocal in expressing their displeasure to the players but for manager Jim Smith, things were more complex, "I felt immensely proud that my team had made it - Oxford not Q.P.R." That was a comment by a reflective Smith given in a recent interview with an Oxford-based business magazine, "We were in the tunnel for an age before the game and there was more banter between me and the Oxford lads than my current team, I knew them a lot better than my own lads. I didn't really lose that day...." For the record, the Rangers line-up that afternoon consisted of Barron, McDonald, Dawes, Fereday, Wicks, Fenwick, Allen, Robbie, Bannister, Byrne, Robinson.

Ex-Swan Charles had been a Rangers player between November 1983 and February 1985, prior to switching to Oxford and so his path did cross with his former colleague prior to United becoming his final club before injury curtailed his career. Charlo had played at Loftus Road on New Year's Day and had scored a half-dozen times this season and was used at number nine and as an emergency centre half for a club with lowest average attendance in the division.

Robbie collected his third goal as a Rangers player in a 1-1 home draw with Sheffield Wednesday on 2 November. He had entered the proceedings as a substitute and saw his strike produce a point for Rangers in a game watched by 12,123 spectators. Away at West Bromwich Albion, on 9 November, saw a narrow 0-1 providing three points but from a game that had little to offer as a spectacle. It was the team's first away goal for more than two months against an Albion side managed by former Preston boss Nobby Stiles. He had been involved in that massive game against Swansea which sealed the fate of both clubs only a few seasons back. But like many from the World Cup 1966 winning side, his managerial career was not so good. After fifteen League games, Rangers had gathered fourteen points more than Albion who were situated at the bottom of the Division One table and would be relegated come the close.

Post Cup Final found Rangers heavily-defeat away at Spurs by 5-2 and then home to Coventry on the final day of the season against a team which found Q.P.R's recent form against them being poor. The team closed their campaign in thirteenth position having won fifteen out of a possible forty-two games and losing twenty.

Despite the rigours of a hard season, many of the Rangers squad headed to the sun-kissed West coast of America, as invited-participants in the 'Coca-Cola Classic International Soccer Series 1986'. Accepting an invitation of former Super Hoops star Rodney Marsh, he had proven a great success in the American Soccer boom of the late-1970s and was now working as coach with Tampa Bay Rowdies, based in Florida. Back in the 1976/ 77 Football League season, he and George Best, both in their thirties, were playing for Fulham in Division Two, and prior to heading off to the sunshine offered by the States to gain stardom in front of a new audience.

Lots of British footballers played in America, both names in the UK and workmanlike players, including Wrexham's Arfon Griffiths, Trevor Francis and Robbie's Swansea team mate Eddie May, the latter using it as a summer fitness boost in preparation for a new season back home. Past star names such as Bobby Moore, Gordon Best, Pelé, Cruyff, Beckenbauer and his fellow German, Gerd Müller, and also made the trip over. But by the mid-1980s the glory days of the N.A.S.L had folded before Robbie and colleagues including Chivers and Wicks were temporary additions to their squad for five games across a little over a month. Commencing with a 1-0 defeat of

Irish side Glentoran on 7 June, Dundee United were then defeated 2-1 a week later, with the games attracting a disappointing 7,303 and 2,787, respectively. The Canadian national team beat the Rowdies 0-1 on 21 June before the biggie, a 4 July encounter with the N.A.S.L All-Stars. Coached by Pelé and with future Stoke team mate Alan Hudson in opposition, the Rowdies were beaten 3-4, in front of a considerable crowd totalling 29,755. In between the final two games, the Rowdies/Rangers side gave an exhibition match against Orlando Lions which they won 3-2. In American sport, there simply has to be a winner and soccer was no exception, with the Canada game seeing a penalty shoot-out required to find a victor. Visiting British clubs were not a novelty to the Americans, as many had visited previously, including Nottingham Forest, Manchester City, Hereford, Luton Town and Leeds United.

The 1986/ 87 pre-season for Robbie and his Rangers team mates saw a Scandinavian tour with fixtures against Hoganos BK and Osterlenlaget plus a friendly back home, at Fratton Park, with Portsmouth. Rising England goalkeeping talent David Seaman signs from Birmingham City this season whilst other new arrivals include Alan Brazil, Sammy Lee and Les Ferdinand. Robbie had previously scored against Seaman in a Milk Cup game in his debut season as a Stoke player.

Southampton away was the prickly challenge for the opening game of the new season. Three goals down on twenty-five minutes, things got progressively worse and the game ended in a resounding 5-1 defeat. Smith immediately bemoaned his woes to the sports press, stating that the lengthy injury list at Loftus Road had a direct effect on the resulting hammering. Robbie had played at number four in that game, which was attended 14,711.

A crowd totalling several hundred less came to see what Rangers could do in the first home game of the campaign, a 26 August meeting with Watford. It produced a great 3-2 win and found Robbie wearing number eight, something that he would do on a number of occasions this season, when not at his regular number four.

Aston Villa provided the third opposition in the space of a week when they were beaten by a narrow 1-0 which pleased the Rangers boss more for the three points rather than his team's performance in front of a 13,003 gate.

Sustaining a decent run of form, the team travelled up to Newcastle for a mid-week fixture attended by a handsome 23,080. They saw the visitors take away a 0-2 victory against a team that Robbie usually did well against.

Above: Robbie recognised as the Q.P.R Man-of-the-Match
after an exciting Milk Cup game with Liverpool.

Also in September, Robbie scored one of the goals in a 2-3
defeat at home to West Ham, a match day ticket cost £9. A
Rangers Select traveled to Wales on 25 November to play in a
fund raiser for Merthyr Tydfil at Penydarren Park. It is
unknown whetheror not Robbie made the trip but the game
was abandoned mid-way through due to a flooded pitch. But
something that did definitely occur this season was the thrill
given to Rangers fans upon seeing their team's photo appear
in a centre spread of the much loved football magazine Shoot!

December 1986 was a busy period for Robbie and the Q.P.R.
playing staff as they had to meet five fixtures across the
month. Also, they would be required to play on Boxing Day
and the following day before a break until New Year's Day
when the League recommenced. That prosperous Christmas
period saw a 3-1 home success against Coventry before an
away journey to rivals Oxford came the very next day. It
would be at this fixture that Robbie collected the winner in a
1-0 win at the Manor Ground. The goal proved to be his
penultimate contribution.

Robbie's final goal as a Rangers player proved to be a
memorable one, it came against Leicester City in the third
round of the F.A. Cup. Played in the second week of January
1987, Q.P.R. had visited Filbert Street 25 March and been
beaten 4-1. They had also played each other back in
September, with City winning 1-0 before a crowd of 10,021.

Funnily enough, it was the first League match for Leicester after their recent Cup win over Swansea City. Returning to Robbie's goal, Foxes fanatic Rob Pressier remembers the moment well, "(It was) a rip snorting effort from twenty-five yards in a terrible 5-2 defeat for City. He played centre midfield for them alongside Sammy Lee."

That same month, both Robbie and his manager would vent their anger at a Daily Express article which had claimed that the acting club skipper was refusing to sign a new contract and had fallen-out with Smith. The truth was that Robbie remained under contract until June 1987 which was when he chose to leave the club. At the time, Robbie had made twenty-three appearances, including three as sub battling for selection against some stiff competition from team mates Martin Allen, Lee and Fenwick, who all saw themselves selected in the same during the season.

An early, drawn away game at eventual Champions Everton was held as being the strongest team performance of the campaign but the season concludes poorly with Sheffield Wednesday smashing in seven against Rangers before Arsenal hit another four and Charlton a further two, in the final three League games. It resulted in Q.P.R finishing sixteenth in Division One; three places above the relegation zone. Having accumulated fifty points, despite a terrible mid-season run which saw nine games without a win, the total sufficed to keep them up whilst Leicester, Man City and Villa were relegated. A proposed merger between Rangers and Fulham was finally rejected as Robbie departed to join his fourth club, Leicester City.

Fans writing on wearetherangersboys.com, one of the many online club boards, 'qprted' recalls Robbie's cracking Cup goal against Leicester, "He was a superb player but we had, at that time, a very talented team, so used to play him at full back. His greatest asset, his ability to score goals, was never used by the club but I do remember him hitting a fabulous goal from thirty yards into the top, right-hand corner. I met him several times. He was a deep thinker but with his several times broken nose, he looked a very tough sort; not the sort of bloke you engage in conversation in a pub, he gave off that vibe that he just wanted to be left alone. I wouldn't like to have seen him lose his temper...he had a sort of Kirk Douglas look." The final words go to Robbie himself, speaking in an interview after leaving, "The artificial pitch...was tough on the joints and the atmosphere could be so strange sometimes that often it didn't feel like a competitive match but I still enjoyed some good times with the club."

Leicester City

Founded in 1884, the club had enjoyed four seasons in Division One before relegation came at the close of the 1986/87 campaign when Robbie signed for them in summer 1987 for a fee of £100,000.

He linked-up with his new team mates for a Scandinavian tour which incorporated a dozen games. Robbie scored in their fourth match, against Tomelilla I.F and in all, City notched up five wins and a solitary defeat, putting in twenty-four goals and conceding only three. He was one of four new signings made by manager Bryan Hamilton; others included future Swan Nick Cusack and keeper Paul Cooper (pictured above with Robbie). The club already had a mix of experienced players including ex-Ipswich defender Russell Osman, Steve Moran and a young Gary McAllister coupled with established City names Paul Ramsey and Ian Wilson.

By then well-established at their Filbert Street ground, it was here that Irish international Ramsey made his initial professional association with Robbie; with the two later playing at Cardiff City together. Cusack, then twenty-one, made the advancement from non-League football and would later work for the Professional Footballers Association, aka the P.F.A. He also advanced to spending five years at the Vetch as club captain and was briefly involved as a player-manager but not when Robbie was there.

This season found twenty-three clubs in Division Two and the First consisting of twenty-one. This was because of restructuring which would change the total of clubs in the First to twenty, and twenty-four in the Second, respectively. This meant that for every week one Division Two side would not have a game and each club would have two empty Saturdays.

Managed by former Northern Ireland international Bryan Hamilton, who took charge of the club in the summer of 1986, Walkers Crisps became the new shirt sponsors of the Foxes, with the firm employing 1,500 people in the town. The Belfast-born Mr Hamilton signed Robbie to add a bit of experience to the team. Capped on fifty occasions for Northern Ireland, his new manager had been forced to retire whilst a midfield player with Oxford, due to a persistent and insurmountable injury in April 1985. He had played against Robbie in his Everton days and like him, had been at Q.P.R. Season ticket cost from £115 to £85, with a standing equivalent priced at £52. Match tickets averaged £5.00, dependant upon who the club was playing (just like today, City added a premium to watch visiting teams that could demand higher gate receipts).

Robbie, as a Queens Park Rangers player, had seen his side compete against City on three occasions last season; twice in the League (winning and losing) and once in the F.A. Cup. So clearly Foxes supporters could hardly fail to remember him for that stunning Cup goal scored against them in January 1987. Funnily enough, that match came after Leicester had eliminated Swansea City from the League Cup, across two legs, via a 5-2 aggregate.

For the 1987/ 88 campaign Robbie went on to play across twenty-eight games, both in the League and various Cup competitions. But he now found himself in a Leicester team competing against sides such as Barnsley, Plymouth and Swindon whereas the previous season Manchester United, Arsenal and Spurs were some of the tastier opponents. Not that coming down a division was going to be an easy ride, as it contained some well-established clubs including Sheffield United, Leeds, Birmingham and London sides Crystal Palace, Charlton and Millwall. However, it would be against another big club which enjoyed tremendous support, Middlesborough, that Robbie prevented a certain goal at Filbert Street on 5 December. His goal line clearance helped City share the points against the then-current table toppers thanks to a 0-0 encounter watched by under 10k.

Returning to the start of the season, Shrewsbury Town arrived on Saturday 15 August. Only in the Football League since 1950, they could attest to registering the lowest gates in Division Two, despite being established there for the past nine years. A crowd of 8,569 attended the match and watched on as a poor 0-1 finish by the visitors spoilt the day. Wearing their new Admiral-made kits, everyone at Leicester City was disappointed at their recent relegation back in May and collectively, there was a keenness for a swift return to Division One. Alas it would not arrive for some time, as the club would spend a number of years in the second tier.

Robbie would wear the number two, three and nine shirt across the campaign and the Leicester side for his League debut consisted of Ian Andrews, Simon Morgan, Robbie, Russell Osman, Steve Walsh, Paul Ramsey, Gary Ford, Gary McAllister, Nick Cusack, Ian Wilson.

September saw an impressive 10,288 turn out to see them against Midlands rivals Aston Villa, who had surprisingly been relegated along with them and Manchester City last season. Termed a 'miserable' display, it was a weak performance by a sluggish, unimaginative Leicester side, leaking a goal in each half. Robbie showed his endeavour, battling hard and causing the defence some concern with his headers. Doubly frustrating, injuries were also picked up by McAllister and Osman as the gate peaked at 10,288.

After six games, they had only recorded a single victory, a 1-0 against eventual Champions Millwall and lost the rest. Hamilton believed that his team had played well in all their away games but defensive errors had cost them dearly. A return to Stoke's Victoria Ground proved a disappointment for Robbie, as his new side lost 2-1. "I am the first to admit that our performances at home so far have been disappointing."

offered the under-fire manager in his programme notes for a September meeting with Oldham Athletic. "Both the players and the supporters need a win to give them a lift, and hopefully tonight the team can relax a little and play the way we know they can." The last time that Oldham came to Leicester, City won 2-1 and that was not going to change after this result: 4-1 to the Foxes.

An improvement followed, thanks to wins at Filbert Street against Plymouth and then Scunthorpe in the League Cup with Robbie bedding-in well at number three. The latter game was a Tuesday evening encounter which Leicester won 2-1. Curiously, in both Cup games thus far, the Foxes had initially slipped a goal behind in both. Hamilton would acknowledge by the next month that he needed to strengthen his squad. Unfortunately, he was finding it a task to locate players.

Bournemouth proved a thrilling game away at Dean Court, with a penalty save from Cooper, who had made a habit of blocking them throughout his career. His previous save in the Oldham game had helped turn things for Leicester. He also stopped another against West Brom.

Surprisingly relegated along with Villa and Leicester, Robbie and his team mates travelled to Maine Road, home of Man City and suffered a 4-2 defeat. Robbie was seen venting his

frustration as the cameras caught the fourth goal going in after a previous 1-1 with Ipswich. Leicester took the lead in the first five minutes, using a sweeper system that had taken them down the season before! The result ended a five match unbeaten run with Cooper now their preferred goalkeeping choice. The fences around the ground were taken down from this game onwards with the visitors managed by Leeds legend Allan Clarke. He was the United boss who brought his Leeds team to the Vetch for Swansea City's inaugural match in the First Division and we all know what happened that day.

Leicester completed a League double over Scunthorpe in October and grabbed four points via a draw at home to Barnsley and a comprehensive 3-0 victory against West Brom was sealed by a super Moran volley. Robbie failed a fitness test which meant that he was absent for a 2-2 at Boothferry Park, home of Hull City as a crowd of a little under 9,000 attended endured a yo-yo of a match with both sides having opportunities to win an entertaining game. A third round replay against Oxford in the Littlewoods Cup scheduled for a midweek evening affair on 4 November, was required after the sides played out a 0-0 at United's ground at the end of October. Tickets for away fans were priced at £4.50 and I wonder if any of the travelling fans were wearing the new replica shirt priced at £17.99? The replay saw Leicester performing well against First Division opponents and almost took the spoils via two last minute rocket shots from Moran and Robbie both of which narrowly missed. Unfortunately, the visitors knocked City out of the tournament thanks to a 2-3 score line. It was not to be the final meeting between the sides as they were drawn against each other for an early January F.A. Cup encounter. The most recent meeting recorded a number nine in their team by the name of Dean Saunders. His father, Roy, coached Robbie at Swansea earlier and 'Deano' would establish himself as a decent goal scorer, full Welsh international and present-day manager. City found them selves rooted in the lower depths of Division Two all season, positioned in seventeenth at the time of the Cup replay with Oxford and having lost a League fixture with Blackburn Rovers in between time.

Swindon had been beaten 3-3 at Filbert Street before visitors Huddersfield Town had also been swiftly dealt with in a 1-0 Cup fixture at home. Robbie did not feature in that game but he would be involved in the subsequent League clash with them a couple of weeks later. He also missed a hardy 2-2 draw at St. Andrews against hosts Birmingham City. Attended by 8,666, they watched as Leicester advanced to being a goal up initially before being pegged-back. Robbie's future employers and the present division leaders, Bradford City beat his side 0-2 at Filbert Street next before he made an appearance as a substitute a week later, away at Leeds Road in a 0-1 League victory recorded against Huddersfield.

December is always a hectic time in the life of a professional footballer and this year was no different for Robbie. Leicester played five matches across the month, with Robbie featuring in all of them. An away win at First Division strugglers Charlton Athletic in a Simod Cup fixture attended by a small crowd of 1,327 was followed by a worthy draw with a vastly superior Middlesborough, as previously mentioned. The Simod Cup had formerly been known as the Full Members Cup, and was viewed as a money-making opportunity for the lower League teams. Reduced admission prices for the Huddersfield match failed to bring in the crowds but at 3,440 was an improvement on the away game at Charlton. Middlesborough had cobbled together an experienced managerial team consisting of ex-players, with Bruce Rioch filling the managerial role with Colin Todd and Brian Little utilised as coaches. There was little to cheer off-the-pitch, when it was revealed that the average attendance at Filbert Street meant that the club was failing to break even, financially-speaking. It meant the end for Bryan Hamilton who had his contract terminated. The Leicester board was unhappy with recent results and the lack of progress: City had won eight of their twenty-six fixtures this season and that proved decisive. "The trouble with the game of football," surmised Chairman Terry Shipman, "is that when things keep going wrong they have a habit of needing a change to put them right..."

Consecutive defeats by Oldham, away and Harry Redknapp's AFC Bournemouth at the Street, on Boxing Day, saw the latter record the highest attendance at home so far: 11,452. A terrifically well-supported affair, it was usually the case for games played at this time of the year. Back in late-September, a visit by Ipswich Town had seen the next best gate, 11,533, who watched a 1-1 played out. Turning back the clock, a bumper crowd of 19,500 had seen the Foxes face Brighton & Hove Albion in 1980 whilst in comparison; the gate for the visit of Bournemouth totalled a still-impressive, 11,452 for this traditional mid-morning kick-off. Wearing the number four shirt in an opposition found three places above their hosts at the time, was Tony Pulis, an old Wales Youth acquaintance of Robbie's. The former would advance into management but at this time he had recently been playing for Newport County.

Two days after the Bournemouth loss, City travelled to Plymouth, a side that they had already beaten 4-0 this season, only to lose 2-0. Then on New Year's Day they were defeated 1-0 away at Millwall. The Football League fixture makers decreed that Leicester should play the next day also; this time at home to Crystal Palace. The match proved to be Robbie's final appearance in the blue of a Leicester City shirt. A pulsating 4-4 was enjoyed by a 10,104 Filbert Street crowd.

With a change of management at any club it often necessitates the sudden departure and arrival of both playing and backroom staff and this was the case when David Pleat became the new Leicester manager early in early January 1988. Naturally seeking to begin to mould the team in to his way of thinking there are always casualties involved as a result and Robbie was one of them as former Luton Town kingpin Pleat set about shaping the team to his style of play. He didn't last long. Robbie's services had been seen as being surplus to requirements after he had played a total of twenty-eight games, including five Cup matches for the Foxes but did not score in a competitive match. At the time of his departure, City could be found in the lower third of the table, where they remained all season. Robbie played fifteen times at Filbert Street and across thirteen away matches; being on the winning side in ten matches, four draws and losing the rest. The club would retain its Division Two status by concluding its season in thirteenth spot whilst Robbie's former club Stoke City, settled in eleventh.

So all in all, his time at Leicester was not that inspiring. "Desperately lacking in pace and in many City fans eyes, just going through the motions," recalls Foxes nut Rob Pressier in a forthright correspondence with the author. However, for someone regarded this way, Robbie had been shown good faith by Bryan Hamilton in selecting him across twenty-eight games out of a possible thirty-two; subbed in six and entering the game as such in two.

Despite the abruptness of his departure, Robbie confirmed that he appreciated his brief time living in the Leicester area, coming as it did as a direct contrast to London life whilst at Q.P.R. He was returning home to Swansea City, for a second spell at the Vetch and to a club now playing in Division Four alongside Cardiff City, Wrexham and Newport County.

A return to the Swans

"There is a great team spirit at the Vetch."

Terry Yorath

After being discarded at Leicester under the new rule of David Pleat, a January 1988 return to Swansea for Robbie was facilitated by Vetch manager Terry Yorath and Chairman Doug Sharpe. It came after numerous telephone calls between the player and the club and after they had managed to get his suggested fee reduced to £35,000.

No sooner had he signed than he was back in west Wales training with his new team mates on Thursday 14 January 1988 in readiness for a home game on the coming Saturday against Scarborough in the Barclays-sponsored Division Four. Yorath, in his second year with the club, was pleased with his acquisition and told the Western Mail, "He will put a bit of steel into the side. He's a good organizer and a good talker." The style of play implemented at Swansea was not one that all supporters cared for as it used the offside trap and stifled many a game in its midst. But his side proved to be one of the more skillful teams in the lowest division.

Recent form for Robbie's new/ old club had been abysmal, losing 2-0 to Merthyr Tydfil in the Welsh Cup and with a dire home form recently which had totaled five games without a home win. That was amended thanks to a 3-0 victory against Scarborough. Watched by 4,366, Robbie was in a team alongside Wales internationals Alan Davies and Colin Pascoe, the latter in at number six, replacing veteran midfielder Gary Emmanuel. Alan had been with the club since August and would fulfill a major part in the success enjoyed by the team by the season close. Gary's father, Len, was a former Swansea player but his son was struggling with injuries this season which meant his continued absence from the first team. He left to join Merthyr and was later at Llanelli, just like Robbie, only when Wyndham Evans was the manager of a side that included ex-Swans Glan Letheren and Alan Waddle. Pascoe is now a successful coach and in recent times has been at Liverpool with former boss Brendan Rogers, after following him there from Swansea. He was a sixteen-year-old apprentice at the Vetch in 1981 and by 1994 had advanced into the Wales team, playing alongside Robbie in the majority of his ten full caps. Unfortunately, he was sold to Sunderland for a bargain fee during the transfer period this season. Only Dudley Lewis was still with the club from Robbie's former days. Coincidentally, the Swans wore an Admiral branded kit just like his previous club. The team for his debut was Hughes, Harrison, Lewis, Dudley Lewis, Knill, Robbie, Davies, Raynor, Davey, Pascoe, Andrews.

A super-fit Robbie was immediately given the captaincy and would play in all of the remaining nineteen League fixtures and beyond. He would be substituted in one game, a 0-3 away win at Cambridge United and start in all other fixtures. The drop down of two divisions meant that it took him time to adjust. The win was followed by a draw with Halifax before a special moment arrived for Robbie in an away fixture with Hartlepool on 30 January: he scored his hundredth goal for the Swans after a six year wait! The goal came via his head, after meeting a cross from former Newport player/manager John Lewis, now a Swansea team mate. County would sadly be lost to the Football League by the end of the season. Robbie and Davies played well together in midfield and the 0-2 win put the team in ninth position in the table. Not too far away, his old team mates Alan Curtis, Terry Boyle and Nigel Stevenson were all part of a soon-to-be-promoted Cardiff City side, also in the same division. A goal less affair with rivals Burnley was added-to by a 1-1 at the Vetch Field with Stockport County, where a last gasp equalizer salvaged a point for the Swans. Robbie had a couple of chances in the Burnley match within a squad that struggled to cope with a multitude of injuries. Subbed at Cambridge for the only time since his return, the Swans won 0-3 before defeat arrived via Colchester next.

The club performed much better away from home this season and continued their good form with a 1-2 win at Somerton Park against Newport. A header from Robbie flew over the bar and would have brought the score to 1-1 if it had gone in. It didn't matter, as the win was their seventh away success of the campaign and their third consecutive victory. Meanwhile County was a club in dire financial turmoil at the time.

Wales' manager Mike England was sacked in the first week of February and David Williams, later to manage Newport, took temporary charge in a Caretaker capacity. He selected Robbie for a fixture with Yugoslavia at the Vetch Field on 23 March following a number of inevitable withdrawals: the game would mark his final appearance in a red shirt.

The Racecourse was a ground well-known to Robbie both as a League player and at international level and there it produced a decent 1-2 win for the Swans against Wrexham. This March fixture saw a typical Robbie shot from twenty yards and he also got the winner, a stunning diving header with two minutes remaining. Alas, this Welsh derby was only attended by 1,916.

Played on a soggy Vetch Field, a later strike against Bolton Wanderers was rewarded with three points for the Swans and it distanced a run of four games at the ground without a win, by being their third consecutive points-taker. A dreadful team performance was produced in a 3-0 defeat by Orient which Yorath was honest about in his furious post-match summary.

The Swans would meet Torquay on six occasions this season, commencing with an away defeat in the League Cup, a 1-1 at the

Vetch in August and another draw in mid-December. They also lost away at the end of March before facing them in the Play-offs.

An awkward defeat by lowly Rochdale ruled-out a decent first half showing by the hosts which included Robbie perfectly setting up a wasted scoring opportunity for a team mate. The 0-3 loss put a dent in the club's promotion challenge, with the first coming at the end of the first half.

Soon back in action during the Easter holidays, Swans hot shot Joe Allon scored his eleventh goal of the season nine minutes before full time in an away win at Peterborough; then managed by future BBC football pundit Mark Lawrenson, wjho had played against Robbie during the Swans' two seasons in the top flight. Meantime Yorath was announced as the new Wales manager. He was selected after Old Big 'ead, Brian Clough, was muted as a candidate before the idea was vetoed by his club, Nottingham Forest. A former hard man and Wales captain, Terry felt that he could remain as Swansea boss and control things for Wales on a part-time basis. Although, he later conceded in his autobiography that perhaps his club Chairman was right in feeling that he could not do both.

A 1-2 reverse by Tranmere Rovers at the Vetch proved to be a shocking result for the club, coming after they had played three games in the last eight days. Robbie contributed his third and final goal of the season since his return in January. The recent spell of one away win and two home losses was explained by the manager, who pointed out that his players seemed afraid to make mistakes at the Vetch Field but were a different beast away. The loss put the Swans down into seventh place with four games remaining: away at Wolves and Carlisle and home to Scunthorpe and Darlington.

The Wolves manager was complimentary about the Swans after his side produced a strong 2-0 win at Molineux. It took them to within a point of sealing promotion as Champions, thanks largely to the goal scoring prowess of Bull and Mutch. More than 12,000 had been at that game but a little under a third of that attended a 1-1 draw at home with Scunthorpe a week later. It was two points dropped but it did produce a rare treat for Swansea supporters: a first half goal for them to enjoy. It also saw the return of old head Tommy Hutchison and young talent Chris Coleman to the first team. Significant in that the forty-year-old Scot and teenaged Coleman would contribute much as the season reached its climax. Alan Knill, described as "Swansea's lanky midfielder", he was a Robbie team mate at the Vetch and elsewhere, and it was his goal against Carlisle that proved to be the winner. United played poorly and consequently had their own fans boo them off the field at full time! Robbie wore the number ten shirt for the only time this season, after filling the number six jersey across all the other games that he was selected for.

In the final League fixture of the season, Swansea needed a win against Darlington to push for a place in the newly-introduced Play-offs which guaranteed the winners a final promotion spot. Robbie produced a shot that was pushed around the post by the keeper during a game which saw the Swans pile on the pressure against their rivals at the Vetch on 7 May. Involved in much of the pivotal action, Robbie contributed to two of the three goals scored by his team in what proved to be an important win. It was his header that found Davies who struck the second and a foul in injury time led to Robbie tapping the ball across to Andy Melville, who sent it back in the centre for Sean McCarthy to put in his own flying header to seal a 3-0 success. The North Bank supporters invaded the pitch after the final whistle prior to the players returning to the centre circle to acknowledge them. The victory meant that the club would advance to two games with Rotherham commencing on Sunday 15 May, with the return the following Wednesday.

A McCarthy goal proved enough at the Vetch where a 1-0 was achieved in readiness to take to Rotherham for the return leg. Some 9,148 watched the first game whilst 5,568 attended the subsequent 1-1 away. The success saw the Swans advance to the final and further games with Torquay, thanks to a 2-1 aggregate.

Welcome to the Vetch
BARCLAYS LEAGUE DIVISION 4

PLAY OFFS - FINAL FIRST LEG

TORQUAY
WEDNESDAY, 25th MAY, 1988
Kick Off 7.30 p.m.

The SWAN

Today's Match Sponsored by
LEYLAND DAF & S & G TYRES

SPONSORED BY DIVERSIFIED PRODUCTS

OFFICIAL PROGRAMME

DP
Fit for Life   50p

The clubs had already met on four occasions this season, twice in the League and twice in the League Cup. The first leg of the final occurred on Wednesday 25 May and recorded a 2-1 win for Robbie and his team during an evening game attended by 10,825 at the Vetch. The Swans had stormed to a 2-0 lead before leaking a very late goal in front of the largest gate of the 1987/88 campaign. Robbie contributed to both goals, the first via a free kick and the other found him starting the move. The return leg arrived three days later and ended in a thrilling 3-3. Sadly safety concerns saw severe restrictions in the number of away fans allowed entry into Torquay's tight little ground. The Swans twice took the lead against a team that finished their season seven places above them. Advancing to 2-3 up by half time, Davies added to the earlier Raynor and McCarthy strikes. Into the second half and the visitors battled to hold on to their lead as the rain came down and saw a rapid deterioration in the playing surface. The Swans had on-loan keeper Peter Guthrie as a recent, enforced replacement for Mike Hughes, who had to retire on medical grounds. Robbie and Hutchison, neighbours away from football, provided a steadying influence in the team and Guthrie performed admirably as the game ended all-square. "I was surprised that Torquay came back at us so well," reflected Robbie, "it was a nail-biting game, but we really should have sewn up promotion before the Play-offs." The draw meant that Swansea City won 5-4 on aggregate and took the vacant promotion spot and with it entry up into Division Three. For a change, Robbie had joined a team that was going up a division rather than his recent battles against relegation whilst with Leicester in Division Two.

After being promoted via the lottery that was the Play-offs, in the 1988/89 season, the Swans would prove unable to build upon this success despite being heralded as the best football-playing side in Division Three. Robbie was selected at number six but would also make a couple of appearances at number eight during the season. Elsewhere in football, the Hillsborough tragedy mars the new campaign for all.

The season commenced with a trip to Gillingham and a 2-3 success on Saturday 27 August which saw a brace from Robbie. Playing in midfield, he was also involved in the opening goal scored and managed to get himself booked on ten minutes! Robbie's first goal was a stunning thirty yard effort which flew in to the corner of the net to put his team 2-0 up. His second was the result of a penalty. It brought his total to five goals scored since his return. The game attracted 4,437 spectators but was to be bettered three days later when the Swans made a visit to Ninian Park to face a Cardiff side that had gained automatic promotion at the close of the previous season. Marvelously, the visitors took away three points thanks to a 0-1 win. Now finding themselves playing alongside Wigan, Reading, Notts County and both Bristol clubs, they would meet the Bluebirds on five separate occasions; twice in the League and in the League Cup and Sherpa Van trophy.

Following that fruitful away gathering at Cardiff, Robbie contributed his side's only goal in a 1-1 with Bury, the first game of the new 1988/ 89 campaign to be staged at the Vetch. An improved 5,137 watched the fixture and saw the points shared after a 1-1. Robbie's goal was created by clever interplay between Davies and Krill, which was polished off by his twenty-five yard rocket. A familiar face in the Bury side was his former Stoke team mate Sammy McIlroy. A long haul to Roots Hall, home of Southend United followed, with a 0-2 win for the Swans making the visit worthwhile. The following Saturday saw Brentford come to west Wales and contribute to another 1-1.

Following the previous win in south Wales, Swansea City conceded twice at the Vetch in front of a bumper 6,917 gate and kissed goodbye to any advancement in the League Cup this season in a disappointing 0-2 defeat. Old team mates Alan Curtis, Terry Boyle and Nigel Stevenson could now be found in the Cardiff team facing their former colleague. A Robbie shot struck the bar in the first half and he also had a penalty saved by in-form keeper George Wood. The game saw a pitch invasion when Cardiff scored one of their goals, in what was their first win at the ground in thirty years.

That defeat started a run of two successive losses; a hefty 2-5 by eventual-Champions once more, Wolves; at home and a 2-0 at Ashton Gate by Bristol City.

Robbie scored the winner, his fourth of the campaign, at the Vetch against Bolton in an evening game in the first week of October. His twenty yard shot was deflected off a Wanderers player to beat the keeper but was to be cherished due to the win being his club's first home success of the season after five attempts. Terry Yorath would later reveal that he could have left the Swans this month, as well as in March of the following year. A Sunday game at Aldershot produced a 0-1 victory, something that was repeated against Northampton and concluded a run of three games all seeing 1-0 wins. A home win against Fulham then saw two more points after draws with Huddersfield and Preston (a game which Robbie was absent from).

November provided a hefty eight fixtures and began with a midweek game at Wigan which produced a 2-1 win. A 1-3 loss at Chester saw Robbie wearing the number eight shirt, something that he would do on several occasions this season. Victories in the F.A. Cup and Welsh Cup, over Mansfield and Merthyr Tydfil, the latter at Penydarren Park are contrasted by a draw at Blackpool and defeat at Port Vale. A welcome 1-0 success against Torquay, at home, in the Sherpa Van trophy closed a busy month.

December was the same, starting off with a decent share of the points with eventual division runners-up Sheffield United before a short trip to Cardiff for a midweek meeting with the Bluebirds in the latest Sherpa Van fixture. Again another Cup competition which stimulated little interest from supporters, the game attracted a gate of 2,896. The Swans enjoyed a 2-2 away at Colchester in the F.A Cup before a midweek replay at the Vetch saw a 1-3 defeat.

The recent Cup meeting between Cardiff and Swansea was soon forgotten as Robbie and his colleagues paid a Boxing Day morning visit to Ninian Park. A mighty 10,675 endured another tense derby and saw a 2-2 completed with the opening Cardiff goal coming in the first minute of play. Robbie was Swansea captain in this feisty Division Three battle where all the goals arrived in the first-half. New Year's Eve fell on a Saturday this time around and it necessitated an away trip to Eastville, home of Bristol Rovers, to realize a 1-1 in a match that the Swans should have won. Robbie proved a nuisance, seeing his shot cleared off the line.

An immediately busy New Year diary started with Reading coming to the Vetch on 2 January only to be beaten 2-0. "Robbie James did very well. You don't see a lot of him but when he does come into a game he's very effective." That was a quote from Reading manager Ian Branfoot after seeing Robbie score against his side in their defeat at the Vetch. The run of good form for the Swans continued with a 2-0 against Notts County, also at home, before a trip to Bury ended in a 1-0 defeat. Another Robbie blaster put his team into third in the table after the County win due to his twenty-five yard net buster being made possible after he found space to put in a shot. His goal came just after the half hour mark and he also set-up team mate Wade for the other goal.

Central Wales League part-timers Caersws provided the Tuesday night Welsh Cup opponents at the Vetch Field which ended 0-0 in front of 2,055. Another home game saw Southend dispatched 2-0 before the Swans travelled to Caersws for a replay which closed with a 0-2 win for them. A header from Robbie had almost broken the deadlock.

Robbie started off February 1989 with the home side's only goal, via a late penalty, in a 1-1 with Bristol City watched by a not insignificant 6,523 gate. It proved remarkable due to the turmoil at the club following Yorath's recent exit to take up a managerial post with Division Two side Bradford City. The news was revealed before the game and left Swansea Chairman Doug Sharpe fuming. He demanded £250,000 compensation for his club, a figure not presently offered by the Bantams. Terry had not been interested in signing a new three year contract at the Vetch and he reasoned that the job at Valley Parade would be convenient for him to be close to his family which was still living in Leeds. He had been assistant manager to Trevor Cherry during the 1984/85 season when the Bantams won the Third Division. Cherry had played in the Leeds side demolished 5-1 at the Vetch previously. Sharpe proved successful in obtaining an initial injunction preventing him from taking charge at Bradford following his exit from Swansea City.

After defeating Bolton back in October, the Swans fell to a 1-0 defeat at their place next in an exciting, drama-filled affair producing lots of goal-mouth incidents before the late winner. Present Swansea player Tommy Hutchison, was acting Caretaker manager and playing well in the team. It was a position that he had previously filled following the departure of John Bond.

Wrexham are swiftly dealt with in a 4-1 Welsh Cup success at the Racecourse which in turn offers two games with Barry Town in April. A League double is completed over Aldershot in a Friday night encounter at the Vetch on 17 February, in advance of a long hike to Northampton which saw a defeat.

By March, with three months of the season remaining, things start off badly in a 1-0 loss at Craven Cottage to Fulham before 1-1 draws are produced against Chester and Preston. Former Wales international Ian Evans is installed as Robbie's clubmanager but he would last only until March 1990.

A Sunday evening encounter with Gillingham sees the Swans produce another 'double' due to a 3-2 win, the same score line in their opening game of the 1988/89 season. Watched by a 4,075 crowd, Robbie scored from the penalty spot in a vital 1-0 home win over Huddersfield at the start of the third week of March. Regrettably they then lost at Reading before hosting a visit from Cardiff in the closing fixture of the month. Bluebirds captain Boyle, soon to join the Vetch playing staff, got himself sent off in an Easter Monday derby attended by 9,201 ended 1-1.

April saw the Swans play eight times, including twice in the Welsh Cup, as the season reached its most important month. An

April Fools Day loss at Chesterfield found Swansea beaten by two second half goals, despite dominating much of the match. The defeat leaves them seventh in the table but things do not improve with a 1-0 defeat at Notts County added three days later. The Swans lose 2-1 at Eastville, and with this being their fourth defeat in the last five games, their manager declares that any Play-off hopes are over. Now ten games in since Evans has taken over from Yorath, Robbie got himself sent off during the game and was facing an automatic, three-match ban. An incident had occurred in the seventieth minute where punches were thrown involving himself and 6'4" Rovers man Guy McLean. Due to Robbie retaliating, he was given a red card, as was the opponent. The Swans had taken the lead after Melville got his head onto a cross from Robbie, in a move initiated by Davies and Raynor.

With dire form in the League, a Welsh Cup semi-final meeting with Barry must have been a blessed distraction. Sandwiched between a defeat by Wigan, with only seven League games remaining the team lost 1-2 at the Vetch in a tense affair. Evans was dismayed by his team's performance whilst Robbie played in the match as his ban had not yet been activated. Swansea won the first leg 1-0 before the return saw a 3-1 win in front of 2,338 at home. The fixture saw Barry take a surprise lead but the win meant that the Swans would face the winners of Hereford versus Kidderminster in the final.

Wolves started a spate of three games all seeing draws: Robbie's ban meant that he missed an impressive 1-1 away draw against the subsequent Champions who had beaten them 2-5 at the Vetch, previously. Port Vale saw a 0-0 at the Vetch Field with the Swans battling effectively against visitors that had remained in the top four all season. Situated in eleventh position, the team had admirably produced draws with two sides in the higher reaches of the division.

The final month of the season started with a visit to Mansfield. Following on from the Swans win back in November, the clubs had not played each other since spring 1979 when John Toshack was then manager. Coincidentally, Robbie played in the away draw with them back then and scored one of the goals in a 2-2 finish. This time, a crowd of 2,550 gathered to see a goal less encounter. The current Swansea City squad had conceded forty goals across forty-three games whilst scoring forty-eight times. Sheffield United added to this with a 5-1 hammering which saw Robbie come on as a second half substitute. Back after his three-game absence, he had scored eight times this season, a little behind Melville on thirteen. Astonishingly 4-0 down at one point, the Swans failed to enhance a 2-2 achieved previously.

In the penultimate League fixture of the campaign, a Tuesday night trip to Brentford finished 1-1, again repeating the score from their September visit to west Wales. However, an unfortunate 1-2 reverse to relegation-threatened Blackpool spoilt the closing home game of the season with Hutchison playing against one of his former clubs. Robbie entered proceedings as a sub after struggling to break back into the team since his enforced absence. The defeat saw his side conclude their endeavours in twelfth position on sixty-one points gathered from fifteen wins and sixteen draws.

Having reached the Welsh Cup Final, to be played at the Vetch on 21 May, the Swans faced Vauxhall Conference part-timers Kidderminster. Selected in the first XI, Robbie succeeded in setting-up the first goal before his own came next to put the Swans 2-0 ahead. His twenty yard strike occurred after he was allowed time to wallop the ball which sent the keeper the wrong way. A gate of 5,100 saw Swansea take the Cup, their first in six years, thanks to an emphatic 5-0. The team, shown below (thanks to Ian Garland for the photograph), consisted of Bracey, Melville, Coleman, D Lewis, Knill, Thornber, Robbie, Davies, Raynor, Wade (Legg), Hutchison (Hough). Robbie, as captain, starred in a moustache-tastic team and is shown kneeling, centre. Tommy Hutchison is shown to his right and Alan Davies, third right, top.

"Playing in the European Cup Winners' Cup when I was forty-one, we came up just short. It was a pity that we never had a little more cash to spend on players. We always had to sell our best ones and didn't always get the price they should have demanded: all a bit frustrating for the fans." That was former Swans player, friend and neighbour to Robbie, Hutchison, in a correspondence with the author. He would see Robbie play in thirty-four League matches across the 1989/ 90 season, some as sub, like himself. The duo would again link up at Merthyr when Robbie subsequently took the player-manager role and found his friend there as assistant. They also played in charity matches in and around Swansea.

A 19 August haul up to Huddersfield saw the first League match in the new division and with it a 1-0 defeat in front of a 5,775 crowd. Robbie would fill the number six shirt in the first four League games, in a team with a number of old heads, including Terry Boyle, alongside youngsters such as future Wales boss Chris Coleman. Boyle had played in the 1976 Wales youth side alongside Robbie and would see his career mirroring Robbie's; both being involved with Cardiff City, Merthyr and Barry Town. Arriving at the Vetch in July 1989, he would be gone by the same time the following year.

Supporters had to wait until the sixth game of the season, at home to Chester City, to see the first win of the 1989/ 90 campaign from their team. They had lost to Exeter and Birmingham whilst also recording draws with Northampton and Exeter City (in the League Cup) previously.

Robbie missed the next couple of games, defeats against Fulham and Reading with the team conceding eight times and scoring only once, most of the goals coming in a 6-1 thumping by the latter at the Vetch.

Due to their success in winning the Welsh Cup at the close of the previous season, it meant that Robbie would once again play in the European Cup Winners' Cup, this time facing Greek giants Panathinaikos whose team included many internationals. Not underestimating the Swans, their manager and his assistant had been over to watch them play during pre-season and in an early League match.

The squad traveled to Athens for the first round, first leg tie on 13 September which enabled the visiting team the thrill of playing before a humongous 53,500 crowd. In contrast, 3,495 had watched Swansea's opening League fixture at the Vetch with Northampton, in mid-August. The Greek side raced to a 3-0 lead before an admirable come back from the Swans

almost ended in success: they narrowly lost 3-2. On Wednesday 27 September, the return tie took place in Wales. Attended by an 8,364 gate, Robbie was subbed during the game, an enthralling 3-3 affair, after he had scored via the penalty spot. He had now struck thirteen times for the Swans in his second spell with them. A 0-0 with Notts County, a club that would gain a lucrative promotion thanks to the Play-offs, closed an underwhelming month which had seen one victory in seven games for Swansea City.

Alan Curtis rejoined the Swans in the first week of October and began his third spell with them. Signed by Evans, he joined Robbie and Hutchy in midfield, at a time when Doug Sharpe was keen to sell the club. Appropriately named, he was held as being a tricky character to deal with as he allegedly meddled in team selection and tactics. Ask most managers and they will concur that the last thing you want is for anyone to interfere with your job whilst you are trying to do it. But he had also saved the club from extinction back in 1986, after joining the board back in 1981, so credit to him for that.

Wins over Crewe and League runners-up Bristol City, where the home supporters applauded the Swansea players off the pitch, came before a defeat at Bury and success at table-topping Tranmere. A heavy loss at Mansfield was cast aside thanks to Robbie getting his second goal of the season and the match winner, before being substituted in a 1-0 away win at Walsall. It would pre-empt a prolonged absence from selection for him running right through to January 1990.

He missed the embarrassment of a 0-3 Welsh Cup defeat at the Vetch against future club Merthyr Tydfil at the end of the first week of November, as well as a Boxing Day visit from Cardiff City. In addition, he would sit-out the advancement in the F.A Cup with another win over recent Welsh Cup opponents Kidderminster.

After a New Year's Day away draw at Shrewsbury Town, minus Robbie, Liverpool arrived at the Vetch Field for a third round tie. Miraculously, the subsequent Division One League Champions would be held to a goal-less draw before a tremendous 16,098 crowd. Back in the 1981/ 82 First Division days, the Reds had attracted 24,500 to the Vetch. Robbie was one of the two listed substitutes for this exciting home game with Liverpool on 6 January. Alan Hansen and his old Wales team mate Ian Rush played in the draw before the replay at Anfield produced quite a different result. At theirs, Robbie filled-in for Curt in a terrible 8-0 battering seen by 29,194.

After the whitewash in Merseyside, the Swansea team had to face an away trip some four days later. Robbie again replaced his old mate, whilst Curt would play quite a few games at number eight, as would Robbie. Our Mr James kept his place in the team for the next two consecutive home games against Reading and Huddersfield Town and scored a consolation goal in the latter, thanks to a penalty on forty-nine minutes, in a 1-3 loss. Former Swan Dudley Lewis was then a Town player and he would be rejoined by Robbie at Merthyr, where he was club captain when Robbie took on the player-manager role there for the 1993/ 94 season. In between times and later on, he played some games for the Reserves, as would Curt, with Robbie scoring a goal against Yeovil in a 3-0 win.

Absent for the away defeat at Chester, February would see Robbie used as a sub in its initial three fixtures: Fulham, Birmingham City and Rotherham before he missed the games against Reading and Bristol Rovers.

By March, Terry Yorath would make a surprise return to Swansea City F.C, after being sacked by Bradford. Replacing Evans, Yorath had broken his contract whilst with the Swans originally, to take the vacant job with the Bantams. However, he had taken the unusual step of paying-up his remaining contract with Swansea to do so. The first game back in charge was at the Vetch, a 0-5 defeat watched by 2,582.

Robbie had no involvement with fixtures concerning Leyton Orient, Notts County or Mansfield but would subsequently see himself selected at right back for the first time this season, in a 1-1 with Crewe on 17 March. He featured in a hefty 0-5 defeat by Bristol City, playing at number five and doing the same in a 0-1 defeat, also at home, against Bury. Sub in the game at Tranmere, things didn't improve: the Swans lost 3-0.

With nine League games remaining in April, Robbie began an extended run in the team, at numbers six and eight. He would play in all the remaining matches: Orient, Walsall, Shrewsbury Town, Cardiff City, Wigan, Preston, Blackpool, Brentford and Bolton.

The Swans faced a struggling Cardiff on Easter Monday, a noon kick-off, with both clubs battling in the relegation zone. The Bluebirds were beaten 2-0 in a dire match and by the season close, they would be relegated.

Coming immediately after that holiday encounter, Robbie scored a brace at the Vetch against Wigan, in front of 3,141spectators. The win overturned a 2-0 away loss back in mid-December. He would remain at number eight for the season.

Defeat to Preston by 3-0 on their plastic pitch felt a million miles away from that famous promotion-clinching afternoon that sealed Swansea's rise up into the First Division back in May 1981. A 2-2 with their Lancashire cousins Blackpool was followed by a 2-1 loss at Brentford in the final away fixture of the season. Robbie and his team mates now faced high-flyers Bolton at the Vetch on 5 May in a crucial match for both. For the Swans, a win was important to keep them in the division whilst their visitors sought points to seal promotion. It was to be the final time that Alan Curtis would wear a Swansea City shirt and as the whistle

blew for full time, he was thrust upon the shoulders of supporters. Curt had been approach by Barry Town and Robbie too would make the switch to the same club soon enough. The Swans finished their campaign seventeenth out of twenty.

Robbie's second spell at the Vetch had produced sixteen goals across two and a half seasons before he bid farewell to his beloved Swans in August 1990, to join Bradford City.

But before he left, he responded to a request from former Swansea Schools man Gareth Williams, a teacher at Sketty Primary school in the town, to contribute to their project to raise money for a guide dog. He answered their "My Biggest Thrill"project with the following. "There have been a few big thrills in my career: making my debut for Swansea, playing for Wales, playing in the Milk Cup Final for Q.P.R but my biggest thrill was when I won promotion with Swansea to the First Division. When I first started, playing for Swansea it was always my ambition to play in Division One with them. Many people thought I was mad to think that we would ever get out of Division Four, but as time went on we went up from Division Four, to Division Three, to Division Two and finally made it to Division One on May 2nd 1981, nine years after making my debut as the age of sixteen."

183

Bradford City

"Robbie was a very good player at a difficult time for us.

He was nearing the veteran stage when he joined us
but both his energy and experience was superb.

He was popular with the fans and earned respect
for his never-say-die performances."

Bradford forum Claret and Banter.

Robbie had played against Bradford on many occasions
during his career prior to joining them in August 1990. He
and his second wife had recently welcomed their newborn
son Luke into the family in May 1990 before his father's
footballing travels took the James clan to Yorkshire. Calling
Valley Parade home, most football fans will recall the terrible
1985 fire there which was seen live on television as the final
scores started to roll in on that particular Saturday afternoon.
Advancing to summer 1990, several players left the
club and five new faces came in, including Robbie,
who himself arrived as part of an exchange deal
after he had fallen out with the Swansea
City.Chairman. Known as the Bantams and playing
in claret and blue, City had come down to the Third
Division after five years in Division Two.

Wearing an ugly, Bukta-made kit; the same company that had designed a much-liked Swansea kit worn in the late-1970s, the Bradford one had a collar and two poppers down its front, utilizing a combination of thicker and thinner vertical lines running down the chest. These were accompanied by single-coloured shorts and socks. A replica shirt was available at a rather expensive £24.95. Robbie had his kit sponsored by local firm Universal Pricing Systems. Other club-related branding included playing cards, bum bags and belts amongst a host of commercial items. Robbie's former manager Terry Yorath, had been sacked by Bradford in March 1990 when the club was in Division Two and his replacement, John Docherty, had ten games to keep them up: he failed. Across the year, the club made a loss of more than £600,000 after suffering relegation and seeing Yorath spend £1m on transfers whilst in charge. Docherty already had a long association with Bradford from his playing days. An ex-Millwall name, as manager there, he led them up into Division One for the 1988/89 season. It was at this time that Robbie was with Leicester and he played against the team that his future

manager was then in charge of. A familiar face to Robbie from back at the Vetch and international duties was Leighton James, who was working as a coach at Bradford when he arrived.

The division saw forty-six League fixtures needing to be fulfilled, against teams that included Birmingham City, Stoke City, Preston North End and Crewe. There would be three automatic promotion places available; with another one offered from via a Play-off final.

Pre-season found the squad competing in the Yorkshire and Humberside Cup against Grimsby Town at Valley Parade, which was when Robbie made his home debut. The ground had a capacity of 16,072 but would not see anything near that in the two seasons that he played there (although some games, especially local derbies, reached five figures).

The new Barclays League Division Three 1990/91 season started with two home games within four days. Commencing with a disappointing 1-2 reverse to Tranmere Rovers, the City players had received a hearty ovation from the 7,970 fans, in readiness for the new campaign. The defeat was swiftly followed by a 2-0 success against Bury in the new Rumbelows League Cup which now offered a tantalising U.E.F.A Cup place for its winners.

Robbie was installed as club captain and would wear number four throughout the season until a switch to right-back, and the number two shirt, from 2 February, a 3-0 win against AFC Bournemouth. Joining ex-Vetch team mate Sean McCarthy in the team across all forty-six League games, Robbie advanced to playing in a staggering fifty-seven fixtures (inclusive of the various Cup games). He would contribute five goals; beginning with a strike at Luton Town on their plastic pitch, in mid-September. Although, it would be his second, away at Rotherham United in November, that he truly left his mark in the minds of the Bradford City diehards.

With the Bantams defense looking decent, September got off to a strong start thanks to a 0-1 win at Bolton. Thankfully the result had broken an eighteen month period of no away wins for the club! It was followed by a Tuesday night game at Bury in the second leg of the first round proper of the Rumbelows Cup at Gigg Lane. Bury, who had Alan Knill, an ex-Swansea team mate of Robbie's, had last tasted success with promotion from Division Four in 1985 when Bradford had won the Division Three title. City lost 2-3.

Despite a good performance from the Royals keeper, City succeeded in beating his old Wales youth colleague Eddie Niedzwiecki's Reading side by 2-1, going 1-0 up via a penalty. Grimsby had provided the first-ever Football League opponents for Bradford back in 1903 and next shared a 1-1 with them at the start of the third week of September. At Bournemouth, a 4,942 crowd observed the visitors lagging a goal behind on twenty-two minutes before equalizing just before half time. By the final whistle, Bradford slipped to a 3-1 loss. Funnily enough, their keeper was someone known by Robbie; namely Peter Guthrie, involved with Swansea in their recent Play-off success.

One of the highlights of the season came with the visit of Swansea City to Valley Parade on 22 September. Attended by the second highest gate of the campaign, 7,724, the fixture saw the return of ex-Bantams boss Terry Yorath, Alan Davies and Lee Bracey in his new Swansea team, some six months since the former had been sacked by the club. Now twenty-eight, Davies had returned in July 1990 to the Vetch Field club, after spending a season with Bradford under Yorath. He had signed for them during summer 1990 sometime after moving in the opposite direction a year previously. An understated John Docherty observed in his managerial programme notes, "It will certainly be a special day for these two players." The clubs had last met at the ground back in January 1985 when they played out a 1-1. The present meeting was their thirty-ninth and Bradford had a slightly better win average: seventeen to Swansea's thirteen. After five League fixtures

Bradford were tenth in the division, with seven points collected, whilst the Swans had only taken four points. So far this season, Robbie had played in all seven League games for the Bantams, wearing the number four shirt. Although enjoying most of the play, ironically, it was his mistake which led to the only goal of the match which allowed the visitors a narrow 0-1 victory. It happened on fifty-five minutes, when he blocked a shot on the edge of the goal with the ball spilling advantageously to a Swansea player.

September saw Robbie score his first goal for the club away at Division One side Luton. Visiting City fans paid £4 for tickets to see a 1-1 in this Rumbelows Cup second round, first leg tie. Town had recently suffered a 6-1 mauling at Q.P.R on their artificial playing surface, known well by their former player Robbie James. A 2-1 defeat at Orient had seen the O's 2-0 up before Bradford pulled one back on seventy-three minutes.

A home win against a Chester side containing Robbie's future Cardiff team mate Carl Dale, was smothered by a subsequent 0-1 defeat by Brentford in October prior to Luton being the third home game for the club in the course of a week. The teams had already drawn in the first leg and they repeated the score line in the return. However, Bradford went through following penalties after extra time. Their reward for seeing-off the Hatters was an exciting away trip to White Hart Lane, to face a resurgent Tottenham Hotspur on the last day of the month.

A point at Exeter was added by three more gained from a 0-1 win at Mansfield's Field Mill ground before Stoke City and Wigan came to Valley Parade in successive fixtures. Stoke had been relegated down into Division Three with Bradford at the end of the 1989/ 90 season whilst the week before the fixture, the Bradford squad had been enjoying a break in Torquay. The home crowd was behind their team on the night but could only watch the players being thwarted by an in-form Peter Fox in the Stoke goal. The Bantams conceded a poor goal in a 1-2 defeat with Mickey Thomas' latest club which was managed by former World Cup winner Alan Ball. He commented that along with Tranmere, Bradford was the best side that his team had played against. They were eight places from bottom of the table and some six points behind their next visitors Wigan. Robbie met up again with his former Leicester boss Bryan Hamilton, now in charge of the club. The game saw the visitors defeated 2-1 in front of a 6,803 crowd; a slight drop from the Stoke game. The Mansfield win was significant as it recorded eight points collected for Bradford away, startlingly equal to the whole of last season.

With stars Gazza and Gary Lineker playing well in a Terry Venables-managed Spurs side, an impressive 25,451 were there to see Bradford put in a very good show in the third round meeting with them. Tottenham could be found in third spot in the top division and had recently beaten Bradford's fellow Division Three counterparts Hartlepool 7-1, on aggregate, in the previous round. Robbie and his team even took the lead on thirteen minutes before losing 2-1. Memories must have been evoked as Robbie had scored against them back in a 1978/79 League Cup game at the Vetch which although ending in a draw, the replay at the Lane was won by the Swans in a big Cup surprise of the day. A more recent flashback related to Spurs and Wales defender Pat van den Hauwe, known to Robbie in his time at Q.P.R.

After their Cup exploits in London, the Bradford squad had to return to normality with an away trip to Rotherham United next. They managed to raise their game and produce a decent 0-2 win watched by 6,057. One of the goals scored came from Robbie and it proved to be a classic. A strike from well outside of the area, it is still remembered by fans today, here's how one of them saw it, "[It] came from a cross from the right wing, followed by a bit of pinball between attack and defense before the ball ran out for a powering Robbie James to thump it on the move. The ball ballooned up and in to the net into the keeper's top left-hand post, delighting the fans behind that goal!" His manager also made mention of it in his programme notes for their next home game, "I thought we deserved a win," summarised Mr Docherty before adding, "and I am sure, like me, you enjoyed Robbie James' blockbuster of a goal late in the game. Down the years Robbie has made his name with that type of goal and I am delighted he managed to score one like that for us. It certainly got me out of my seat for the first time this season." Rightly considered the strike of the season, 'Robbie's rocket' came after eighty-four minutes: have a look at it on You Tube.

Other November games saw a 1-1 Cup draw with Huddersfield and a win against Preston, who had Robbie's old Stoke pal Sammy McIlroy in their squad. Robbie and his team had won three of their last four games but had taken more points away from home than at Valley Parade so far this season. They added to this with a 1-2 win.

City had won the F.A Cup in 1911, reached the quarter-finals in 1976 and found them selves facing a struggling Shrewsbury side in a first round tie that ended goal-less. A swift replay saw them exit the competition 2-1 before the end of the year. That loss was repeated at Crewe, opponents that would finish their campaign in the bottom three.

December 1990 opened with an away success at Huddersfield, coming soon after the recent Leyland Cup draw between the clubs. The side was then beaten by a single goal at the Valley by Cambridge United, a team which had recently won promotion thanks to the Play-offs and would storm towards winning the Third Division title this season. Bradford had not had a home League fixture in almost a month but then had two across a single week and an impressive 4-0 away win over Hartlepool sandwiched in between. They again faced Shrewsbury, their third mach against them across the 1990/ 91 season in a six goal thriller unfortunately ending 2-4 to the visitors in a fixture completed some three days before Christmas. And they still had to play them come April. A Boxing Day draw with Fulham was completed before picking up a point away at Southend United in a 1-1 against the subsequent division runners-up.

With thirty games played, Bury made the short trip to Valley Parade on New Year's Day. The Lancashire rivals had already played each other twice in the Rumbelows Cup but a fine 7,174 were in attendance for this traditional mid-day kick-off which resulted in a welcomed 3-1 home win. A tough trip to face Birmingham City was watched by a gate of 6,315, as the Blues went a goal up on four minutes and thus frustrating the Bantams supporters until seventy-three minutes when an equaliser arrived to see the game finish 1-1.

Bradford and Bolton had first met each back in 1903 and by the time of playing them in January 1991, Robbie had played in all thirty-three games of the current season, always in the number four shirt (except for away at Mansfield Town, where he wore the number two). City was a club perched in tenth position in Division Three, with thirty-three points gathered across twenty-three games played, when they played Bolton on 12 January at the Valley. The 1-1 was watched by the highest of the season: 8,764.

Tranmere, current holders of the Leyland Daf trophy, beat the Bantams 2-1 in Birkenhead before City met Hartlepool in the competition. With the pressure for Robbie and his colleagues to do well against a team from a lower division, fortunately they beat them comfortably 3-2 after creating a number of scoring opportunities on a cold evening. Robbie registered his fourth goal of the season in this rearranged match. That game started a run of four consecutive home games, with mixed results.

Grimsby, to be promoted by the season close, had been enjoying decent form and was firmly positioned high in the table when playing Bradford, themselves a little lower down, in eleventh. Coming four day after the Hartlepool game, the attendance shot up to 8,314 but the home fans must have been disappointed, as Robbie and his team lost 0-2. This was added to by a Leyland Daf Cup quarter-final encounter with Burnley which saw the unlucky Bantams miss plenty of chances, including a penalty, in a 0-1 defeat.

A cold spell across the country resulted in many February fixtures being postponed due to frozen pitches back when few clubs had under soil heating. Bournemouth, also relegated with Bradford and Stoke at the close of the previous season had beaten Bradford, at Dean Court 3-1 back in mid-September. A Luther Blissett penalty led to a 3-1 defeat for the visitors in that game and the fixture found Robbie playing against the former England striker who had been a Watford player in a Graham Taylor-team heading up the leagues, previously. Two points separated the clubs in the table and this time, it presented a 3-0 win for Bradford and saw Robbie switched to number two and facing his former Q.P.R. team mate Wayne Fereday. A similar points difference separated Birmingham and Bradford when they reconvened at Valley Parade after recording a 1-1 at St.Andrews in January. This time out, Robbie's lads won 2-0 in their fifth home game in a row. A League double over Preston followed, after a 0-3 win at Deepdale saw Bradford produce three wins without conceding a goal.

Robbie's excellent March performance in a local derby with Huddersfield was acknowledged by a Man-of-the-Match award. Now finding the Bantams on a lively run, with their last three games all won and eight goals scored, Robbie's late goal in the match would no doubt have been appreciated by the supporters, keen to put one over their west Yorkshire rivals. An encouraging 9,697 supporters attended and saw Town initially go 1-0 up before Robbie's goal on seventy-five minutes was complimented by the winner, from Sinnott, on eight-one minutes. Trivia fans might like to know that both Robbie and team mate Lee Duxbury favoured beans on toast as their pre-match meal. Robbie would have his around the mid-day mark, without having had breakfast earlier, and he had been doing so since his early days with Swansea! The game ended 2-2 with both Huddersfield goals scored via set-pieces. Disappointment came at Chester away with a 4-2 defeat, erasing a recent run where only two points from a possible twelve had been dropped by Bradford. The team immediately returned to their winning ways with a sparkling 4-0 win at home against Orient and a Wednesday evening meeting with Exeter, again at the Valley, seeing a super 3-0 success.

On Robbie's birthday, 23 March, Brentford provided a thumping for his side with a 6-1 which not only upset the supporters but also those within the club. Docherty termed his players as all being to blame for the loss, whilst Robbie, interviewed on the club line, expressed regret. "We let everyone down...we all felt sorry for the fans who made the long trip and must have gone home totally miserable..."

With only five home fixtures of the season remaining, they beat Crewe 2-0 before drawing with Fulham, when they came to Yorkshire and enjoyed a share of the spoils in another goal less encounter. In the Cottagers side that day was a certain Phil Stant, soon to join Robbie at Cardiff City.

Southend are defeated 2-1 next, prior to the team traveling to Bury where nearly 2,000 City fans contribute to 5,285 there to see a 0-0. In the penultimate fixture at Valley Parade, a 1-0 against Mansfield completes the double over a team that would finish at the bottom of the table, a massive thirty+ points behind Bradford.

Now with six games remaining, Stoke City did the double over them this season. Robbie scored one of the two goals in a 1-2 win against Reading, recording another League double before a low 1,934 crowd. Sean McCarthy got the other goal. His sixteenth of the season for the club. He had turned professional at Swansea and spent three years with them. Somehow, the Bridgend-born striker managed to both score and get himself dismissed on his Bradford debut, previously.

The closing month of the season commenced poorly with a 3-0 defeat at Wigan after previously beating them at home in mid-October. The loss was followed by another, this time at eventual Champions Cambridge before Robbie made an emotional return to the Vetch Field, only now as a Bradford City player, to see a goal in both halves enough to take away a 0-2 win. He enjoyed a couple of noteworthy moments on the ball during the game. Rotherham provided the opposition for the final home game of the campaign, producing a 1-0 win, days after the Swans game.

After concluding the 1990/91 season in a respectable eight and narrowly missing out on the Play-offs, Robbie and his Bradford City colleagues kicked-off the new 1991/92 Barclays League

Division Three campaign with a visit by one of his former clubs, Stoke on 17 August. A 1-0 win was appreciated by a great 7,556 gate which would see the club finish five places above the visitors come May.

The financial purse strings at Valley Parade had been severely tightened and this meant that wage bills had to be reduced and any new players could only come in on-loan. Pre-season had seen the squad win five times against such diverse opposition as Huddersfield, Leeds and a Spanish side. They had enjoyed some early success with victory in the West Riding Cup, a regional affair but otherwise hadn't won anything since being Division Three champions in the 1984/85 season. The club had new shirt sponsors and it meant that they had to hastily produce a new home kit to incorporate their involvement.

Robbie had completed fifty-seven appearances across his first season and had scored five times but in this his second campaign with the club, he would be struck by injuries. This would not dent his reputation amongst the diehards, "He was a class apart. His vision and ability with the ball made him stand out; a great bloke by the sound of it and no doubt missed by many, including of course his family. That goal at Rotherham United and a performance at Huddersfield Town summed him up for me: top player!" A quote from The Master on claretandbanter.co.uk.

Next meeting Stockport County away in a 1-1 League Cup tie prior to losing to regional rivals Huddersfield 1-0, before an impressive 9,234 gate. Stockport came to the Valley and were soundly beaten in the second leg of the League Cup following extra time being played. Success meant that Bradford would play West Ham across two games, in the next round. Recently promoted Hartlepool made the trip to Bradford for a 1-1, the first of three such consecutive draws for the Bantams; something they would repeat this season. Fortunately, a last minute penalty salvaged a point.

September saw seven fixtures played by the club, beginning with an away draw at Leyton Orient, in the battle of the ugly kits. Former Stoke and Wales colleague George Berry surfaced as a Preston player on their plastic pitch against Robbie in a 1-1 draw before it was added to a week later with the same result, at home, with Chester. Three players received their marching orders in a tempestuous 4-4 with Bolton; a game remembered by supporters for its dramatic content and Man-of-the-Match showing by Robbie. Across the campaign, Bradford would record twenty-two draws. A break from League affairs came after a promising 1-2 away win at Reading with a visit by West Ham in the second round of the League Cup on 24 September.

Played on a Tuesday night, a non-descript Hammers team made their hosts work hard in a physically draining encounter for Robbie and his colleagues as they played out a 1-1 draw watched by 7,063 prior to the return leg in October. The Bradford style of play at this time might not have been the best to watch from a spectator's perspective but changes would soon occur within the club. Future Swans manager John Bond brought his woeful Shrewsbury Town to Bradford in the final game of the month and left pointless thanks to a 3-0 thrashing. The Shrews would be relegated by the end of the season.

Having already drawn with, and beaten Stockport this season, the teams met once more in October only this time County won 4-1 at their place in Bradford's thirteenth game of the new campaign. Although this was not to be their heaviest defeat, that arrived at the Boleyn ground, in a 4-0 loss to West Ham next.

Standing tickets for the visiting away fans cost £7 whilst to sit, they had to pay £12 for entry into a ground similar to the Vetch, in that the fans could almost touch the players on the pitch before them. Fulham, a team that would complete a League double over them this season, added another defeat at Valley Parade for City in a 3-4 win. The defeat marked twelve goals concede to four scored in their last three fixtures.

A home game with Torquay on 19 October not only produced a 2-0 win but was also significant in that it marked the 700th League appearance by Robbie. Now aged thirty-four and having lost much of his earlier pace, he put in "an inspired display" and was presented with an inscribed silver salver to mark the achievement. Throughout his playing days, Robbie received many accolades and awards and by now possessed a backroom full of trinkets. Returning to his early days with the Swans, you might recall that he recorded his hundredth League start against them back on St Valentine's Day 1976.

Defeat at Hull in the Autoglass Trophy, which used to be the Leyland Daf Vans Cup, was forgotten thanks to a 1-3 success at AFC Bournemouth at the end of the month. Their hosts had beaten both Swansea and Cardiff this season but couldn't do the same against a Bantams side consisting of lads mainly under twenty-three years of age: Robbie excluded, of course.

A 2 November noon kick-off with soon-to-be promoted Brentford resulted in defeat and was added by another, again 1-0, at Exeter City. Robbie's former Leicester team mate Steve Moran was in their side, playing for an opposition that had seen some strange results this term. A third defeat reared its ugly head at Peterborough, as a 2-1 loss was watched by an esteemed 9,224 gate. Bury would exit the Third  Division in May 1992 and also saw any advancement in the F.A Cup dashed by Bradford.

The second of three meetings with Hartlepool arrived next in a 3-3 Autoglass Cup meeting at the Valley which saw striking performances from both Robbie and his team mate Phil Babb. Those two Cup games with West Ham might have been roused most fans during the current campaign but it was to be a mid-November match with bottom-of-the-table Swansea City that proved the most remarkable. In an incredible ten goal thriller, the visitors came off the bottom of Division Three in some style: with a 4-6 win! They surprised everyone by overturning some lackluster away form which saw them 1-4 ahead at half-time. Coincidentally, Leighton James was acting Caretaker manager for mid-table Bradford, following the departure of John Docherty and had scrapped the sweeper system which Robbie had been fulfilling. Proving to be a strong central presence in the team, he was still selected for this astonishing match, which did little to favour Leight's desire to be appointed full-time manager. After the ten goals shared between the clubs at Valley Parade, the return League fixture at the Vetch at the end of March produced four more, in a 2-2. Finally this month, away at St Andrew's saw a tough test against Birmingham prove too much, with the Bantams defeated 2-0 in front of a 10,468 gate against an opposition that would gain promotion.

By the end of the first week of December, Robbie and his team mates travelled to Bolton only to lose 3-1 in the F.A Cup. That was their third consecutive defeat before returning to the Valley where they next faced games against Bobby Gould's West Brom and then, Huddersfield. Once again, both produced 1-1 draws, with crowds totaling 7,195 and 10,050, respectively. The derby game with the latter kicked-off at noon and found City on twenty-one points and their visitors on a much healthier thirty-five. In the squad of the away side was Dudley Lewis, a team mate of Robbie's back at Swansea.

When thinking of Robbie James, most people picture him with a moustache but a demonstration of his thoughtfulness saw him shave it off this month. Why? It was part of a charity fundraiser to help a young baby with Cerebral Palsy. It would seem that off the pitch, Robbie was also quite the gentleman. Sheriff_Lobo, a supporter writing on claretndbandbanter remembers, "During the early 1990's the local schools in Bradford used to have a penalty shoot out competition at half time down at Valley Parade. Luckily for my school we used to have some decent footballers so we got to the final at least a couple of times. We used to play in a distinctive green kit and we would walk past the players as they were coming off at half time and then back on for the second half. Robbie recognized us every time because of our kit and he used to wish us luck and gee us up as he walked off the pitch; he would then always ask how we got on at the end of half time and used to congratulate us when we won. It was such a buzz as a young lad to have a player take interest in your little game and he used to make us feel like a million dollars. I will always have fond memories of Robbie and I was deeply saddened by his death."

Boxing Day found the squad fulfilling another fixture at Hartlepool. A 1-0 defeat for City, it proved to be Robbie's twenty-ninth and final appearance in the number four shirt as he picked up a hamstring injury late in the game. He would miss the next four matches, being replaced by new arrival Frank Stapleton. Announced as their next player-manager on 9 December, as an Arsenal and later Manchester United player, the Irishman had faced Robbie in a Swansea team and had seen the present club captain score against his United side during the illustrious 1981/82 season in Division One. Robbie would miss draws against Stoke, Orient and Bury, in addition to a defeat at Wigan. Before returning to first team duties, he played a single game for the Reserves this month.

On 18 January, he returned to selection, now at number two, in a disappointing 2-1 loss at Wigan. Unfortunately for Robbie, he strained his neck muscles in the game and would also injure his forearm whilst playing for the Bantams. Colin Todd was announced as Stapleton's new assistant and past Manchester United star Mike Duxbury was came in on loan.

Swansea old boys, Robbie and McCarthy, produced the goals in a 2-1 win at Valley Parade a week later, against Hull. Scoring from the penalty spot, his third goal of the 1991/ 92 season, Robbie would advance to play in all sixteen remaining games.

A draw at Torquay on 1 February was added-to by a repeat 3-1 defeat of Bournemouth before Birmingham achieved the double over Bradford with a 1-2 win at the Valley next. Sadly, also this month came news of the death of Alan Davies.

West Bromwich Albion provided Stapleton's first game in charge and was a tough task away at the Hawthorns for the club's twenty-seventh fixture of the campaign. The Baggies sat on top of 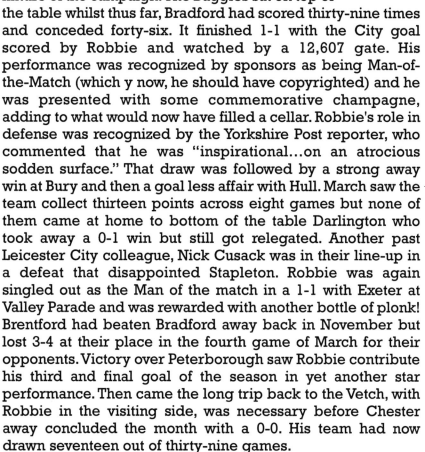 the table whilst thus far, Bradford had scored thirty-nine times and conceded forty-six. It finished 1-1 with the City goal scored by Robbie and watched by a 12,607 gate. His performance was recognized by sponsors as being Man-of-the-Match (which y now, he should have copyrighted) and he was presented with some commemorative champagne, adding to what would now have filled a cellar. Robbie's role in defense was recognized by the Yorkshire Post reporter, who commented that he was "inspirational...on an atrocious sodden surface." That draw was followed by a strong away win at Bury and then a goal less affair with Hull. March saw the team collect thirteen points across eight games but none of them came at home to bottom of the table Darlington who took away a 0-1 win but still got relegated. Another past Leicester City colleague, Nick Cusack was in their line-up in a defeat that disappointed Stapleton. Robbie was again singled out as the Man of the match in a 1-1 with Exeter at Valley Parade and was rewarded with another bottle of plonk! Brentford had beaten Bradford away back in November but lost 3-4 at their place in the fourth game of March for their opponents. Victory over Peterborough saw Robbie contribute his third and final goal of the season in yet another star performance. Then came the long trip back to the Vetch, with Robbie in the visiting side, was necessary before Chester away concluded the month with a 0-0. His team had now drawn seventeen out of thirty-nine games.

April would see six fixtures for the club, half of them at home and the other away games. A decent-sized crowd of 6,896 saw the 1-1 with Preston at the Valley with seven games remaining of the season. A point difference separated the clubs and spectators enjoyed a strong first half display from their team that proved pleasing to watch. Captain Robbie James was again given the Man-of-the-Match award. Darlington were beaten 1-3 at their ground prior to a draw at Bolton for City within which Robbie produced much creative play.

By the time of entertaining Reading at home, Bradford City had played all but four of their forty-six League fixtures. Found in a lower mid-table position, as were the Royals, the Bantams won 1-0 in front of a 5,492 crowd. Defensive mistakes allowed Shrewsbury three points at Gay Meadow before Stockport provided the final visitors at Valley Parade for the season. City sat in thirteenth whilst the visitors still had all to play for, as they were competing for the Play-offs. Their hopes were dashed with a 1-0 defeat whilst Bradford looked to their final game of the campaign, away to Fulham on 2 May. They lost that 2-1 and concluded their endeavours in sixteenth. For the record, Swansea could be found three places below whilst Brentford won the Division on eighty-two points collected (to Bradford's fifty-eight).

Robbie left Bradford for Cardiff City in 1992 via a £17,500 transfer fee; an amount subsequently needing to be set by a tribunal and not the first time such a decision was need to place a value on him. His legacy with the club remains intact."I remember him playing for us at right back, bombing down the wing, overlapping the winger." Remenisced Phantom_Bantam

responding to the author on the www.claretandbanter.co.uk fans forum. "He had one hell of a shot on him." Another adds, "I suppose Robbie was similar to Gary Jones in a way when he played for us, nearing the latter stages of his career but although he'd lost a bit of pace, he more than made up for it with his enthusiasm! A skillful player with plenty of flair, I would love to have seen him play for us when he was in his prime but he still graced the Valley Parade pitch with his silky passing skills."

This is complimented by one other fan, who writes: "I would echo what has already been said about him being like Jones! Although he was slightly rotund, he could show a great turn of pace, hurtling through the center of midfield, just what we need now. He scored a cracker of a goal against 'udders (Huddersfield Town) away, when we won at Leeds Road, he smacked one in from twenty yards out and celebrated by doing a forward roll. He was a very good passer of the ball and had good vision and never stopped." Skyebantam commented, "Robbie was playing just as I started going to see City. I saw him play a few times, and even though the number of games is less than some fans, in those few games he left the same impression on me. He was a crowd favourite but he was more than just heart and determination; despite his age you could see the skill he had. Shame I only saw him for a brief time in City colours. My dad really liked him; in those early days when I went with him he used to point out what a good player he was."

Bantams fans also say that Robbie ran a pub whilst at Bradford, supposedly the Lord Rodney, at Church Green, Kayleigh but I wonder how this could be true. Of course, many ex-pros were known to move in to the licensing trade once their playing days were over but not during. Ex-team mate Eddie May ran a pub for a short while before getting back in to the game and former Swans stopper Tony Millington did so too. Mel Nurse owns a hotel and Robbie did briefly take over the license of a Swansea city centre bar when he was their part-time player-manager at Llanelli but here, this seems somewhat unlikely.

Even in the latter part of his playing career Robbie was still a big draw in the game, as the programme cover for Bradford's away visit to the Hawthorns, home of West Bromwich Albion, demonstrates.

Cardiff City

*"…along Sloper road, we make our way, to Ninian Park,
where the Bluebirds play!"*

Old grounds like the Vetch and Ninian Park, the latter being the much-loved home of Cardiff City for many years, may now be sadly lost, both since demolished but they will forever linger in the memories of supporters stretching across many seasons. It seems wrong that football heritage does not have its value protected, with the game today now driven more by financial necessity than anything else. At Ninian, a private housing estate now stands, with the modern Cardiff City Stadium gleaming but a breath away from its former home. Similarities between the clubs and their grounds are numerable, and lots of players, managers and coaches have made the switch between the clubs over the years. Names that immediately spring to mind include Ivor Allchurch, John Toshack and Nigel Stevenson but there have been many, many others. When Alan Curtis quizzed Robbie about an offer that he had received regarding signing for Cardiff, Robbie told him to take it and not worry about the rivalry between the clubs. It was no coincidence that later he would do the same, signing for Cardiff after being a long-established Swansea great.

With its name taken from Lord Ninian Edward Crichton-Stuart, Member of Parliament for Cardiff between 1910-1915, the inaugural match played at Ninian Park occurred on Thursday 1 September 1910.

Advancing to the 1970s, £225,000 was spent on the main stand extension; including its seating total being raised to 4,500. The playing surface had also vastly improved. Ninian Park suffered as a result of the Safety of Sports Grounds Act (1977) as did Vetch Field, as the former was deemed unsafe and necessitated major reconstruction work. Costing £600,000, a third of which came from the Football Grounds Improvement Trust and the much-maligned Football Association of Wales (F.A.W) contributed £27,000. The ground capacity fell to 10,000 and the act saw the demolition of the Grangetown roof/ banking.

By the 1980s, Ninian Park had a long-established reputation as an intimidating place for players and visiting supporters. Cardiff fans had been banned at the Vetch in this hooligan-strewn decade and thus the ban was reciprocated at Ninian Park. Television footage of the 1984 Boxing Day fixture with the Swans shows the ground looking decrepit.

Stepping in to the 1990s and things had improved, Robbie who would sign for Cardiff City in 1992; a couple of years after the main stand enclosure had a freshly-installed, extended roof put on. The Popular Bank (always known as the Bob Bank due to its former price of entry) now had an upper section of seating but retained a small standing-only section. Former Swans youth coach and Wales legend, John Charles, was the V.I.P in October 1994 during the home game with Crewe, wherein he officially opened the John Charles Suite housed in the Grandstand. We should remember that a certain Mr. Toshack learnt much from "Big John" whilst both were players at the club back in the 1960s. Much of it being extra heading practice which proved so significant for Tosh when a Swan.

As regards the playing fortunes of Cardiff City Football Club, they had been relegated down into Division Four at the close of the 1989/ 90 season, along with Swansea, and finished thirteenth in the division in the next campaign. Defeats by Isthmian League side Hayes in the FA Cup, and to Merthyr Tydfil in the Welsh Cup, capped a mediocre season for the Bluebirds and saw manager Len Ashurst quit. He was succeeded by former Swansea and Wrexham player, and past team mate of Robbie's, Eddie May. After previously being the youth coach at Ninian Park, Eddie made the step up into his first managerial position after some years as a coach. He and Robbie were good friends and that was reflected in his autobiography, wherein big Eddie felt the loss of his old mate greatly. The 1991/ 92 season saw a vast improvement in fortunes as the club climbed to an excellent ninth position by its close.

Having been voted club Player of the Season across both the 1990/ 91 and 1991/ 92 Barclays League Division Three campaigns, Bradford City were not keen to allow Robbie to join Cardiff without some recompense. They were still paying his wages even though he was in south Wales training with the Bluebirds in late summer 1992. Robbie felt that as he was now out of contract that Cardiff should not be required to pay them a fee but Bradford wanted something for him. It was another ugly financial wrangle involving Robbie resulting in a tribunal hearing to fix the amount payable. Funnily enough, by the time of his subsequent departure from Cardiff in 1994, the Bluebirds would be demanding compensation from his new club, Merthyr Tydfil, but more of that later.

Robbie was clearly detached of any emotions towards Bradford after declaring that he had fulfilled his contractual obligations as a professional footballer and that he wanted to move on. With his family residing near Caswell Bay in Swansea, the prospect of plying his trade in Cardiff had its obvious geographical merits.

Eddie May recognised Robbie as a perfect fix to introduce some professionalism and experience into his Cardiff side but almost gave up the pursuit to sign him. Initially seeking to take the former Wales star on-loan, Bradford valued James at £30,000 whilst May was getting impatient at the stalemate. It proved unhelpful in his quest to reinforce his squad and to register all new arrivals in anticipation of a long League season and first round entry into the European Cup Winners'

Cup. The matter went to an FA tribunal, held on 3 September and Cardiff City had to pay £17,500 to the Bantams.

Major structural improvements had been made to Ninian Park during the close-season, seeing seats on part of the Bob Bank and a new terrace in front with seating added. The Canton stand, where families would be accomodated, was made in to an all-seating area with the primitive wooden benching discarded. Cardiff also had a new shirt sponsorship deal with local newspaper the South Wales Echo. Wearing a somewhat busy and unattractive shirt with its two button collar and neck, some City fans loved it whilst others not so.

Pre-season friendlies with clubs in higher divisions saw Oxford United, Bristol Rovers, Plymouth Argyle and Darlington come to Ninian Park but Robbie was ineligible for selection in any of them due to contract/ registration wrangles. It was during this time that he played as a guest in a benefit match against a Manchester United select XI, in aid of the family of Alan Davies staged at the Vetch on 11 August. Sadly, Alan, a very talented player, took his own life whilst with Swansea City in February 1992. The two had been team mates at Swansea, Bradford and for Wales.

Robbie, now thirty-five, eventually signed a contract with Cardiff on 14 August 1992, in readiness for the start of a memorable season which would see the club complete a promotion and Welsh Cup double (not repeated since). May was delighted. "He will be an asset to us because he can fill a number of positions and he has a good pedigree. He has impressed everyone in training and his experience will be invaluable." George Smith, a colleague of both Robbie and Eddie's back at Swansea in the mid-1970s, remembers a younger Robbie not all that keen in this department. "I was surprised with Robbie's attitude to training, at times, because he would give far less than was expected of him." Now living back in Middlesborough and running a football coaching academy, Smith, in a correspondence with the author, adds "However, in matches he was a different animal; strong, competitive but not arrogant, a pleasure to play with."

The bookies made City favourites for the Division Three title after the club had won the Welsh Cup in May 1992 thanks to defeating Hendesford Town. Robbie felt that if the team could gel well then they could challenge for promotion. He agreed that the team was lacking in experience and hoped that by being added to the squad that he could help in that area. After making some 484 appearances, his modesty was endearing.

Some twenty years earlier, before Robbie broke in to the Swansea first team, he was rejected by Cardiff City whilst being on their books as a schoolboy. The Bluebirds were then managed by ex-pro Jimmy Scoular and his decision came despite a scout saying that they should sign him. That man was Harry Parsons, known as 'Mr Cardiff City', he was the kit man in later years and was still with the club when Robbie joined them. New Chairman Rick Wright offered a more direct incentive, dangling a bonus for each player if they won promotion/ the Welsh Cup this season totalling almost £40,000.

Robbie rejoined some familiar faces at City, including old team mate May and also, captain Paul Ramsey, who had been an established player at Leicester City when he joined them in late summer 1987. Ramsey was a dedicated pro that had been a part of the Northern Ireland squad at the 1982 World Cup finals and had signed for Cardiff from Leicester. The debonair Irishman was loved by May because he regarded him as his right hand man on the pitch.

It was a year in which the new back pass law was introduced into the Football League and it caused a great deal of consternation to many clubs, including Cardiff, with mistakes being made in many games by both players and referees. The new rule was meant to prevent time wasting as it prohibited a keeper from picking up the ball if it had intentionally been passed back to him.

Robbie went on to play in every match, mainly in the number two shirt, across this glorious season and added a fifth medal to his Welsh Cup winning tally at its close. He is pictured below in the Cardiff City squad, immediate left, top row.

An excellent 8,399 crowd attended the opening game of the season on 15 August for the visit of Darlington to Ninian Park. The attendance was the highest recorded in the division that day and the Bluebirds regularly repeated this throughout a testing campaign. The City supporters are arguably the best in Wales, with due respect to Swansea, and despite much mixed fortunes on the pitch and problems off it, their dedication in following their team never faltered.

A drab 0-0 against a freshly-relegated opposition wasn't the most inspiring beginning but City was a club known for being slow starters. Only three players in the starting line-up remained from last season and there was a place for former Manchester United player Derek Brazil and another new arrival, Nicky Richardson. The team selection was a strong one:Grew, Robbie, Searle, Richardson, Perry, Brazil, Ramsey, Pike, Dale, Blake. Player-coach Roger Gibbins, selected as substitute, would compete against Robbie when the latter was a Barry player and May, manager there, during the 1994/ 95 season in the Konica League. Like Robbie, Roger played for both Cardiff and Swansea City during his career and coached at Merthyr Tydfil and Weston.

Robbie slotted in perfectly at right-back and although his pace had lessened considerably, he added much to a City side that created chances and looked secure at the back against one of many teams that season that adopted a 'defend-first' strategy when visiting Ninian Park.

As well as League duties, Cardiff competed in a number of Cup competitions across the season, namely the FA Cup, European Cup Winners' Cup, Welsh Cup, League Cup (sponsored by Coca-Cola) and Associated Members Cup (aka the Autoglass Trophy). The first of these saw the arrival of rivals across the Severn, Bristol City, in a League Cup meeting in August. To be played across two legs, City boss May was not overly concerned with progression here as the League and Welsh Cup were his priorities. The Robins had drawn 3-3 with Portsmouth in their opening game of the season but were beaten 1-0 by Cardiff, thanks to a Dale goal. It was his opening strike of the new campaign and saw the former Chester man building on the success of his partnership with Pike from the previous season. Robbie's new team mates were the Little & Large of the side and played well in a good team performance seeing the strikers and midfield players working effectively and helping defend when necessary. May was pleased with the result and happy to chalk up the first win of the season. Dale had played against Robbie whilst with Chester when Jamo had returned for a second spell with Swansea City.

With Hurricane Andrew causing mayhem in the United States, Cardiff continued with matters in the League and an away fixture at the Bescott Stadium, home of Walsall. A commanding performance from Robbie saw him enjoying exchanges with Ramsey during his forays up field from defence. City scored twice in the space of eight minutes in a match that recorded several bookings and a 2-3 win. The final score flattered Walsall as City dominated. It was regarded as the best team performance that Eddie May had seen.

Robbie needed treatment to his knee during the game and was looking doubtful to play in the away leg of the Coca-Cola sponsored League Cup match at Ashton Gate some three days later. It was the first time that the clubs had met in the competition since in 1945.

The mercurial Nathan Blake, a Cardiff-born power horse of a player, and a precocious talent, was in trouble off the field during his early days at Cardiff and before. But on the pitch, he was playing well this season and soon to step up to becoming a full Wales international. 'Blakey', along with Dale and another star this year; Phil Stant, are remembered for scoring many goals for the club and remain much-loved.

A hat-trick from future Man United star Andy Cole flattened an under-strength Cardiff side in a 5-1 drubbing that saw May furious with his players. Nearly 10k attended the match and watched as the veteran legs of Robbie James failed to compete with the strength of the much-younger Cole, as poor defending put the Bluebirds out of the competition.

The atmosphere in the City dressing room after the Bristol defeat was tense and so the players were keen to bounce back as soon as possible with an upcoming home win against Halifax Town desired. May was as passionate a coach/ manager as he was a player and if his team did not perform, then they got quite an ear bashing: he was not a man that you wanted to disappoint!

Tickets for the match against a Jimmy Case led Town on a wet August Bank Holiday weekend were priced at £7 and £8 for the Grandstand and £5 for either the Bob Bank or Canton Stand. The fans that did decide to venture out saw Robbie get his name on the score sheet just after the half-hour mark thanks to a trade mark rocket shot which was the first goal in a game won 2-1 by City. The match that saw Ramsey sent off and the players seeing a £200 bonus kick-in as the result saw them placed in the top three of the division despite facing a side intent on stifling their play. Robbie declared that he would be even better once he was fully match fit and his goal, one of two that he collected this season, came from a classy twenty five yard rocket. He saw a similarly struck shot fly just over the bar in the recent Bristol City game.

Games at Cardiff City were priced in differing categories and a later strategy saw higher prices being charged if the team was winning, and so the Northampton Town game, a 2-1 win, on the first day of September cost slightly more to watch. The victory took City to second spot, behind York City, and saw team mate Cohen Griffiths thanking Robbie for his guidance during games. The affable Griffiths, known as 'Co' to his friends, was a Guyana-born player that struggled with injury during the 1992/ 93 season, his fourth year with the club but when he did play, often in front of Robbie, he greatly appreciated the on-field guidance from the older pro. City fought back from being 1-0 down to equalise and saw a Robbie-inspired corner reach Blake only for a defender to 205 concede a penalty put away by Ramsey. Robbie was also instrumental in the move to get the winner.

In another team photograph below, Robbie can be found second left in the middle row. The Welsh Cup is shown in front of manager Eddie May. It was a trophy that Robbie would win on five ocassions, whilst at Swansea and Cardiff.

However, a number of away fixtures proved problematic for the club this season, with restrictions at some of the smaller grounds also hampered by numerous improvements being made at stadiums across the country resulting in a temporary limit on ground capacities. The away match down in Devon against Torquay was a case in point, with only 1,000 tickets made available to travelling supporters for a trip usually much-enjoyed by fans. Local police there were rightly worried about hooliganism concerns as a club like United simply could not cope with teams such as Cardiff City who generated much larger travelling support. The day proved a calamity all round with City losing 2-1 and fighting recorded both before and after the match. On the pitch, a peculiar incident involving Torquay player-manager Justin Fashanu resulted in a broken cheekbone for City player John Williams. In the subsequent mêlée, Robbie, Eddie May, Fashanu and Williams all got involved. The more talented Fashanu brother was rightly sent-off and the City manager almost arrested for trying to break up the incident. Robbie had played against the troubled Fash whilst a Swansea player in the old First

Division and scored three times against the latter when he was at Notts Forest during the 1981/ 82 season. Cardiff performed poorly in the first half and were lacking in quality, rushing and not playing the way that they could. Dale missed the match, his first in more than a year for the club.

A 2-2 with visiting Carlisle came the night before Wales thrashed the Faroe Islands at the National stadium in Cardiff, with the game seeing a rare, off-night for Robbie.

There always seems to be certain clubs that are regularly drawn against each other in Cup games as well in corresponding League fixtures and this season that could be said for Cardiff, Hereford United and Wrexham. A 1-1 away at Hereford's Edgar Road ground on 13 September saw that match switched from a Saturday to Sunday and City's Chairman Rick Wright furious with Hereford for agreeing to the change to allow police to deal with the considerable City contingency. He asked supporters to boycott the match but they went anyway and the gate was sufficiently swollen to 4,039 (more than half of the total being travelling City supporters) and saw a late Blake equaliser. They would also meet in the Autoglass Trophy in December, again seeing a win for Cardiff: Wrexham would come later.

As a Swansea City player, Robbie James had played for the club in the European Cup Winners' Cup against the likes of Lokomotive Leipzig, Sporting Baraga, Paris St. Germain and Panathinakos and this season would add Austrian side F.C Baumit

Admira Wacker to the list. Unfortunately for him and Cardiff City, an unspent suspension accrued from his Swansea days meant that he was ineligible for selection in the September home fixture. That game resulted in a 1-1 and he was free to play in the return leg at the end of that month.

May had watched Wacker before their first meeting and his City team played well at Ninian Park before a gate of 9,624. Positioned in ninth position in the League, their opponents were more used to playing the likes of Rapid Vienna and Sturm Gratz than the Bluebirds of Cardiff. The City manager had stressed the importance of not conceding at home but could only watch as an entertaining game was played out, spoilt only by an error to give the visitors a valuable 'away' goal. A ticket for the tie at the Sudstadt Stadion, Vienna, could be purchased for £6 and Wright had offered free admission to Ninian Park for all away fans but not many travelled. The ever-industrious Chairman chartered a plane and offered supporters a ticket/ flight package for £179.

Admira now play their football in the Austrian Bundesliga alongside Rapid and Sturm Graz, but at the time of meeting Cardiff they had recent European tournament experience in the U.E.F.A. Cup and the present one.

Robbie and his team mates flew to Austria on 28 September for the game which was being played the following day in front of 4,700 fans. Starting in place of young Anthony Bird, Robbie was switched to midfield, where he linked up with Paul Ramsey for the first time since their Leicester City days. Alas City lost 2-0, with both goals coming in the second half and so ended their involvement in the competition this season. "I went over to Vienna hoping but not expecting," offered Rick Wright before adding that he saw an upcoming League win against Rochdale a necessity.

Although wanting a win from their Chairman, City drew 1-1 with Rochdale as the season advanced in to October. Missing many chances, Rochdale manager Dave Sutton was impressed by Cardiff and believed that they would be promoted. This was a view echoed by a number of opponents.

In a new initiative, Robbie was named as the most consistent Third Division player for September by a French football boot manufacturer. He was awarded a commemorative scroll in recognition by the sponsors.

Next electing to use a sweeper system, a tactic and role familiar to Robbie, it failed to work in a poor away defeat at Gresty Road, where Crewe beat the Bluebirds 2-0 and saw the

Welsh team drop down in to seventh in the table after ten games played. A total of sixteen points had been collected, a dozen behind leaders York City, and it proved to be a poor collective effort from Robbie and his team mates against a side that were four places above.

Grouped with Shrewsbury Town and Hereford in the early stages of the Autoglass Trophy, City next made the short journey to Gay Meadow for a League fixture with the Shrews. Sent away via a 3-2 defeat, the loss continued a shoddy run of form, with only a single win in the last nine. However, the Cup meeting would in December would produce a different result.

Being the current holders of the Welsh Cup, Cardiff sought to retain it this year with Robbie playing in all six rounds of the competition against a mixture of teams from various divisions. First opponents Ton Petre, then unbeaten in the Abacus League, would kick start a total of twenty two goals scored by the Bluebirds, with just the one returned. Swansea City fell out of contention after losing 2-0 to a Merthyr Tydfil side led by Terry

Boyle. He was a former Cardiff player and captain that had led the Bluebirds to a Welsh Cup final victory and League promotion back in 1988. Terry had also been the joint player of the year with Alan Curtis that year.

Meanwhile the present Cardiff City team would advance to beat Caerau, Maesteg Park, Wrexham and Rhyl in the current tournament. But beginning with Petre, that tie was played on a heavy Ynys Park pitch and in wet conditions, with two late strikes seeing them off in a game which saw a sparkling performance from Robbie at a tight little ground. Despite goals from Millar and Ramsey, the need for a new striker was proving acutely obvious for City if they were to do well in the League. But with main man Dale unlucky to pick up an injury which would keep him out for a huge chunk of the season, salvation was to arrive in the peculiar guise of an ex-Army bomb disposal man.

New loan striker Tony Kelly came during October for a run of five games alongside Robbie and had been registered as a Stoke player in 1986/ 87 when Rob was with the club. They would not

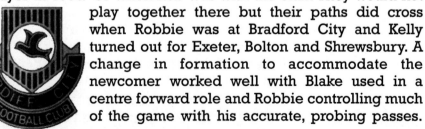

play together there but their paths did cross when Robbie was at Bradford City and Kelly turned out for Exeter, Bolton and Shrewsbury. A change in formation to accommodate the newcomer worked well with Blake used in a centre forward role and Robbie controlling much of the game with his accurate, probing passes.

Kelly got one of the goals on his debut before a 3 November away game at long-ball merchants Chesterfield saw a rare James goal proving insufficient to avoid a 2-1 defeat. Made captain for the game in the absence of stalwart Ramsey, he also took over the midfield role usually taken by the Irishman. Producing a good individual performance and a goal from twenty yards out, the Bluebirds' away form was poor. Frustrations abound after the game at Saltergate, with Robbie booked and expressing his irritation, "The worst thing is that we are giving away easy goals," conceded the former Swans player to the local press. "We are giving bad goals away and we are creating chances and not scoring them. We have to sort it out now!" The string of bad results was putting pressure on manager Eddie May who was unafraid to vent his frustrations in the local paper, as he had already relayed to his players that mistakes needed to be fixed. City had leaked five goals in their last two outings against poor opposition. The fans were also expressing their own dissatisfaction with them by booing as the team left the pitch.

Remaining in November, a welcome 3-1 home win against Colchester United was seen by a crowd totalling 5,505, the lowest of the season at Ninian Park all season. It again displayed the fact that the errors being made were only countered by City strikers Dale and Blake scoring at the other end. Roger Gibbins made a rare start in a game played exactly a week before the next home fixture, an F.A. Cup meeting with Bath City. Then of the Vauxhall Conference, it was a game which was to prove the catalyst for the season. Cardiff had been knocked out of the competition in the previous season by non-league opposition, including Weymouth, and you might well foretell what was to happen this year.

Merthyr Tydfil manager Wynford Hopkins had given Eddie May the low down on their West Country opponents, after the exiles had played them twice that season: winning once and drawing the other. His summation of Bath was not glowing, "Very competitive; a no-nonsense side who are very committed. They have had more or less the same team for some time and are very basic." But what he failed to say was that Merthyr had played them some while ago and Bath City had improved greatly since then. Hopkins felt that the Bluebirds would beat them whilst the Bath manager Tony Richards simply said that his team of part-timers would enjoy the game, regardless of the outcome.

The English visitors shocked the home supporters by taking a 1-0 lead after twenty minutes before City responded well with goals from Millar and Blake which took them in at half-time with a 2-1 lead. However, this being a Cup game where anything can and sometimes does happen, Bath City equalised just before the hour. The defensive frailties shown by the hosts proved their downfall and astonishingly, the final score was Cardiff 2 - Bath City 3. "It was a sad day for Cardiff City," lamented an embarrassed May at the time and still bitter about it some twenty years later. The crowd, numbering 4,506, was not so passive; once again booing their team off and chanting for Eddie's head in between bouts of "What a load of rubbish!" Rick Wright was away on another extended holiday but did state that he would not be sacking his manager, despite the outcry. Wright was unconcerned about exiting the competition but accepted that losing to non-League opposition was unacceptable.

Following the debacle of the F.A. Cup exit, Robbie and his team mates were made to watch a recording of the game with their irate manager and it must have been quite the 'video nasty'. Their

victors exited the Cup in the next round after a replay with Third Division side Northampton Town.

City skipper Paul Ramsey asked supporters to stay with them as they would make amends for that embarrassment. Facing Barnet next, they looked tense and lost 2-1 managed by the charismatic Barry Fry who felt that his side along with City and Wrexham deserved to fill the automatic promotion places. And he would prove to be spot on with his assertion. It was City's fourth consecutive away defeat. A rare error from Robbie led to one of the Barnet goals, with his lack of pace capitalised upon.

Less than a week later and the City players looked stiff in the first half of a game against Bury, the first home fixture since the Bath City debacle. Nevertheless, a 3-0 win put Cardiff into eight in the division, with Welsh rivals Wrexham five places below. The game was an ugly encounter to watch but produced a valuable win and succeeded in upholding an unbeaten home League run stretching across eight fixtures played at Ninian Park this season. The Bury match recorded the lowest attendance seen at home this season: 4,348. It also marked the final appearance from speedy youngster Kelly.

After a League defeat away at Shrewsbury in mid-October, City made amends with a 1-3 away win back at Gay Meadow in the Autoglass. The result pleased May despite one of the goals coming from a back pass decision made by the match referee.

In the closing month of 1992, Robbie's former Swansea, Bradford and Wales associate Leighton James made the sports headlines, after declining the vacant managerial vacancy at Beazer Homes club Weymouth.

Featuring in his second Welsh Cup game of the season, Robbie took part in a 0-9 routing of Caerau before Hereford Town followed a few days later in a busy December, which continued with Autoglass Trophy duties. Playing their second of three matches against each other this season, Cardiff met Hereford in the Autoglass aka, Associate Members Cup and twice came from behind to run-out eventual 3-2 winners. A cross from Robbie was controlled by Stant and he used both feet on the way to scoring from a volley just before the hour to take the sides to 2-2. Bolton-born Stant, then aged thirty, was tremendous this season in a Bluebirds shirt.

Meanwhile back in the League, a long trip to Doncaster Rovers saw a gutsy performance by Cardiff City at Belle Vue with a solid defensive performance and finding Robbie in great form. It was only City's second away win of the 1992/ 93 campaign and was played at a time when Robbie was struggling with a knee injury. Ex-players are often physical wrecks after years of hard-wearing seasons and this period saw Mr James requiring cortisone injections, coupled with rest, to enable him to soldier on. The Rovers game saw the full League debut for Phil Stant, signed for earlier in the month from Mansfied Town at a bargain £100,000. Known as 'Stanty', this much-travelled hot shot proved an instant hit and a crowd favourite. So much so that the fans would chant, "Who needs Cantona when we've got Stantona" (it was the time when Man United had Frenchman Eric Cantona in their team). In his career so far, this dedicated and hard-working player had scored eighty eight goals and would push that into three figures during his time with the Bluebirds. Cracking in thirty one goals across all competitions by the end of the season, sadly his legacy at the club proved a sour one, with money issues proving his downfall against the might of Rick Wright. So much so that when the club moved to its new stadium in recent years, Stant was noticeable in his absence from opening celebrations.

Interviewed in the press, Robbie, a football "general with a sweet pass" reflected that Cardiff seemed to perform more effectively against the bigger clubs in the division, such as Wrexham. He also felt that the 18 December game with the Robins would set Cardiff up nicely for a Boxing Day meeting in south Wales with York City. Often Cardiff City would win games but not play to their full potential in games this year.

The comedy adventures of Del Boy and Rodney in Only Fools and Horses was the Christmas Day telly highlight of 1992 but the City player had to forgo all Yuletide spirit as they prepared for the visit of York. After spending the morning with their families, the squad rendezvoused at a hotel in preparation for the match. An away journey to Sincl Bank and Lincoln City on 28 December would soon be followed by entertaining Hereford on 2 January.

Youngster Lee Baddeley was surprised at getting a game for the Bluebirds against Lincoln and it proved a frustrating game as City looked to have control but conceded a 1-0 and 2-1 advantage before losing the match 3-2. Ordinarily scoring two goals away from home would be sufficient for a win but their inability to keep a clean sheet was causing much concern within the club. May was worried that he might lose his job as individual mistakes cost his team the points. Robbie switched to playing as a sweeper and gave another solid performance but the necessity for reinforcements to the squad was clear. City had conceded six goals in their last two matches as they faced Hereford at Ninian Park. Scoring in each half against a United side that included a number of ex-City players, the match was played out on a bitterly cold day and with the Bluebirds missing key strikers. An admirable 2-1 win was their first victory recorded over the last four matches. It was the third meeting between the clubs and City had won twice and drawn the other. Sadly, the home attendance was down by almost 4,000 since the Boxing Day meet with York.

The club was placed eight in the division, a massive eleven points behind leaders York, at this time. That Boxing Day encounter produced a half dozen goals but the previous season's 3-0 victory was not to be repeated. Andy Gorman made his only League appearance this season in a City side ravaged by injuries and containing Robbie alongside teenager Baddeley, in defence. He and Robbie played together across eighteen matches during the two seasons that the latter was at the club. Whilst Robbie and Andy would go on to briefly play for Barry across the subsequent 1994/ 95 season. A goal from Gorman and a super Stanty bicycle kick set up the Bluebirds to race to a 3-0 score line at half time (with an added own goal bonus) but the second half saw their sweeper system fail and manager Eddie May furious with his team's display in allowing a final 3-3 score.

A cold Friday night in Cardiff could not have been anybody's idea of a fun time and it certainly would not be the cases for the

6,832 diehards watching City relinquish their unbeaten League run of thirteen matches at home. The Bluebirds had a four point advantage on Wrexham reduced to one after Brian Flynn and Joey Jones, both past Wales team mates of Robbie's, brought their team from north Wales. City skipper Paul Ramsey missed a penalty, after netting his four previous attempts, and two great goals from the visitors could not be wiped out by a single Nathan Blake strike.

Also in January 1993, City would meet an opponent known all too well to Robbie: whisper it, "Swansea City". Then of Division Two, confirmation of the second round Autoglass tie between them was released this month. It helped fuel a massive amount of interest in the media and in the minds of rival supporters. Back in the previous season, Ramsey had received his marching orders at the Vetch in a 0-0; whilst a 1-0 friendly fixture was played at Ninian Park in between a 1-0 away victory in the Welsh Cup. However, the Swans had put City out of the F. A. Cup that season too!

The Welsh Cup meeting with Caerau on 5 December was especially memorable as former soldier Stant nabbed a hat-trick, one of two that he would collect this season, and hotshot Dale hit four across a game in which City players seemed to be queuing up to score. Caerau, unfortunate to be facing such a red hot City side, did manage a shot on goal but had fallen 3-0 behind by half-time, in front of a decent-sized 2,579 gate.

For those supporters unable to travel to such far off places as Halifax, where Cardiff had an away fixture on 26 January, a new initiative was launched: the "Bluebirds Line". For a not-insubstantial 36p or 48p a minute, fans could listen to a live commentary as Stanty put in goal number twenty-nine for City this season in a 1-0 victory that took the team up to fourth in the table. It was a repeat score line from their recent away game in Kent with bottom-of-the-table Gillingham achieved three days earlier. City only managed to score once despite having lots of attempts during the game which was watched by a small gate of 1,339. The Halifax manager reiterated that the visitors were the best team that they had played against this year. Robbie was involved in setting up the winner, after running down the right wing and hitting a low cross past the keeper and defender for Stanty to finish off. Somewhat ungallantly, in their programme notes, Town criticised Robbie's perceived limitations whilst with Bradford, commenting on his infrequent forays up into the opposing box whilst with the Bantams. A little unjust in that he had been voted their player of the season across the two campaigns that he was with the club prior to switching to Cardiff.

Worryingly for City fans, their Chairman was still declaring his intentions to quit the club at the end of the season, taking his money with him, if new investors were not found. A barmy suggestion of joining the League of Wales was also broached by the businessman this season, too. That was an idea that fans and many involved with the club, found ridiculous.

Walsall at home provided the twenty fifth League fixture of the season, with an additional nine Cup games, which found Robbie playing in all of them. "They have strength in depth because against us they were without their better players, Dale and Stant." Offered Walsall player Kevin Macdonald after seeing his side go down 2-1. "They also have one or two players on the bench. They have to be optimistic about their chances of getting promotion and if things go right for them they could even be Champions." Prophetic words from Macdonald, an-ex Cardiff City name who found himself lining up directly against Robbie in the game. This was City's fifth win on the trot and saw Stant hitting more goals and Robbie and Irishman Paul Millar combined in showing themselves as a useful pairing when controlling play. The team was on a roll.

An undefeated run of five League matches in January saw a debut goal from new arrival Kevin Ratcliffe against Carlisle United on a bumpy Brunton Park pitch in windy conditions. Aged thirty-two, Kevin joined the club on a pay-per-play basis after the astute Eddie May noticed that Everton were seeking to off-load their unwanted former captain. Ratcliffe had spent fourteen seasons with them and won almost every possible trophy. Capped on fifty-eight occasions for Wales, this north Walian had played a number of times with Robbie on international duties, one of the most memorable being a 1-0 defeat of England in Wrexham back in 1984. "Rats" had drifted a little before signing for City, following a one month loan with Dundee where he failed to agree personal terms. May was delighted at securing his services and was hugely complimentary about the level of experience that he would bring to aid the younger players, enhancing Robbie's own contribution. Now acting club captain, Robbie was also impressed, "He looks comfortable on the ball, he reads situations and that is something that perhaps we have been lacking." Ratcliffe enjoyed a blinding debut, scoring a rare goal, one of only three in his career, which came directly from a ball delivered from a corner. Talking up a central defender role, Robbie was switched to right-back with the ever-present Damon

Searle on the left. United also had problems in defence, leaking seventeen goals this season; although that was nine less than Cardiff! On a mud-strewn pitch, Rats joined up to make an all-Welsh City defence.

After playing in Europe with Everton, Ratcliffe, ineligible for Cup appearances, could only watch Robbie and his new team mates continue to advance through the rounds of the Welsh Cup with a visit by Konica League side Maesteg Park in mid-January. The sides had met in the previous year's quarter-finals and here put in dogged resistance despite the deceptive 4-0 score line, with a hat trick from the sensational Stant. So far City had scored fifteen goals in the competition and not conceded.

There had been great public interest when the Autoglass Trophy match between Cardiff City and Swansea City was to be screened live in January by the newly-merged BSkyB satellite company. Although not the most glamorous of cup competitions, fixtures had managed to draw audiences of about a million but despite concerns that it might affect the gate attendance, the tie attracted a crowd of 13,516 and Robbie found himself in the Cardiff team playing in the wind and rain on a waterlogged pitch. It was the only time this season that the Welsh cousins faced each other, as the Swans played in a higher division. Swansea had recently drawn with Robbie's former club, Bradford and there was a buzz amongst supporters excited by another 'Cup final' meeting between the great rivals.

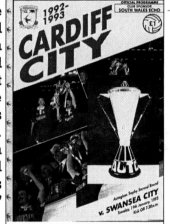

Violence before the kick-off around Cardiff centre by travelling hooligans was minimalised at Ninian Park due to a strong police presence and the bad weather curtailed problems in the city environs afterwards.

In a match that saw seven bookings, this exciting, drama-filled game ended 1-1at full time, thanks to a late Andy Legg goal for the yellow-shirted Swans. But the Bluebirds went out 1-2 following extra time. Added to the melodrama was a late goal from Cardiff being ruled offside. Robbie was voted Man-of-the-Match and was photographed with Wales manager Terry Yorath presenting him with a bottle of champagne. As a Swan, Robbie had shared a case of whisky with team mate

Alan Curtis donated by a manufacturer, after both had scored a hat-trick in the same match (against Hartlepool). The hooliganism made the news across the country but it was nothing new, as previous problems had occurred as recently as 1991. After beating Cardiff, the Swans were put out by Exeter City. Despite the Cup defeat, Robbie's manager Eddie May was awarded the Barclays Manager of the Month for January (with a cheque and over-sized bottle of champagne as a reward).

One thing City's Chairman Rick Wright did succeed at doing was getting young supporters involved with the club. By February 1993, 7,000 of them had joined the Junior Bluebirds, one year since its inception. Linked with shirt sponsors the South Wales Echo, free membership was offered and coupled with reduced admission to Ninian Park. The playing surface there had been receiving quite a battering due to the adverse weather and the amount of games played upon it resulting in it being churned up and heavily sanded in the centre. With a two week break until the next home fixture, Reserves matches were postponed to give the pitch a break as City were known as a side that liked to play the ball along the ground. The manager joked that with the amount of sand on the pitch, they might as well play on Barry Island beach! This coming from a former player that had trained on the beach with Robbie back in their Swansea days, as well as running up the dunes in Aberystwyth during the rigours of pre-season training with Wrexham. Older fans will remember grounds like Derby County and Q.P.R. having terrible pitches which lost all its grass well before the end of each season. Both Ninian Park and Vetch Field struggled with overtired pitches.

In February, the Chairman was once more repeated that he would no longer continue to plough in more of his own money into the club after investing £2m, half of that immediately being eaten up by outstanding tax and debts. He devised a player sponsorship initiative which for a monthly fee, would allow a business to use City players for publicity purposes and see the investor being named in the club programme and possibly have an advertising board around the pitch. Today such an approach is common but back in 1993, money was tight. Wright publicly disclosed that outgoings exceeded the funds generated by attendances by some £36,000. Always transparent in his views and actions involving the club, often to the chagrin of others, he realised his limitations.

A brace from forgotten man Chris Pike, in his final season with Cardiff, saw a 0-2 away win at Darlington, on a muddy pitch and in front of another small crowd, this time recorded at 1,775. That total was vastly less than in the previous August when the sides met in a 0-0 at Ninian. It continued the excellent extended run of form, with City winning their last six League outings. Pike came on as a sub and transformed the fortunes of a game that looked to be heading for a goal-less draw until his brace late on. Robbie and Millar one again gained the initiative on the pitch for Cardiff to exploit.

On the day before Valentine's, Cardiff smashed Torquay United 4-0 at home, with the goals added to a total of forty nine scored this season by the Bluebirds. Thankfully there was to be no repeat of the unsavoury scenes down in Devon back in the 2-1 September defeat.

Switching to midfield in the absence of Paul Ramsey, a 1-2 win at Northampton's County Ground gave Robbie and the players a boost in confidence as by now, they were feeling as if they would win every game and had no thoughts of defeat or simply playing for a point. Battling against a strong wind in the first half, team mate Stant vocalised his view that Cardiff could not simply turn up and play teams like Northampton and expect a win to be a foregone conclusion. Two second half goals succeeded in a win despite a late penalty going in against them. It put City second in the table and saw them raring to meet Crewe at the end of the month.

A super gate of 10,012, the second highest of the campaign, watched a 1-1 played out as City's impressive run of being unbeaten in their last nine matches continued. Alexandra boss Dario Gradi had not been looking forward to visiting Ninian Park, describing it as "a very intimidating place." Away fans would also agree with that. Crowd problems the previous season had concerned the long-serving Gradi but he need not have worried as the home supporters were fine towards him. However, some idiots in the crowd were unable to show their respect for Bobby Moore, who had recently passed away, during the minutes silence. Having lost 2-0 to Crewe in the previous October, Cardiff competed well and the match finished 1-1. It was a decent game to watch and a fair result for both, keeping City second in the table. An under-par Robbie did not shine.

March saw City having to complete seven fixtures, six of them in the League and the other, a Welsh Cup encounter with Wrexham. "It's all about bottle and attitude now," proclaimed Eddie May in the South Wales Echo. Whilst Paul 'Gazza' Gascoine was off in Italy playing for Lazio against the likes of the cheating Diego Maradona, Robbie found himself featuring in matches against the less-than glamorous Rochdale, Scarborough, Carlisle and Bury. With thirteen games remaining in the season, he hit the post, featuring in a side getting closer to scoring even without four first-team names. They did well in a 1-2 away victory at Rochdale, followed by a decent 1-0 win against Scarborough, thanks to the defence succeeding in halting the impressive away goals tally being added to by their visitors. The sides would meet again in April when City would complete the 'double' over the seaside club. The win took Cardiff to three points off the top of the table but saw acting captain Robbie pick up an injury, a dead leg, during the game. A dramatic goal-line clearance in the dying minutes meant that points were chalked up Cardiff City's favour.

Overexcited visiting supporters invaded the pitch at Colchester United when Chris Pike hit the first of four Cardiff goals during this Friday evening kick-off. A recent mass invasion at Maine Road during the Manchester City v Spurs game had been reported in the press but there was no violence intended here by the City followers. The victory saw Cardiff perched on top of the division with sixty three points collected across thirty one games.

A much-needed break from League concerns arrived with the first leg semi-final of the Welsh Cup with Wrexham the following Tuesday. Rhyl faced Connah's Quay in the corresponding tie. Cardiff won their match 2-0 with one of their goals coming from a returning Carl Dale in a game which was not the best spectacle to watch. During the game, Robbie had a shot which tested the Robins keeper before the City goals, one in either half, set-up the return leg nicely.

Former Wales great Trevor Ford was a regular at Ninian Park this season and warned his former club to be careful about going to the Racecourse and thinking that their passage to the final was already booked. City had by now become a strong physical presence, equally adept as a good goal scoring side. This saw so the odds of them winning the League title and the Welsh Cup double shortened by book makers. City defender Kevin Ratcliffe was delighted to be selected to play for Wales in against Belgium at the National stadium (which they won 2-0).

But before the second leg at the Racecourse ground, a stadium that Robbie played in many times during his career, his attention returned to the League and an upcoming encounter at Ninian Park with Chesterfield.

CARDIFF
CITY A.F.C.
NINIAN PARK
SLOPER ROAD

Probing effectively down the right-side of midfield, he contributed much to a 2-1win which wasn't the most electrifying team performance but nonetheless collected the three points. 2-0 up thanks to Dale and Richardson, a goal from the visitors meant an uncomfortable final spell for City. A stern challenge would be provided by an away trip to Bury in the penultimate match of the month. Bury were eighth in the table and worked their sweeper system well, as it frustrated Cardiff who managed to pass the ball around well but were unable to break them down. They lost 1-0 and Bury completed their own 'double' after winning at Ninian Park in November. The game was noteworthy in that in only one further game (against Wrexham) did Cardiff not manage to score. The Bluebirds were acknowledged as the top scorers in the league with sixty one goals; they would close the season on seventy six but failed to add to this against Bury. It was their first time since October, against Crewe, since no City player managed to hit the back of the net. Despite this, Cardiff had collected thirty seven points out of a possible thirty nine and their Chairman felt that they could gain promotion if they could accumulate eighty points (they presently had sixty six). With eight games left, four of them at home, the season run-in was a tense one for all the teams involved. City would meet table-toppers Barnet, Scarborough, Doncaster Rovers, York, Lincoln, Wrexham, Shrewsbury Town and Scunthorpe United as their campaign reached its climax.

Barnet was a club in dire financial straits, but with the chirpy Barry Fry as manger they were serious contenders for promotion this season. They had defeated Cardiff in November at Underhill and Fry acknowledged the strength in depth of the Bluebirds supporters and he believed that his club, City and Wrexham deserved to fill the automatic promotion places. The Barnet side that faced City in late March 1993 was in a poor run of form. A huge 16,073 gate, the largest of the season, and biggest in more than a decade, would witness a 1-1 draw. Robbie played well and put in his familiar surging runs in an action-packed encounter seeing City drop two points rather than gaining one.

In spring 1993, the Welsh public was debating the merits of Sunday shopping whilst City began the first of a half-dozen April fixtures commencing with a long trip to Scarborough. Their hosts, having recently sacked its manager, were a club in turmoil whilst the Bluebirds enjoyed a midweek break in preparation for the game, with the exceptions of Messrs

Ratcliffe and Searle; both away on international duty with Wales. Formation changes found Robbie switched to right-back across a season where he was also utilised in the centre of defence and in a midfield position. City won 1-3 on a springy pitch across a windy afternoon with Ramsey and Robbie combining to play a passing game so recognisable to the team.

A Tuesday evening match with Doncaster ended in a 1-1 with the City boss acknowledging that away teams coming to Ninian Park realised that they would need to put in an exceptional performance if they wanted to avoid being beaten there. York, next to play the Bluebirds, had drawn with Chesterfield on the same night and had done the same with Cardiff back on Boxing Day, with Cardiff collapsing after being 3-0 up before the final score of 3-3. The match had been seen as a stern test for City but both teams had defended diabolically that afternoon. York made no mistake at their place, winning 3-1 and pushing Cardiff back to second in the table, a point behind leaders Barnet. Robbie was fulfilling a midfield role as well as at right-back where he was just as efficient, using the ball well wherever he ventured around the pitch. A late goal from Griffiths was little consolation despite the visitors having more possession of the ball. The second Cardiff City goal arrived via the endeavours of Stant who got the ball out to the right where Robbie then floated in a beautifully crafted cross that was met by a Gorman header powered into the net. Poor Robbie also played a part when the Bluebirds were 3-1 up and a York shot on goal rebounded off the post and a lunging tackle by Jamo was not enough to prevent the striker from putting in a goal.

An impressive 2,000 tickets had been allocated to City fans in anticipation of a derby match away at Wrexham. It was the last League fixture between the Welsh cousins but they had two additional meetings in the Welsh Cup still to play out. Safety concerns at the Racecourse meant that the close proximity of terracing in front of the Cardiff fans remained empty. The first away game with Wrexham was on a Saturday followed on the coming Wednesday evening by their second leg of the Welsh Cup semi final. The games produced quite differing results: City won 0-2 in the League but lost 1-0 in the Cup meeting. The former was attended by 10,852 whilst the latter fixture saw only 5,735. As both clubs were promotional rivals, the tension was palpable but City overpowered their hosts with two first half strikes. Robbie put in a blinder of a performance. Although supposedly having 2,000 away tickets allocated, Cardiff took twice that figure. Manager Eddie May who would be presented with the Barclays

Manager of the Month Award for April, had made his name at Wrexham across many seasons and returned there with much anticipation. The hosts had been in a confident mood before the game and this worked in galvanizing Ed's side. Nathan Blake scored a brilliant header from a Robbie cross, as the team put their best performance in of the season and outplayed Wrexham. His City players were so good in the first half that May didn't want the referee to blow his whistle at half time! Well before the end, many home fans made for the exits as elated City fans did the now-famous Ayatollah, hereby used as a gesture of delight, seeing the patting of both hands on the top of the head. Joined by Messrs May and Wright upon the final whistle, it was a cracking ninety minutes, with two excellent goals sending Cardiff top of the table.

Wrexham were poor in that first meeting and their players intended to come back strongly for the Welsh Cup game. No one in the City squad believed that their path to the final was already theirs, despite winning the first leg 2-0 at Ninian Park in March.

Regrettably, some so-called supporters showed their hostility to the wives and partners of many of the Cardiff players at the Saturday match and made things most unpleasant for the invited guests. This irked the Cardiff boys and only succeeded in spurring them on. Even Rick Wright's wife Marie was mistreated by officials at the Racecourse on the same day. Returning hero May was also spat at by fans and Blake was the target of some ugly racist abuse. An important save from keeper Gavin Ward helped keep the score down to a 1-0 defeat and so it meant that Cardiff made it through 2-1 on aggregate to a meeting with Manweb Cymru Alliance side Rhyl on 16 May. The traveling City support was glad to see the back of the Racecourse.

Wales boss Terry Yorath had a sports column in the Echo this year and he commented that the experienced pros would be needed to be relied upon during a promotional push and that Cardiff were a club well stacked in this area with Ratcliffe, Robbie, Ramsey and Dale all well-established.

A visit from a John Bond-led Shrewsbury Town came a week before the final League fixture, away at Scunthorpe. The Shrews game was another all-ticket affair whilst the other match saw a massive ticket allocation of 5,000 made available to City fans at £6/ £7 each.

Cardiff City Football Club had seen a 110% rise in attendances since the previous season but the fans were demanding, as ever, during the final home game of the season. The players showed their intentions within the first minute with a Ramsey shot that involved Robbie in its build-up. Playing at right-back and demonstrating his skillful passing, it didn't prevent the fans singing "All we are saying, is give us a goal." The goals did flow, the first via a Perry header, his third goal of the season, and the second from a Robbie James throw-in knocked on to Richardson then to Brazil and put in the net by Blake: and all this within ten minutes of the second half.

Eddie May had read every connotation of his name being utilized in a match report whilst he was a player and so the Echo's "Eddie May Day" must have come as little surprise after an impressive 17,253 were sent delirious thanks to the 2-1 score line. The fans had waited a long time since the club had last won a League title but that was looking a distinct possibility of being corrected after the victory put City a point clear of Barnet. May, with the supporters chanting "Eddie May's Barmy Army!" was

right in saying that it really did prove to be "an unforgettable day." A troop of a half dozen mounted police officers moved on to the half way line briefly, after City fans prematurely swarmed onto the pitch two minutes before the end due to a joker in the crowd having brought along a whistle. The hugely imposing horses made their way past Robbie as he stood just to the right of the half way line, hands on hips and caused him to move out of their path! Anticipation oozed from the fans gathered within touching distance of the players, as they waited on the edge of the pitch in scenes reminiscent of Cup finals in days gone by. Desperately trying to contain themselves whilst amassed along side the goals, the whistle was a false alarm and everyone was made to get off the pitch, including a request made by the manager, before the game was eventually restarted. When at last full time did arrive, the players made a dash for the dressing rooms, situated beneath the Grandstand as a throng of City supporters chased after them in celebration! With a party atmosphere sought by Mr. Wright before the game being fulfilled, his players were hoisted on the shoulders of the fans, their blue shirts emphatically removed as souvenirs by supporters. A recent Reading v Swansea game had seen hooligan problems with Swans fans coming onto the pitch and engaging in all kinds of nastiness. However, there was no such malice aforethought this afternoon: just euphoria.

The team had put in a workmanlike performance and as Barnet and York both lost that afternoon, promotion was sealed for the Bluebirds with their win. But they wanted to have their fate be in their own hands and knew that victory at Scunthorpe would see them go up as Champions.

Robbie and his team mates would be well-rewarded for gaining promotion, thanks to a generous £20,000+ bonus provided from their Chairman. It would rise to more than double that amount if they were to be crowned Champions but that would be decided after the outcome of their final game. Wright was a happy man too, after the victory had sealed promotion. At the start of the season he had calculated how much he could afford to pay out if Cardiff went up and placed the money with insurance broker Lloyds against that happening and had netted himself close to a cool £1.5m!

With promotion fixed, the City players were back in training on the Monday following the game, with a plea for fans not to make the journey up to Humberside if they did not have a ticket. However, with such a high density of City support subsequently present, the players remarked that their fans made the game feel more like a home match. One of the squad acknowledged that for many of them, the day was going to be the highlight of their playing careers and it was all in their hands. A brace from Griffith and a strike from City legend Stant, returning for the game, saw Cardiff City becoming Champions of the new Third Division. Already 2-0 up by half-time, a third arrived in the second half, with the traveling supporters peacefully invading the pitch at the end. City went up on eighty three points collected, followed by Wrexham, Barnet and York. The team had scored 109 times, many of them coming from the talented Blake/ Stan/ Dale trio.

 After a mammoth fifty-five matches completed across the season, there was one game left to play: the Welsh Cup Final against Rhyl on 16 May. City were the present holders of the trophy, after beating Hednesford Town by a single goal in a midweek final played at the National Stadium on 7 May 1992.

May had former Swansea and Wales player John Mahoney watch Rhyl and report back to him in anticipation of playing them. The two had a brief spell working together at Newport County previously until a lack of finances saw Eddie manage the club for only a short period when they did not play a game. He departed whilst 'Josh' remained, filling the managerial slot and he later managed Carmarthen Town F.C. Mahoney and Robbie were former Swans and Wales team mates. Tickets for the final, staged at the old National Stadium in Cardiff, cost £6 and attracted a crowd of 16,443. Played on a Sunday, the team was presented with the League championship before the kick-off but behind-the-scenes there was much ill-feeling amongst the players due to promised bonuses being cancelled. The game finished with a convincing 5-0 win for Cardiff thanks to a hat trick from Stanty and a brace from a resurgent Griffith. Robbie was one of many players with attempted strikes on the Rhyl goal as their non-League opponents put in a good performance but were unable to compete with City. Within the club, chaos ensued with Stant having to be informed by his dejected manager before kick-off that the striker could not be selected if he did not agree to a bonus restriction. Some while later, Stint won his appeal against this but not before being ostracized by Wright. On a personal front, Robbie had played in all six Cup games.

After playing in fifty six matches across the League and various Cup competitions during the 1992/ 93 season, Robbie scored twice to cap a terrific footballing campaign. Selected as the recipient of the Player of the Year award from the Cardiff City Supporters Club, Robbie and a number of the playing and backroom staff attended the ceremony a few days before the Welsh Cup final. Receiving the accolade, the Swansea-born star displayed great humility. "It is lovely to receive awards like this especially at the end of a successful season. But the season is all about a squad of players. The support was terrific, this year, home and away. Without the fans we would not have achieved what we did."

The 1993/ 94 season saw financial complications on a lease for Ninian Park proved frustrating for Rick Wright after talks with the council, as his self-imposed deadline for leaving the club was approaching (original time line being September 1993). Wright wanted to sell the club for £2m but no buyer was forthcoming. His legacy with Cardiff is one that still divides opinion today, with the multi-company owning businessman putting the club up for sale via an advertisement in The Times newspaper immediately upon taking over control at Ninian Park. There was no buyer then and the situation remained the same after the 1992/ 93 'double' season. A business man first and foremost, he had no knowledge of professional football upon arrival and surrounded himself with those that did: people like Eddie May. His position as coach/ manager often came up for scrutiny but Wright stuck with him. As for players like Robbie, he and many of his team mates continued on weekly or monthly contracts, a situation that proved problematic for some as it undermined futures.

Some £250,000 was spent on ground improvements during the close season and it was publicly revealed that the club was paying a wage bill of £120,000 to its playing staff across June and July. Little surprise that Mr Wright did not insist that his players put in stints as Bluecoats at his Majestic holiday camp on the nearby Barry Island resort!

A summer tour in Ireland continued with pre-season friendlies including a 5-0 over Briton Ferry in readiness for the 1993/ 94 Endsleigh Insurance League Division Two campaign. In his twenty-first season as a professional footballer, it would see Robbie looking at fixtures against the likes of Fulham, Plymouth, Brighton and Reading. Winning the Welsh Cup meant that an appearance in the European Cup Winners' Cup would surface via home and away tie with Belgian side Standard Liege in September. However, Leyton Orient provided the opening day opponents at Ninian Park on 14 August before ensuing Cup commitments. A little-less than 10,000 attended the match, an increase on the previous season and a total acknowledged as the highest opener since 1974. Robbie was back in a starting XI that was not much different from last season: with the noticeable exception of new striker and former Q.P.R player, Garry Thompson.

Now captained by Kevin Ratcliffe, whose form would dip dramatically this year, calls for the return of terrace favourite Phil Stant, dispatched off to Mansfield Town after his fall-out with Rick Wright, emanated from supporters and would regularly feature in press reports. The visitors were favourites to win promotion this year but second half goals from Blake and Griffiths set the season off to a decent start before a Cup trip at Bournemouth.

Sloppy in defence and having teenagers on the bench, May once again needed re-enforcements to his squad after failing to secure loan deals and City went down 3-1. Funds would soon be available after the startling recent departure of Paul Ramsey to St. Johnstone for £75,000. Robbie and Rats did well but the fragility of a skeletal squad was a concern that needed correcting before its weakness was exposed.

After winning promotion as Champions and their emphatic Welsh Cup Final win, the fans, media and players all anticipated further advancements. The Chairman made a lot of money from his association with the club, which cost a huge amount to run but funds were not released on bringing in new players in the way that everybody might have anticipated or assumed. Wright would spend money on players but they had to be at the right price, this meant that May had to do his homework on any prospective signing but at times he was flabbergasted by his Chairman. We all know that the people who fulfil these roles are often dogmatic individuals whose visions for their club are not always pleasing to the supporters. Wright was never concerned with worrying about speaking his mind, however offensive to fans, those involved in the game or the players that he employed.

Representatives from Liege visited Ninian Park to view facilities in advance of their fixture in September and also to view them in a Cup game. Their manager would also pay the club a visit later on and the City boss traveled over to see them play, also. At City, opponents would always be watched in advance of meeting them. Liege had finished runners-up in the Belgian League, behind Anderlecht and would provide a stern test for the Bluebirds across the two games.

As controversial as ever, the City Chairman, away on holiday again, proclaimed that if the fans really wanted to see Stant return, then they should put their hands in their pockets and pay for him to be bought back! His reckoning was that they should buy season tickets, accounting to several hundred, within the next three week across a rigid, three-week deadline in mid-August. He made it clear that personally he did not want the player to return to the club but if the supporters did, and his manager, too, then this would be possible. He revealed that Robbie's team mates Perry, Searle and Blake had been on a weekly wage of a £1K. This had been increased this season once projected bonuses were included.

With many players feeling uncertain of their long-term futures, there was much consternation within the squad which ultimately manifest itself by a number of departures. The fans were unhappy at the public revelation and it did nothing for the players, either, after an unsettling summer break.

A super 1-3 win at Fulham, recorded amidst scuffles between fans, found the team in good shape. Robbie, Blake and Thompson all put in strong showings as the side marched to a 0-3 score line at Craven Cottage. The game was chalked up as being the 775th appearance by Robbie. Poor policing and stewarding errors at the ground made the likelihood of crowd trouble inevitable as a small number of away fans were allowed to enter a family stand filled with home supporters.

Back at Ninian Park, Bournemouth put City out of the Coca-Cola up after a 1-1 saw them progress via 4-2 on aggregate. Despite seeing a poor team performance, a succession of scouts watched the game, casting their eyes over players such as Nathan Blake. Manager Eddie May would find it impossible to deter offers for his players due to the nature of their short-term obligations to the club namely weekly and monthly contracts. City offered a particular contract that was presented to players with no leeway for manouvere. Both Blake and Robbie James, made captain for this game and the following two, put in sterling shows but the 3-1 from the first leg was a hurdle too far. This Cup competition was not proving popular with fans, and it showed in the 4,459 gate (the corresponding fixture from last season attracted a little less).

The Seagulls of Brighton & Hove Albion flew down to meet the Bluebirds of Cardiff City in the third League match of the new season on 28 August. And despite Robbie carrying an injury his side shared the points via a 2-2 finish. That scenario was a common one as players like him and Thommo had to play when they should have been rested.

The Chairman had revealed that as a business, Cardiff City Football Club needed gates of an average 4,500 for the club to break even. The Albion game, a frustrating encounter to watch, saw 7,687. With only fourteen fit players to select from, the team played exceedingly well in the first half but were woeful in the second, with a goal just before the final whistle saving things.

A battling but uninspiring show meant that City took another point, this time at Exeter City, whilst some travelling City fans had a hairy departure from the town after being set upon by local hooligans. In the absence of Kevin Ratcliffe, Robbie took on the captaincy in a match that saw the visiting defense put under unrelenting pressure. The barrage meant that City could not show how well that they could play as Exeter stifled them. An early away goal, scored in the first minute, was not capitalised upon once again.

Another trip away, this time to promotion-favorites Port Vale, saw City march to being 0-2 up at half-time before a dynamic Vale resurgence in the second resulted in the match concluding at 2-2. The away support was phenomenal, with a strong contingent there to roar on their team.

After five games, City sat in fifth position in Division Two, above Bradford City and Swansea City; two of Robbie's former clubs. It was the fourth fixture that found Cardiff unable to hold on to a lead. Regrettably, Blake, scorer of City's opening goal, was faced with a couple of racist-spewing louts running towards him before stewards dealt with them. After the incident at Ninian Park at the close of last season, police on horses intervened as visiting fans celebrated their team's goal strikes. Tickets to watch the game were made available at the turnstiles for City supporters at £7 each. Blake would leave Cardiff by the end of the season following a career-defining performance against Manchester City in the F.A. Cup.

After a trio of draws in the League, Phil Stant made a surprise return to the fold in the second week of September after having taken the club to a Football League tribunal and getting win bonuses awarded for the endeavours of last season. Dale signed a new contract also but was out for an extended period due to injury. The City diehards gave Stant a warm welcome upon his 'debut' at Hull City and joker Robbie James bowed to him upon running on to the pitch for a warm-up prior to kick-off! Stanty went on to score twenty goals in total upon his return. The high-scoring Tigers continued with their four goals-per-match ratio and beat City 3-4 in an exciting spectacle. Five goals came in the second half amidst feeble defensive errors as Cardiff added to their eleven scored thus far (against eleven conceded).

The final League game of September saw visitors Plymouth Argyle taking away a win. City found themselves in the unenviable position of being 0-3 down before Stant and Millar restored a bit of credibility to see the game close at 2-3. Bury centre back Alan Krill, another ex-Swans player that had played with Robbie, came in on a month's loan but failed to usurp a dominant Argyle midfield. Cardiff had now gone nine games without a win, losing their last four and leaking goals.

A break from the rigours of domestic football arrived on Monday 13 September with the City squad flying out to Belgium, in readiness for the midweek encounter with Standard Liege at the Stade de Sclessin. For this European Cup Winners' Cup tie, Robbie was switched to form a part of a three man midfield consisting of Richardson, Blake and himself. Ratcliffe was used in a sweeper capacity as a tactical manouvere by the manager. Things looked to be promising as City held Leige at 1-1 by half time, following a Bird equalizer on 39 minutes (one of his two goals). Liege had not scored many goals recently but that would change as they won the game 5-2. However, a bright twenty minute spell in the first half gave much hope for Cardiff until later with the score at 2-2 and the balance radically changed. City would have an opportunity to make amends with a quick return leg back in Wales at the end of the month. The away leg was Robbie's penultimate appearance in the tournament. The Cardiff City line-up was Kite, Perry, Ratcliffe, Baddeley, Searle, Richardson, Griffith, Robbie, Blake, Stant, Bird. Over a thousand City supporters made the easy trip to Belgium but the game was marred by a number of hooliganism incidents. Cardiff has for many long years been known within these circles as having a major 'firm' and so opposing set-ups would often seek to confront them. On a lighter note, the City team received strong support, with their fans doing a rare, bouncing version of the Ayatollah!

In the return fixture the Bluebirds lost 1-3 in front of 6,069 despite a stunning goal from Robbie just before the hour mark. City fell 0-3 behind before Robbie's twenty yard strike in another Man of the Match show. Some impressive passing of the ball and movement from the visitors proved telling and May was furious with some of his under-performing players. Problems with individuals in the crowd saw abuse being hurled at the Liege keeper and some unsavoury spitting. Two nil down by half-time, City exited the competition 8-3 on aggregate. Losing to Standard was no disgrace; as they went on to reach the final.

That game was the the penultimate appearance for Robbie in a City shirt and came before City returned to domestic matters with a lengthy trip up to Bloomfield Park, home of Blackpool F.C. The Seasiders played well, resisting a heavy bombardment by City in the second half and winning the game by a single goal. Robbie switched to midfield and worked efficiently by bossing the second half but it wasn't enough, with another mistake by Ratcliffe, the defeat put Cardiff eighth from bottom of the division. Eddie May was desperate for new troops and sought to bring Paul Ramsey back from Scotland. Ramsey's presence on the field was much missed but he was subsequently proven to be unable to return due to restrictions in same-season movements by players imposed by the League.

On Saturday 2 October, Rick Wright passed the ownership of Cardiff City Football Club over to the 9,000 Echo Junior Bluebirds, via shares, when his first team was away at York City. Wright switched to being their representative on the City board whilst money owed to the Inland Revenue reared its ugly head. On the field, Robbie's final appearance in a Cardiff shirt was not to offer a fond farewell: they were battered 5-0. But maintaining his consistency, he put in a fittingly majestic show with his class shining through. Match reporter for the local Echo, Robert Phillips commented, "Even in defeat James was magnificent and

the prime reason why City could have had four goals themselves with accurate finishing." By the close of the 1993/ 94 season, the Bluebirds would finish fifth from bottom of the table and the following season suffer relegation.

In all, Robbie played sixty eight times for Cardiff City, scored twice and concluded his time there after playing in 782 League matches across his career. In the second season at Ninian Park, he featured in the first thirteen games, three as captain in the absence of Kevin Ratcliffe (in the games with Bournemouth, Brighton and Exeter).

It was on Tuesday 5 October 1994 that Robbie informed the club of his imminent departure to take up a player-manager role at Merthyr Tydfil F.C, a decision which shook both his manager and Chairman. "He is a really true professional and no club wants to lose that type of person," decreed Rick Wright in the Echo. "If anything I would have liked to see him stay at Ninian Park and go into an assistant manager job in the future." But if that was the case, then why had he not offered him such a future, now?

Robbie had told the press that many players on short term contracts at Cardiff had found the situation unsettling. He added that if he had been under contract with the Bluebirds then he most probably would not have been tempted by the Merthyr vacancy. Just like many others, he lamented his disappointment at not seeing the recent success enhanced with new signings and the fact that the Chairman insisted upon his own imminent departure, it all had an effect upon the playing staff. Wright had recently withdrawn contract offers, at reduced rates, and this was enough for Robbie to seek a future elsewhere. His former Chairman might have been complimentary about him initially but his feelings soon became barbed, accusing Robbie of simply taking the money and not caring at all about the football club. Robbie was keen to thank the fans. "It was not easy being a Swansea boy playing in Cardiff. They [the supporters] made me feel part of the club and very much at home. I wish I could have sorted out a contract and stayed." Despite uprooting himself with the season already into its third month, Robbie was keen to see what life at Penydarren Park could offer him. "I am excited. I have not seen Merthyr play and don't know how everything works at the moment."

He would soon find out.

Alan Curtis played 150 times for Cardiff and it was an odd sight to see this former Swansea team mate of Robbie's scoring for them in a Welsh Cup final with Wrexham staged at the Vetch. Curt also featured in a Barry Town team playing against Cardiff in the 1994 final, too. He was joined in that team by Terry Boyle, and both had previously featured in a Cardiff team that had won the trophy in 1988. He recounts,

with a smile, in his autobiography (see the thanks page for full details) that when Robbie played for Cardiff he would collect his children from school still wearing his Cardiff kit. Only thing being that he was living in Swansea and that was also where his children attended school. Alan chuckles and adds that only Robbie could have gotten away with such a liberty!

WELCOME TO MERTHYR TYDFIL

GM VAUXHALL
CONFERENCE

"The Martyrs"
Wales' Premier
Non-Football League
Club

M.T.A.F.C.

Merthyr

Stepping into the player-manager role

During his playing career poor Robbie had been in the wars: having his nose broken of four occasions, in amongst the other usual problems picked up by a player in the game. This season spent with Merthyr Tydfil F.C. would add to the list.

Primarily known for producing iron, Merthyr became Wales' first recognized, real town. And that lineage continued with the name of their football ground, Penydarren Park. Perched on the edge of the Brecon Beacons, Merthyr has a population of 55,000 and Robbie became the latest player/manager at this self-proclaimed "Wales' premier non-Football League club" in October 1993. He followed the departure of the previous manager who had been criticized publicly by the club Chairman after a spell of recent defeats.

Having his transfer fee from Cardiff set at £100,000 by the F.A.W following much wrangling between City Chairman Rick Wright and his Merthyr counterpart John Reedy, Robbie was set for a new chapter in his career. Wright had made it public that Robbie had been on a basic weekly wage of £1,300 and vented his resentment at him leaving the Bluebirds, stating that the player did not care about his club and just took the money. Robbie rightly did not wish to air such matters in public but did make a comment in the local press, as previously detailed.

The club played in the Vauxhall Conference when he joined them at Penydarren Park, about thirty miles from Swansea. Built upon the top of a Roman fort, the club, formed in 1908, played their first home game at the ground, a friendly with Swansea Town, on Saturday 5 September that same year.

Periods spent in the Welsh League, Southern League and Football Conference never saw the club elected into the Football League, proper but they faired well in various cup competitions over the decades. However, it is in the Welsh Cup that Merthyr have garnered some success. Winners of the beautiful trophy on three occasions, the last being in 1987, that particular victory saw the club qualify for the preliminary rounds of the European Cup Winners' Cup. Pitted against Italian side Atalanta, Merthyr recorded a startling 2-1 win in the first leg at Penydarren but lost the return 2-0 (exiting the competition via a 3-2 aggregate).

A club such as Merthyr had a long-established tradition of former pros coming to the end of their playing days enjoying a final swansong and so the arrival of someone of the caliber of Robbie James was not extraordinary. Indeed, the Swansea connection was well established, with Bob Latchford, who had starred alongside Robbie during their Division One days. 'Latch' was in the Merthyr team that won the 100th Welsh Cup Final in 1987. Mel Nurse joined John Charles as a player when the 'Gentle Giant' was player-manager there in the early-1970s and Robb old boss Harry Griffiths, the true 'Mr Swansea', turned out for them as player-manager in 1965, across an eighteen-month period. Little David Giles, and his brother Paul, both played for, and coached there and the siblings were also involved at Barry Town F.C when Robbie went there; Paul as a player and David as coach. Former Swan Gary Emmanuel, superseded by Robbie upon his return for a second spell at the Vetch during the late 1980s also played for Tydfil, as did stalwarts and past Robbie team mates Terry Boyle and Nigel Stevenson. Gordon Davies, later to establish himself at Fulham, is probably the most well-known player to come out of the club. A full Wales international, he played alongside Robbie for the national side.

Whilst with Cardiff City across the 1992/ 93 and part of the corresponding season, the 36-year-old Robbie, was keen to further his career and so signed for Merthyr Tydfil Football Club. Stepping down into the Vauxhall Conference and into realms of part-time football, the current Cardiff City Player of the Year saw his departure from Cardiff cause a great deal of irritation to the Chairman due to his being on a weekly contract, as many others were, he simply exercised his right to move when an opportunity presented itself. At the end of October, Q.P.R played a friendly at Penydarren although it is uncertain if Robbie was fit enough to have played.

Robbie had starred in a strong Swansea side that had beaten the Martyrs in a January 1981 Welsh Cup encounter with future Tydfil players David Giles, Nigel Stevenson and Jeremy Charles, all in the side that went on to win the Cup that season. Merthyr had won it all the way back in 1949, recording a victory against a certain Swansea Town.

Playing in black and white, chairman John Reddy had been in talks with Robbie at the end of September, whilst on the pitch, his side lost 2-0 to Kidderminster, following a run of drawn games. Also in the Conference this season were Yeovil Town, Southport and Macclesfield Town, the latter being managed by old Stoke City team mate Sammy McIlroy. Clubs such as Kettering, Bath City, Southport, Halifax Town and Macclesfield were familiar to Robbie from his early days with Swansea. Merthyr had already met Southport at home this season. Known as the Sound grounders, they had dropped out of the Football League in 1978. Whilst a Cardiff City player, Robbie had been in the losing side at Ninian Park in a surprising F.A Cup defeat by Bath.

Inheriting a squad which had full-time jobs away from the game, Robbie did have a certain Tommy Hutchison to help him in his first managerial post (and to be sporadically selected in the team). The two had been team mates at Swansea and combined, there League appearances top the four figures mark. Tommy had been assistant manager during the previous season and as professional, he had made many appearances for Scotland but is probably most-remembered as the player to score two goals in an F.A Cup Final: one for his Manchester City side and an accidental own goal for their opponents, Spurs. As someone with over a thousand appearances, he enjoyed spells in the U.S Soccer League and in Hong Kong before retiring in 1994, aged forty six. Also helping out at the club this season, in a playing capacity was former Vetch team mate and club captain Dudley Lewis and ex-Cardiff man Andy Gorman.

Cardiff City chairman, the bumptious Rick Wright, was perturbed at losing Robbie and was keen to recoup the £37,500 transfer fee (which included a handsome £20,000 signing-on fee paid directly to the player) shelled out to bring Robbie to City from Bradford in 1992. In a press conference on Wednesday, October 7, a happy John Reddy unveiled his new acquisition, "Robbie will bring his significant experience to the club and I am sure his enthusiasm for the game will have a positive effect on the team," he told the Merthyr Express.

MERTHYR TYDFIL
FOOTBALL CLUB

NID CADARN BRODYR DDE
OND

"In Robbie James and Tommy Hutchison, we have a management team of two players of international caliber and domestic experience unrivalled anywhere in non-league football in this country."

Keen to utilize Robbie to help promote the club in the community, the new arrival was soon visiting local clubs, schools and groups. This was something that he did throughout his career and he was well-liked by the fans of all the clubs that he was associated with.

Robbie made his debut on Saturday 9 October, in a home game against former Football League club Halifax. Attended by 911, his new team won 2-1 and their new player-manager wore the number eight shirt. Across the season, he would feature in twenty-one matches and score three times.

A massively anticipated third round Welsh Cup tie with Swansea City arrived on Thursday 2 December 1993. This re-arranged replay followed a goal-less encounter the previous week watched by 2,431 at a typically-windswept Vetch Field (a gate which bettered some of their league fixtures). Robbie had missed that game due to hamstring problems and was also absent for the return. Watched by a massive 2,106 crowd, the Swans took away a 1-2 win. The clubs had first met in the Welsh Cup at Penydarren Park way back in 1913, with the visitors defeated that day. And Merthyr had a long-standing record of competing in the tournament against the likes of Cardiff, Swansea Town and later, Swansea City.

By the end of November, the Martyrs had found themselves in fourteenth position in the GM Vauxhall Conference. The division contained twenty two sides, with many teams familiar to Robbie. Merthyr were not keen on playing in the Konica-sponsored League of Wales, as low attendances (the season opened with gates of 643 and 543 at home) and lack of cash there would make the long-term future of a club such as theirs unlikely. Indeed, Robbie said that he had taken the player-manager post with the proviso of not wanting to do so if they were planning on moving up to the Konica. Writing in his programme notes, he also related that he accepted the job because he realized that his playing days were coming to a close and that as he wanted to remain involved in the game, he needed to seize the opportunity to gain some experience of managing/coaching. Although by the time of his subsequent departure from Merthyr, Robbie had publicly stated that he would like to continue playing up in the Football League again. Reddy had told him that he wanted him to bring a greater sense of professionalism to the club, both on and off the field of play. He also acknowledged to Robbie in talks that he had neglected matters a little at the club but was determined to rectify this. Robbie said all the right things and with former Swans team-mate Hutchison as his assistant, his ambition was to move the club forward. Money was available to enhance the squad with the intention to push on and win the Conference. Matters off the pitch were proving tricky, as Cardiff City wanted decent recompense for losing Robbie but the £50,000 and then £40,000 that they sought was nowhere near what Merthyr wanted to pay. Reddy instructed City to take his club to a tribunal to sort matters out. At the end of October Robbie was valued at £10,000 by the Football Association of Wales at the first ever tribunal of its kind. It was a huge difference from the £2,500 that they had wanted to shell out. Incredibly, Robbie was held to have brought the game in to disrepute due to his comments made on the day. He was unhappy that there was no P.F.A representative present but the record fee for a non-league club stood. Meanwhile Robbie sent

a letter to the F.A.W asking for a personal hearing. So overall, the messy conclusion of financial matters produced a disappointing final association with his former club.

Putting all such concerns aside, in his first game in charge Robbie saw his side face Halifax at home, as mentioned. He must have wondered what he had let himself in for upon seeing the ball initially pinging about the pitch at head height. Starting the game himself, he instructed his new charges to play along the ground and succeeded in calming matters. Robbie showed signs of his obvious skill, via a run which saw him beat three players. He played in most of the match, seeing his team win 2-1, until limping off.

In the days following the match on the training ground Robbie pointed out areas of play that needed to be improved upon, including corners and keeping the ball at ground level, as mentioned. Keen to improve his playing squad, it was imperative that new faces should be brought in and the need for signing a striker was singled-out by the former Swan.

A subsequent fixture against Northwich Victoria saw a crowd of just over 600 viewing a 5-0 routing by the Martyrs and Robbie made a plea to encourage the fans to come and support the club. Long gone were the days when they once squeezed 21,000 into the ground for an F.A Cup 2nd Round tie with Reading in 1949. Returning to the present match, Robbie brought in Nathan Jones, a former team mate at Cardiff City and

Merthyr put in three goals in the last eight minutes. Matters away from the football reached boiling point with Reddy accusing the F.A.W of victimizing his club.

By December, Robbie had played in five matches and against Swansea City; he was wearing the number eight shirt in a squad that found a place for veteran Tommy Hutchison against the visitors that included Colin Pascoe in their side. Pascoe would follow Robbie as a subsequent player-manager at Merthyr.

The Tydfil Chairman was peeved with Swansea for charging visiting fans the same price of admission fee as per an ordinary League game: £6.00. And as a consequence, he publicly decreed that they would do likewise for the 500+ Swans fans that made the short trip to Merthyr. Reddy was further agitated by the game having to be re-arranged to accommodate the F.A Cup commitments of their Football League opponents. He was furious because the club had lost vital revenue from advertising due to the original date being changed. The Chairman insisted that the date be adhered too and that if Swansea did not play that they should be thrown out of the competition! Robbie had missed the last four games due to troublesome hamstrings and joked, publicly, that his team played better when he was in the side: not far off the mark as they failed to score in any games during his absence.

But before the games with Swansea, Merthyr had league commitments, the first of which was against Stafford Rangers. Robbie failed to return in time but saw his lads win 2-0.

Now back in training, the fledgling player-manager conceded that he needed more players to be able to compete for promotion but had set a realistic target of a top six finish. Merthyr thereafter had two points deducted and received a fine as a consequence of fielding ineligible players (committed in error before Robbie had arrived).

A 3-3 away result at Bromsgrove made way for the Welsh Cup fixture and by the time Swansea arrived to play the replay at Penydarren Park, Robbie stated that his team had been looking forward to playing their Welsh rivals especially because the Swans had been on a distinctively poor run of recent form. Alas Robbie ruled himself out of contention for playing and could only watch his team lose 1-2 in a game dominated by the visitors. Coincidentally, the clubs had been drawn against each other in the Welsh Cup for the past seven consecutive seasons.

Back in the domestic league, Merthyr fought back from a goal down to beat Northwich Victoria 2-1at Drill Field and had gathered seven points from three matches, two of them being away. Robbie turned out in a December 13 friendly with Southampton at Penydarren Park in a game which saw the Mathew Le Tissier-inspired Saints win 4-0.

Following their tenth draw of the season, the most-recent against Dagenham & Redbridge, Robbie was back in the team and hit the bar in a game that showed much vulnerability at the back by the Martyrs. By the time Sammy McIlroy brought his Macclesfield side to Wales, Merthyr chalked up their tenth game at home without a defeat thanks to a 2-1 victory. The fixture proved an enjoyable encounter to watch, with lots of action on the pitch and Robbie James perched in the centre of the defence. By the close of 1993, the team had played twenty games; winning six, scoring twenty eight and conceding six less.

A 0-3 defeat at home on 3 January by Telford, coming after a 1-1 New Year's Day with at home to Yeovil, found a deflated Robbie describe the match as his worst since being in charge. He played in the game and had an effort on goal well-saved in front of a bumper 1,068 crowd. January saw admission prices into the ground increase by a pound to £5.00; a financial necessity and way of clawing back some of the 1k a week losses being made by the club. Robbie and his players were stunned when Tommy Hutchison revealed in the second week of the New Year that he was retiring after enjoying an extensive professional career.

With their form worsening since Christmas and the League slipping away, Merthyr would fare better in the FA Trophy competition, being drawn against St.Albans City and beating them in a mammoth 4-5 away win. But before that, Altringham defeated their visitors 3-0, putting the Martyrs fourteenth in the table. The small squad as a whole, including its player-manager, was clearly under-performing but did pull off a late win in the above Cup game; with the winner coming a mere four minutes from time. In another Cup competition, Robbie featured in a 8-0 thrashing of Pontlottyn at home, before another bag of goals came in a 4-5 win at St. Albans immediately after!

Fortunes took a further turn for the better, following a victory over Slough, with a Robbie James goal and Man of the Match performance also thrown in. Already 3-0 up by half-time, Robbie's cracker came from a volley on the edge of the area after the opposition had failed to clear a long throw in.

In the next round of the F.A Trophy, Merthyr faced Kingstonians. Known as The K's, they now play in the Ryman Football League Premier Division and would go on to win the F.A. Trophy in both 1999 and 2000. Created in 1969 for semi-professional teams with an opportunity to play at Wembley, the F.A. Challenge Trophy has been won in recent seasons by Wycombe Wanderers, Colchester and in 2013, by Wrexham.

Returning to the Cup, The K's had been in good recent form, scoring sixteen goals in their last four matches but cup competitions do have the ability to throw-up all kinds of results, and the F.A Trophy was no different, the visitors from Wales came away with a 0-2 win and Robbie collected his second goal for the club. Arriving at the end of the first quarter, it was really an own goal, as it went in off a defender but he said that he would still be claiming it!

Upcoming Conference games saw old familiar names to Robbie, away at Southport and Halifax. They lost 3-2 at the former, with Mr. James regrettably giving-away a penalty which put the Merseysiders top of the table.

Poor home support heaped further problems on to a Merthyr side that lost 1-4 at Penydarren to eventual Champions Kidderminster at the beginning of March. The game was a pivotal one in deciding the fate of the team and Robbie, as it saw him going off with a nasty cheekbone injury against the Conference favourites. Dazed and uncomfortable, he was sent for an x-ray which at first did not reveal any breaks despite the event making him feel as if he had "been hit by a baseball bat". Robbie had leveled the scores at 1-1 thanks to a twenty yard net buster and his team had been faithfully adopting his policy of pushing the ball along the ground and employing short passes. Outplayed by the visitors, he went off just after the half-hour mark and it would mean the end of his playing season. A second x-ray, insisted upon by a colleague, revealed that he had suffered a triple fracture of the cheekbone which subsequently necessitated a detailed operation at a Swansea hospital. Robbie was perturbed as the player responsible for inflicting the injury because he had done it with malice aforethought, stating that the former Wales international had, in his mind, deserved it.

Fortunes this season for his two former Welsh League clubs were mixed: Cardiff fought with relegation from Division Two whilst the Swans would win the Autoglass Trophy.

Following a 0-1 defeat by visitors Welling, club doctor Arthur Jones decreed that Robbie was okay to play again. With Merthyr teetering on the brink of relegation, the season would be viewed as its worst in the five years.

Fifth from bottom after thirty-five games played, Robbie, still a novice at managerial level remember, was under tremendous pressure to motivate his players at this pivotal stage in the campaign. He had been closely involved in restructuring salary levels at the club during a month when they were penalized by a points deduction/ fine.

In a hectic season run-in, April saw Robbie having seven games remaining to enable him to move his team away from the bottom reaches of the table. A defeat by Kettering Town was followed by a Monday evening draw away at Runcorn before a Saturday 16 April loss to Welling United at home. Then a short trip across the Severn to Bath City concluded with his new team taking away a much-needed 0-1 victory in readiness for the arrival of Stalybridge Celtic to Penydarren Park on Saturday 23 April: with five fixtures remaining.

Moving to a 1-0 lead into the second half Merthyr ended up losing the game with Stalybridge 1-2, thanks to a dubious refereeing decision for the winning goal. Robbie and his boys struggled and took a battering on the pitch too. Away games at Yeovil and Stafford Rangers came next before two final fixtures in May: home to Bromsgrove Rovers on Monday 2 May and then Witton Albion, on the following Saturday would close the season.

A 2-2 at Yeovil in front of a terrific 2,030 gate, was superseded by a 5-1 battering at Stafford as the Martyrs found themselves fourth from bottom on thirty four points collected. Ahead of Bromsgrove, Yeovil and Witton in the table, with close to forty games played this season, there was much to worry about: could the club avoid the drop? There was added uncertainty regarding which division they might play in if they were relegated. Merthyr had battled hard for the right to stay in the English pyramid system rather than compete in the League of Wales and their projected status was unclear. The sunshine radiated around Penydarren Park as Bromsgrove were beaten 2-1 in the penultimate game of the Conference.

Saturday 7 May 1994 saw Robbie and his team face an already-relegated Witton Albion on the final day of the season. Mascot that day was Robbie's soon-to-be-four year-old son, Luke (pictured). His dad's club, third from bottom, had played two games in the last five days and found itself needing to win and hope that other results went in their favour to avoid slipping out of the Conference. Albion played their part in what turned out to be a highly-dramatic game. Behind 1-3 with twenty minutes of the game remaining, it was not looking good for Merthyr but they fought back valiantly to win the game 4-3. Some feeble defending saw the team leak three goals but a penalty late on was put away by one of their youngsters.

Although Merthyr Tydfil ended their season with a win, they filled the third relegation slot in the table above Slough Town and Witton. However, due to both Marine and Leek Town, the top two in the Northern Premier League being unable to meet regulations to allow them entey into the Conference, Merthyr dubiously retained their status. But football being a results-led game, unless you are Arsenal, Robbie was sacked by his Chairman John Reddy. He was, however, offered the chance to see out his contract but on a player-only basis. "Im completely shocked." He gasped to the Merthyr Express newspaper, "It's the first time I've been relieved of a position and I'm obviously not happy about it." His response was also covered in the South Wales Echo. "I know that we did not do very well and we just about survived. It was my first management job and I didn't expect it to turn out the way that it did. It was a very short apprenticeship."

Official Programme 1993-1994
MERTHYR TYDFIL A.F.C.
"The Martyrs"

WELCOME TO MERTHYR TYDFIL
"The Martyrs"
Wales' Premier
Non-Football League
Club

Main Sponsors HOOVER

GM Vauxhall Conference Saturday May 7th 1994 Kick Off 3.00pm
Penydarren Park, Merthyr Tydfil

V

WITTON ALBION

The Merthyr Chairman issued a brief press statement revealing that he and Robbie had spoken about his future at the club and he told of the opportunity for him to remain on the playing staff with them. Tellingly, it had been reported in the media that Robbie had been linked with a return to a Football League club after he had let it be known that he would like to play there one last time.

After the harsh realities of life as a player-manager, Robbie remained as a player on the books at Merthyr for the commencement of the 1994/95 GM Vauxhall Conference season. Only now, the team was managed by somebody else, namely Gerald Aplin. An uninspiring 2-0 away defeat at Northwich Victoria in the opening game of the new campaign on 20 August 1994 saw Robbie picking up a hamstring injury which would mean that he would miss the next four games. In the previous campaign, the Martyrs had achieved a League double over them. Starting in the number six shirt, he was substituted in the fixture attended by 814 spectators. It had no bearing here, as he left the club to join Barry Town in the League of Wales at the end of the second week of September. There he would find some familiar faces, including his former Swansea team mate David Giles, then in charge at Ebbw Vale. Merthyr suffered relegated by the close the season after a succession of managers failed to stop the rot.

Following the reporting of Robbie's sudden death in 1998, Merthyr Tydfil F.C would honour Robbie with a minute's silence before their match with Burton. The club finished runners-up in the Dr Martens Premier Division that season.

Barry Town F.C.

Oh, I do like to be beside the sea side....

The town of Barry is a mere eight miles or so from Cardiff and has its own football club, Barry Town, today based in the Welsh Premier League. Historically, the club dates back to November 1912, with the first competitive football match taking place in September 1913.

Known as the Linnets, Dragons or Yellow silk man, the club enjoyed a truly miraculous 1993/ 94 campaign, topped off with an outrageous Welsh Cup final win against Cardiff. The Bluebirds had endured a take-over drama which resulted in the departure of manager Eddie May before subsequently returning, all in the space of the same season. In the interim, he managed Barry Town and extended a professional and personal association with Robbie that dated back to 1976 at Swansea City when they were team mates at the Vetch. Eddie was coming to the close of his playing career whilst Robbie was only getting started back then.

In recent times, Barry Town finished eight in the Macwhirter Welsh League Division One but back in July 1994 architectural plans illustrating the projected transformation of Jenner Park in conjunction with the Vale Borough Council were revealed. Barry Town Football Club had recently won the Welsh Cup and were Abacus League Champions with promotion into the Konica League of Wales and their success in the Welsh Cup meant that they qualified for the European Cup Winners' Cup. They also won the Welsh FA Trophy and Cyril Rogers Cup to cap a terrific 1993/ 94 season. A superb record of only two defeats across fifty-six matches in the last season led many to believe that Town would go on to further success in the league when it commenced on 20 August. A sponsorship deal with BT proved useful with the club projecting more than to consolidate their recent endeavours.

Despite all this positive anticipation, there was significant upheaval in the playing staff, with player/manager Andy Beattie and Terry Boyle departing. Terry and Robbie had played in the same Wales Youth team back in the early-1970s.

Robbie became the latest member of the Town squad in September 1994 after leaving Merthyr Tydfil back in April after fulfilling the player-manager role at Penydarren Park. Although suffering with hamstring problems, Robbie's arrival would have been greeted well as the Dragons had been on a dreadful run of results: winning only two of fourteen matches thus far. Club Chairman, the bubbly Neil O'Halloran, a former professional footballer, was still trying to be jolly; stating that despite the start that there was plenty of the season remaining for improvements.

Playing in the Konica League of Wales alongside Bangor City, Rhyl, Ton Pentre and Llanelli it was sponsored by Swansea firm Konica Peter Llewellyn Limited. Formed in 1992, the League contained a total of nineteen clubs in its opening season. However, by the time Robbie joined Barry Town, it totalled twenty and advancing to 2010, it would shrink down to a dozen clubs. Barry became the first club there to turn professional but prior to Robbie making it on to the subs bench for the Cup tie with Inter Cardiff in late September, his new club was already nine games into the season. After stunning the Welsh football world by

defeating holders Cardiff City in the Welsh Cup final in May, a qualification slot in the preliminary round of the European Cup Winners' Cup (on 11 August) was the reward. Drawn to meet Lithuanian champions Zalgiris Vilnius, Town managed to hold them to a scoreless first leg at Cardiff before a 6-0 drubbing in the subsequent return encounter was sandwiched between an away trip to Porthmadog, recording an encouraging 1-4 win in the opening match of the domestic season. This was followed by another away win, a 0-2 against Mold before consecutive home games against Connah's Quay Nomads and Inter Cardiff. These resulted in a 1-1 draw and a 4-2 defeat.

A run of three defeats against the likes of Bangor, Ton Pentre and Rhyl exacerbated the poor form as the second leg Cup game with Inter Cardiff saw a 1-2 defeat. I wonder what Robbie must have made of his new team as he sat alongside a paltry crowd of 130 in Cardiff that day?

Attendances in the League of Wales, with teams consisiting of part-timer players, have always been underwhelming and the 1994/ 95 season was no exception. On 1 October 1994 Robbie made his home debut in his new yellow, with light blue trim, Barry Town shirt via a 2-2 draw with Llansantffraid. Attended by a gate of 236, they saw the former Wales international in the number seven shirt contribute a great deal. Alongside him that day were two old colleagues, Terry Boyle playing at number five and Alan Curtis, who was on the subs bench. Former pros like

Alan and Paul Giles were in the Barry squad, with the by now forty-year old Curt utilized as a substitute. A close friend of Robbie's, Alan had featured in the super achieving 1993/94 season with Barry that was highlighted by winning the Welsh Cup. Like Robbie, he was on the winning side in many finals, this one being his fifth, the same as his old Swans team mate. Curt would soon leave to join Carmarthen Town and made one more appearance in the squad. Boyle had been at Barry Town for awhile and had played in the first fourteen games of the season, four of them alongside Robbie James, before severing his ties with the club and moving on to Merthyr at the end of October after having closed his Football League career with Swansea. The Llansantffraid match was the eleventh fixture of the season and the draw ended the worst run of results for the club in the last sixteen years. The team for the match was: Morris, Gorman, Colcombe, Goodridge, Boyle, Chapple, Robbie, Powell, Evans, Ford, Pengelly.

A 1-3 away win at Flint Town saw Robbie doing well in his new team as former Cardiff City and Inter Cardiff player Paul Giles returned to the fold. The younger Giles brother shone **245** and was clearly better than this level of football but had a bit of a discipline problem on the pitch due to his competitive nature. Overshadowed by the success of his brother, David, Paul remains involved in local Welsh football; a recent managerial post being with Dinas Powis F.C, near Penarth. A pro at Cardiff back when Phil Dwyer was there, big Phil revealed in his autobiography that the nickname given to him by his team mates was Possum: and Paul hated it! The win at Flint was a much-needed boost and Chris Aust, general manger at the club agreed. "It was a very pleasing result but the margin of victory should have been doubled."

After eight games Barry Town had won and lost three, drawing the remainder but charismatic Chairman Neil O'Halloran still believed that the team had the necessary time to foster an improvement in their fortunes. The first week of November saw Terry Boyle sacked whilst Robbie was switched to left-back from midfield and the exchange showed: they lost 3-1 away to Conwy United.

Remaining in that month, ex-Cardiff City and Newport County player John Lewis was unveiled as the new manager and he immediately made Giles his assistant. O'Halloran saw the change as a positive one, as he wanted the club to have a manager that would take control of the playing side of things, rather than just coach. With thirty games remaining there was ample time for a turn around but you are probably guessing that these things are rarely so convenient in football. Jimmy Greaves was often prone to say that soccer is a funny old game and so it proved here. Disciplinary issues for Giles were exacerbated as the talented player shone in the team.

With Robbie now switched to right-back, a home defeat to Porthmadog (2-3) would not have enamored the new boss to the Jenner Park faithful, in this his first game in charge. Lewis said all the right things but he wasn't to last. Robbie strove to be involved in setting up goals but the Dragons missed many early chances in the game. He continued his contribution with a decent game against Mold Alexander, also.

A tricky visit from top-of-the-table and title favourites Bangor City, who had already beaten Town at their ground this season, offered up an excellent 1-0 victory and Lewis decreed he wanted the club to become "a team to be feared".

A Boxing Day fixture with Inter Cardiff at home offered a glimpse of Robbie's skills in the shape of a blistering thirty yard shot that just slipped wide in a 2-2 draw. Another match soon came round, a 1-1 with Ebbw Vale and by the end of January, after only ten weeks in charge; Lewis resigned following a defeat to bottom of the table Maesteg Park. Citing his frustration at the attitudes of some of his players, he might have had a point: the club worked its way through fifty+ footballers during the season.

Into the New Year and by the end of January 1995, a big brash and colourful change was made and who should be announced as the new manager but none other than old Swansea team mate Eddie May. The latter had recently left his job at Cardiff following boardroom upheavals which had made his position untenable. Robbie and his team mates met up with Eddie soon after, whilst preparing for an up-and-coming game with Afan Lido. That match was subsequently postponed but the time gave both parties an opportunity to get to know each other or simply reacquainted, in some cases. May and the Barry Chairman had known each other for a number of years and the new arrival was keen to get started and spoke of his desire to get Town back in to European contention hopefully by the close of the present season. He also acknowledged the embarrassment of his much-fancied Cardiff side losing 2-1 to his new club in the recent Welsh Cup final back in May. Alan Curtis and Terry Boyle were both in the Barry team that day but had left the club before Ed's arrival.

Plans to strengthen the squad were muted as the new incumbent began his reign with an away trip to Cwmbran Town on 4 February.

His arrival naturally galvanized the team and they won 2-3 win before a brace of away fixtures, all featuring Robbie, recorded a 2-2 and 3-2 defeat against Ebbw Vale and Llanelli, respectively. The latter would be a club that saw Robbie feature as a player-manager sometime after. The Cwmbran game had been watched by a spectator total of 271. Attendances in the League of Wales have always been low, as has previously been stated, and the total figure for the whole of the 1994/95 season for Barry fixtures, home and away was 15,330. From 1995 onwards attendances had picked up in the League from around 100 to 500+ for domestic games, and sell outs of 2,500+ for European games. Barry saw 1,914 for the August fixture with Zalgiris but gates of 500-1,000 was a decent level for Welsh domestic football. But how could figures like that prove sustainable for a club with European aspirations? Clearly it would not.

For people of the caliber of Robbie, May and Curt, who had played the game at a higher level and in front of considerably larger crowds than the 600 which had attended the three games against Cwmbran, Ebbw Vale and Llanelli, some might wonder why they would bother. But working with Eddie on his self-titled autobiography, published in 2012, it was all about continuity: the need to be involved in the game in any way possible. That is not to say that any of these three lost any of their ambition or professional standards, but location and opportunity was also a consideration. However, the drop in the quality of play was a hard adjustment for these guys. Robbie was keen to progress and he was aware that he would need to learn the ropes as a fledgling manager at a lower level club like Merthyr Tydfil and Llanelli to gain the necessary experience of man management. He had years of playing experience behind him, but he felt it imperative to develop the necessary skills required to prosper in a managerial role that he was still a novice in. Not all former players make the successful switch into management and past greats such as Gordon Banks and Bobby Moore both failed to enhance their playing pedigree.

But stepping back to the still-growing playing career, he was given the number four shirt, which he would wear in the remaining sixteen fixtures, barring the return fixture with Cwmbran where he took the number two shirt. He also turned out at number eleven, seven and three (as well as twelve and thirteen on the subs bench) across his thirty six appearances since arriving in September.

On the pitch, Robbie was still doing well and a twenty yard drive in the 2-2 draw with Ebbw Vale showed that he still had much to offer. Now, after twenty five games, Barry Town was placed eleventh in the division.

An away defeat at Penydarren Park, home of Llanelli AFC, was followed by a 3-0 win at Jenner Park against Maesteg Park. Sealed by a Batcheler header; the set-up came directly from a Robbie James free-kick. It was an unsurprising result because Maesteg had won only once in their previous twenty five attempts and finished the season bottom of the table. Barry had now collected thirty six points but still quite a way behind table-toppers and eventual Champions, Bangor, on sixty five. Despite that gap, competition between many of the rest of the division was tight but it was a season that saw Barry suffering at times due to defensive errors. Former Wales international David Giles joined his brother, Paul, alongside May as new club coach in March. He and Robbie had long since been professional colleagues from their playing days at Swansea City and Wales. 'Gilo' had played for all four Welsh league clubs (before Newport and Wrexham slipped out of the Football League)

Ed's fifth game in charge, against Caerswys, saw a 3-0 win and also the strongest performance by Robbie thus far: his twenty-second. He continued to show his class by passing the ball adeptly and must have been encouraged by the lapses in defense being addressed. Working well with Giles and Knight, a Robbie through ball saw the latter's shot hit the post. But it was a goal that surfaced a little after the hour mark which stood out. It was a twenty yard pile driver from the boot of Mr. Robbie James. It was to be his one and only goal for Barry and it helped put his side into the lead before being added to by a Giles penalty and Knight strike. With eleven games remaining, Barry found itself fourteenth in the league with a dozen games left and much optimism ringing around little Jenner Park.

Next up came an away game at Afon Lido, soon to be runners-up in the final table, and they beat Barry despite Town dominating proceedings in the first half. It was their inability to get on the end of chances that cost them the points. Manager May stated that if you fail to take the opportunities then you have to keep a clean sheet and he should know, being a former centre half and a decent scorer, too. Collectively, in only seven games across the whole season did Barry fail to score across forty-five matches. A Robbie rocket tested the Lido keeper but the Dragons lost 2-0. The home defeat by Cwmbran on 25 March, a week after Afan Lido saw Robbie wearing the number two shirt against a side that would finish fifth in the League. They featured Roger Gibbins as their player-coach, and interviewed by the local media, he was keen to lock horns with his old Cardiff boss but seemed a little disconsolate in finding the likes of himself and Eddie involved in the lower leagues. In the away match with Cwmbran, a Robbie shot was tapped on to the post by the keeper when the Dragons went 1-3 up and that particular battle of the Towns finished with the visitors successful.

A busy March saw May return for an unfruitful second spell with Cardiff City, and his departure led to the Giles brothers taking charge of team affairs at Barry Town F.C. Neil O'Halloran stated publicly that he felt Eddie had done a great job and that he would be welcome to return if he ever wanted. Cardiff eventually succumbed to relegation after he returned and Eddie left the Ninian Park club for pastures new.

The 1-1 at Ton Pentre saw a fierce encounter with two Barry players and a Pentre player being sent off. Giles was playing well and scoring goals, too. Town had lost 0-3 to them earlier in the season but their luck had been out during the game as Barry hit the woodwork a number of times. The away draws at Ton Pentre and Llansantffraid (later renamed TNS and now known as The New Saints) came at a time when a number of players had been coming and going from Jenner Park but they did demonstrate a slight improvement. A 3-1 home win against Aberystwyth came with a brace from Francis Ford. Signed from Cwmbran Town, the previous September, he added to his eventual total for the season: a lucky thirteen.

The Aberystwyth game was the second in a hectic list of nine fixtures played in just over four weeks. With seven games left, the next couple of home matches, against Flint Town United and Afan Lido, saw a 3-0 win and 0-2 reverse.

Advancing to a busy holiday weekend, with five games remaining, Barry lost 1-0 away at Hollywell on Saturday 15 April but won 2-1 at home against Rhyl on Easter Monday. They had beaten Hollywell, a club that would finish directly beneath them in the final table, back in October but had capitulated to Rhyl, in mid-September.

Rumours of a return for Eddie May proved unfounded whilst Barry had a trio of fixtures to fulfill: Conwy at home, Inter Cardiff away and finally, Newtown at Jenner Park on 29 April.

A 2-1 victory over Conwy, who would conclude their season some ten points less than their opponents, set up a short trip to Inter Cardiff. As for Inter, they had faced them on three previous occasions this season; losing the two Cup ties and drawing at home in front of 263 on Boxing Day. Barry knew much about Inter having brought in a number of players from them including Batchelor, Knight and Paul Giles. Their opponents had signed-up the experienced Terry Boyle, who scored against is former club in the game. In conjunction with his brother, Paul went on to briefly manage the club in October 1999. Inter Cardiff had done very well before this season, finishing second in the last two seasons. Barry beat them 2-3 in what transpired as the penultimate appearance in Town colours for Robbie. The win took them into seventh place in the League after forty four games played (including seven Cup games).

And so it came to the closing fixture of the 1994/ 95 campaign, a home match with Newton played on 29 April before a 197 crowd. Robbie went out with a bang as Town won the match 3-0, a decent result seeing as the visitors finished in fourth spot. Barry closed their campaign on fifty nine points, seventh in the League and some twenty nine behind Bangor City and twenty behind second placed Afan Lido. Newtown, experiencing an underwhelming season despite being much-fancied early doors; were well-beaten on the day, thanks to a convincing 3-0 score line after a 2-2 at their place back in November.

On a personal level, Robbie played in thirty-six games across the season which in all, amounted to forty five including the various Cup matches that Barry Town competed in. As all clubs do, Barry Town had its own season-end awards and Robbie attended the event at a local venue called Buffs Club. From being voted player of the season at many of his professional clubs, Robbie didn't feature so prominently, "Whilst he would reply politely, his body language did let you know that he wasn't too keen on interacting with the fans," recalls Barry fan Stuart Lovering in a correspondence with the author. "For some very valid reason, though I forget why at this distance, there was a third, second and first place. He either was voted second or third. Again I can't remember which - though he was quite rightly well-beaten by a winner who had never played at as high a level as he had. However, in his acceptance speech, he pulled no punches in letting those assembled know exactly what he thought of this."

Llanelli A.F.C as a player

Robbie initially arrived at Llanelli as a player-only for the 1995/ 96 season, prior to returning for their 1997/ 98 campaign, as the new player-manager. No doubt signing for them was partly due to knowing Reds Chairman Robert Jones, formerly involved at Swansea City back in the glory days with him. The obvious convenience of its locality to Swansea would also have been a consideration for Robbie, who was also developing his interests away from the game. His new team mates were all semi-pros, with jobs away from the game.

Llanelli, like Merthyr Tydfil F.C, had a number of ex-Swans join them over recent years and this would continue after his involvement with the club. Reds striker Tony Smolka played with Robbie across both his spells; 1995/ 96 and for the 1997/98 season when he returned. "He was a very nice gentleman. Very professional."

During his first spell, it was clear that Robbie was coming towards the end of his playing days and was not as mobile as he had once been but his vision, passing and temperament was top notch, as Tony remembers today. Robbie joined a very ordinary side which was struggling at the time.

After having left Barry Town who should his debut for his new club come against but Barry back at Jenner Park! That arrived on 22 August 1995 and saw a hefty 6-1 defeat for Llanelli. The team line-up for the match was Thomas, A Evans, G Davies. S Evans, Arthur, N Davies, Myers, Smolka, Fowler and Robbie.

In all, he played in a massive forty-three matches and scored a solitary goal, away at Goytre, in a November Welsh Cup fixture. Unfortunately, Llanelli closed their season at the bottom of the League of Wales and were consequently relegateddown into the Welsh League.

Weston-super-Mare F.C.

Flying high with the Seagulls?

'Ever Forward' is the club motto found under the team badge of Weston-super-Mare Football Club. Prominently featuring a seagull, it is not surprising for a team situated on the coast looking out to the Channel, some eighteen miles from Bristol. As a football club, Weston dates back to 1887 and an early team nickname of the 'Donkey Boys' was not one that seems to have lingered! Reformed in 1948, by the close of the 2012/ 13 season they would be playing in the Blue Square South division competing alongside twenty one other clubs including Welling, Eastleigh, Bath City and Dover Athletic.

However, back at the start of the 1996/ 97 season, ex-Newport County and Cardiff manager Len Ashurst was in charge of the Woodspring Park-based club. Assisted by former County midfielder John Relish, they would work together before finances meant that Ashurst subsequently departed and Relish took on managerial duties from the next season on when Robbie had also left. Robbie had played against John a number of times in the mid-1970s in the Football League and Welsh Cup Swansea City v Newport fixtures (both before and with Ashurst as manager).

Team photo: Robbie at Weston, front row, third from the left.
(Picture courtesy of Mike Williams at TW Publications,
author of the Non-League Club Directory)

The regional, non-League football world can be a small one, as John would later work at Merthyr, another Robbie club. The Ashurst/ Relish axis arrived in February 1996, replacing Keith Christie, manager at the club for several years. Robbie played in pre-season friendlies with Wolves and Calne Town and his arrival did not seem to have received any fanfare at all. New Chairman Paul Bliss was keen for his team to win promotion up into the Dr Martens Premier Division and out of the Southern Division. First, they would have to see off opponents such as Forest Green Rovers, Margate, Havant Town, local rivals Clevedon Town and Weymouth in amongst twenty-two others. A season ticket could be bought for £50.00 to attend all games at the relatively-new ground, in use since 1994.

The super-fit Robbie would need to remain so, as he commenced another football season overflowing with fixtures: forty-two league games and Weston had also entered in the F.A Cup, Dr Martens Cup, F.A. Trophy and Somerset Premier Cup.

Most of the clubs found here were made up of a combination of youngsters, a number of well-established names and some former Football League players; either released or coming to the end of their playing days.

In the Weston first team squad were six players aged twenty or under being joined by a forty-year-old Robbie and aided by captain Paul McLoughlin and goal poacher Dave Mehew. Also coming to the club, from Briton Ferry, was Francis Ford, an ex-team mate at Barry Town with Robbie. He played in ten games but left in November along with a few others. Colleague Lee Jones, an eighteen-year-old from Swansea City, offered a link to Robbie's football heritage. Playing on a relatively-new Woodspring pitch, its tag of providing a poor playing surface had been expunged in anticipation of the coming season.

Home attendances for Weston-super-Mare in the Dr Martens Division Southern League proved slightly higher than those at Barry Town, with a total of 5,295 watching the team across its twenty-one league games and a total of 5,245 attending away fixtures involving the club.

As the season commenced, Robbie made his debut with a trip to Fleet Town, a team that his new club had not beaten before. That did not change: they lost 2-1. "We were easily the better side out there," bemoaned Weston boss Ashurst. That game saw an astonishing nine minutes of added injury time with the Seagulls 2-0 down before a cross field pass by

Robbie was netted by McLoughlin on ninety minutes. Some while later in the campaign and Weston got their revenge thanks to a 3-1 home win which saw Robbie sending a long pass over the opposition defense that reached his team mate Darren Tilley, who cut in and put the ball past the keeper and pushed Weston into a 1-0 lead. The game was not a great one to watch but the result came when points mattered.

Another defeat followed, 1-2 to Weymouth in an incident packed encounter seeing two Weston players and a Weymouth lad, sent off. It also featured three penalty misses, including one from Robbie, in the space of one crazy spell in the first half. The game, his home debut at Woodspring Park, was a strong one for Robbie, and he found himself involved in much of the play. Beginning with a free kick narrowly missing being goal-bound via the head of talented team mate and former Cardiff City player, Paul McLoughlin, Robbie's missed penalty came just after the half-hour mark. A goal up, Weston lost the match by two second half strikes.

An impressive run of ten games without loss followed which took the club up into third in the table. These included a 2-0 home win against Margate, noticeable for the absence of Robbie James due to family illness. But his team performed admirably and recorded their first win of the season on a windy afternoon. A 2-1 away win in Gloucester at Cirencester Town was achieved over the August Bank Holiday weekend and saw Robbie return in the sweeper role. Weston immediately commenced pressurizing the Cirencester defense in a game which Robbie enjoyed being involved in, as he was the organizer of all the set-piece action as his new club took away a win. His thirty yard free kick effort was tipped over the bar by the Town keeper at full stretch.

Into September, a 0-0 with eventual champions Forest Green Rovers was followed by an away visit to Witney Town. There, a dominant Weston-super-Mare advanced to a 0-1 lead shortly after the quarter hour mark against opposition that contained some ex-Seagulls. Most of the fixtures between them had ended in a draw and so it was for this 1-1 played at the Marriotts stadium. Then an F.A. Cup encounter with Bristol Manor Farm of the Screwfix Direct Premier Division came next. Weston had produced an earlier, 2-0 victory against Brislington, the present-holders of the Somerset Premier Cup in what was the first-ever meeting between the clubs. It marked the debut in a Weston shirt for Francis Ford. Current team mate Jon Bowering missed an open goal when put through by an effective Robbie free kick late on in the second half. Both Weston goals came from set pieces, corners, against a Bristol-based opposition regarded as one of the most promising sides in the Western League Premier division. It was their inaugural fixture in the competition. Bristol Manor Farm was easily defeated before Weston exited the competition by losing 2-1 to Trowbridge.

Weston-super-Mare had seen their unbeaten run of ten games at home extinguished by Yate Town recently and so were keen to take the points at Lodge road. Unfortunately, the unlucky Seagulls let in a late equalizer that robbed them of three points. After controlling matters in the first half, Robbie had been involved in a free kick move to set up Bowering but his attempt at goal was eventually blocked by the determined efforts of the Town goalie.

The quaintly-named Tonbridge Angels were effectively dispatched 3-1 at home in a good week for Weston, a win here and then beating Weymouth extended an unbeaten run to six games. The Seagulls twice took the lead and concluded the game via a fine goal from O'Hagan. The teenager had been signed from Plymouth Argyle after the completion of a successful loan spell at Woodspring at the start of the season. Len Ashurst was happy. "That was a competent display at home today and capped by a goal of real quality. We will only get better after this." Robbie was playing well in defense alongside number one Stuart Jones. The Angels keeper had a nightmare game, with an error in the third minute leading to a goal. More than half of the team selected consisted of teenagers, and Ashurst was keen to bring in some experienced players to help out but even a makeshift team proved impressive.

Weymouth had beaten Weston 1-2 back in August but a great 0-3 away win, watched by a 572 crowd saw a solid performance from an unchanged Weston side a few days after a Saturday game with Tonbridge.

Weston and Trowbridge Town must have been sick of each other by the close of this campaign, as they faced each other five times: two League fixtures and the remainder, a trio of Cup competitions. Making the short trip to Frome Road, the visitors went 0-1 up, via a first half header before an equalizer came shortly before the hour mark. The application of pressure by Trowbridge succeeded as they ran out 2-1 winners. The final meeting saw a 2-0 home victory for Weston and it would clinch a League double for them over their Wiltshire rivals. That would occur in mid-December, when the team extended its unbeaten run to eleven games and maintained their third spot in the Dr Martens Southern League. Able to select the same starting XI for a third time, Weston were the highest scorers in the league at the time, after netting forty-three times across twenty games. In total, they would fire in an impressive eighty-two goals and concede forty-three.

On into October and a share of the points away at St Leonards Stamcroft produced an instant improvement. Coming after the 2-1 defeat at Trowbridge, Robbie did not join his team mates in their trip to Hastings to face a side that had recently won promotion from the Sussex County League. St Leonards would gain promotion at the end of the season but shared the points against a makeshift Weston side. Another lengthy trip from Somerset was required to meet lowly Erith & Belvedere, whom they saw off by an impressive 1-5 score line. A midweek 0-0 with visitors Cirencester Town meant that Weston failed to record a League double following an August Bank holiday away win 1-2.

November saw early defeats against Yate Town and Forest Green Rovers in a busy month of fixtures commencing with a 0-1 home loss to Yate. Having scored six times in as many games, Weston conceded a late goal from a header, to record their third defeat of the season, and the second at home. Their away form was much better at this early stage of the season and the Yate encounter could be criticized in that it found Weston rushing their game. Forest Green beat Weston 3-1 next before another positive run of form followed; with victories and draws.

A 3-0 over Erith & Belvedere, a team that would finish their season above Buckingham Town at the bottom of the League, was extended with a 2-0 against Kent-based Dartford. In that game, a strong, attack-minded trio of strikers was selected for the first-ever visit by Dartford to Woodspring. The visitors were forced to select a Reserve team keeper who was kept well-occupied before conceding two second half goals. The win took Weston to third in the table and was their eighth victory in succession. A healthy 4-0 against Trowbridge saw the fourth encounter between the sides this season: the first in the League, came after Weston had lost twice to the Bees and drawn the other time.

Len Ashurst continued with his formation of playing three strikers and the only change from the side that had recently beaten Dartford was at keeper. An early goal set the tone of the game but they could have doubled that score.

On to the final month of 1996, and Weston smashed visiting Fareham Town by 5-1 in an outstanding result in a comprehensive win. Two goals in either half, including a hat-trick for Dave Mehew, one of two this season, saw the total goals tally for the club reach forty. There then followed a 0-3 away win against the same opposition for Weston to achieve the 'double'. A 2-2 away draw on the Isle of Wight, at Newport, came next. At Woodspring, Weston would take all three points thanks to a 1-0, where in the midst of a defence "wonderfully directed by Robbie James" they saw off their island with a goal on twenty minutes. The result continued Newport's woeful run of failing to score there on four attempts. In an enjoyable spectacle to watch, Weston had numerous attempts on goal.

January commenced poorly for Robbie with his side losing away at Margate, 1-0. Watched by a crowd of 251, a dubious goal for the home side came after a disputed throw-in awarded to them was palmed on by one of their players before the Weston keeper saved a shot only for it to rebound into the net via a Margate player's knee! The incident was missed by both the referee and his assistants. Despite the defeat, Weston remained third in the table thanks to favourable results recorded elsewhere. The team enjoyed frequent patches of red hot form and so it was this month when eleven games saw not a single defeat for the Seagulls. Waterlooville, Buckingham, Newport (Isle of Wight), Witby, Tonbridge, Fleet Town and Cinderford were all dispatched and points were shared against Newport and Yate.

An away tip to a team that would be relegated by the close of the season, Buckingham, produced a decent 0-1 win against a side that packed its own half after slipping a goal behind. It was the eleventh clean sheet of the season and saw the Seagulls perched up at second in the League.

An ugly encounter with Cinderford Town was tainted by the dismissal of a Weston player and followed by unsavoury scenes perpetrated by some of the visiting team. Not an enthralling spectacle to watch, Weston were happy to take the points in a game within which they showed much flair demonstrated by their winner; a delicate chip by Tilley.

The next game saw a visit by London side Fisher Athletic who had been beaten by Weston 1-3 back in October. Finishing at 2-2, Robbie and his team were once again robbed for the second week running by a referee who missed a vital incident. When ten minutes remained in this closely-fought match, W-s-M were 2-1 up and pressurizing the Athletic box. Leading scorer Mehew hit the post only for a defender to fall onto the ball and knock it away, using his hand, before any Weston player could reach it. No penalty was awarded.

In the two League games with Havant, both games were drawn: 3-3 in Somerset and a 1-1at their place, with Weston on a run of five games without defeat after the latter result. A crowd totaling 402 braved the rain to attend Woodspring Park for the midweek, top-of-the-table clash with them in a game much enjoyed by the largest crowd of the season. Robbie was taking all free kicks and corners but not the penalties. Weston again conceded late on, on this occasion in injury time by a Havant side that had raced to a fifteen-point lead early on in the season. However, a change in their management had a telling influence on their fortunes and a dramatic dip in form by the time that they came to Weston. Havant would eventually close their campaign in third place; three ahead of Weston-super-Mare F.C. The match saw Robbie testing their keeper via a free kick, only for the ball to be blocked before a stunning thirty-five yard equaliser from Lee Jones saw the score level at 2-2. The share of the points put Weston into second slot in the table. The game was re-arranged and played on a Tuesday evening at home. Havant had been top of the table until being knocked off by eventual champions Forest Green Rovers. By the season close, Havant would finish third and Weston, fourth on seventy six.

Away from League endeavours, the 1996/ 97 campaign saw Weston playing in four different Cup competitions with their resulting fortunes proving mixed. Bath City had seemingly sealed their advancement into the next round with a 4-2, extra-time victory over them at home but regrettably for the Conference side, they fielded an ineligible player and so it was Weston that took their place in the next round as a consequence. Robbie found himself outpaced by a Bath player leading to an eventual goal on just-under forty minutes for the home side. Offering a much sterner test than those provided by many clubs in the Dr Martens League, Bath had been struggling and would be relegated. A February quarter final meeting with Bristol City came after they had recently smashed a team 10-0 in anticipation of facing Weston! Selecting a team of Reserves, Ashurst's team lost 2-0.

A 0-2 with Trowbridge in the inaugural meeting between the clubs in the Southern League Cup continued Weston's repeated failure to advance beyond the first round in recent seasons. With Robbie playing as a sweeper, the Bees scored via a penalty refuted by the Weston players but the claims were ignored by the referee. Town scored their other goal in the second half. The Dr Martens League Cup and F.A Cup had resulted in successive defeats by Trowbridge whilst Yeovil & Sherborne in the quarter final of the Somerset Cup saw the clubs meet here rather than in the final, as of the previous season. In the F.A Trophy, Weston had defeated Worthing but were well-beaten by peculiarly-named Midland League side Raunds Town at Woodspring Park. Levelling early into the second half, the Seagulls again failed to build upon their first half dominance as two further goals went in against them and they exited 1-3.

March recorded the departure of Dave Mehew, due to his contract being cancelled after he proved unyielding towards accepting a wage cut recently imposed by the club. All the other players agreed but Mehew, shortly before the kick-off in a home friendly with Plymouth Argyle, left the club. New signing Andy Beattie was selected for the match and he would demonstrate his class in a number of games, including an away draw with Havant Town. Beattie was a long-established name in the lower leagues and he was at Barry Town during their successful 1993/ 94 season before Robbie arrived there. Andy played in the 1994 Welsh Cup winning side that beat Cardiff City 2-1 in a squad that also included Curt and Terry Boyle.

By the close of March, Weston found themselves second in the table with sixty-nine points collected across thirty-four games. But a subsequent dip in form saw defeats to St Leonards, Clevedon Town and Bashley coupled with draws with Dartford and Cinderford Town.

In April, Weston were beaten 0-2 by their Sussex-based visitors St Leonards Stamcroft in their first trip to a blustery Woodspring Park. It was the first defeat in twelve for Weston and their third at home this season. The loss meant that the Seagulls dropped to third in the table. "We needed to win today, but too many players made mistakes," summarised Weston coach John Relish. "I know the wind did not help, but it was the same for both sides. I felt we gave them too much respect." St Leonards dominated the game but Robbie did manage to put in another of his angled free kicks during the match. He also tested the Zimbabwe-born keeper with an indirect set piece at the close of the first half.

After speeding to a healthy 2-0 lead at home to rivals Clevedon Town, Weston managed to let slip three second half goals and lost the game 2-3. It meant that their chances of promotion were virtually over. The game had originally been scheduled for a traditional Boxing Day morning but had been postponed due to a frozen pitch. Moreover, as it often is in football, the winner came from a former player. That man was

Tony Cook, who a year before had scored a last gasp goal for Weston but against their local rivals. A convincing 0-3 away win at Fareham Town put Weston back into second place in the division. Robbie had a good game, seeing his shot on goal turned away by the keeper and pressing with a corner that was subsequently taken on by a team mate who hit the post.

In the final month of the season, with Weston seeing their form slipping, a surprise 1-1 at home with Buckingham Town, a team that had leaked nearly a hundred goals this season and whose form duly brought relegation (being some twenty three points below their nearest rivals). The closing game of the campaign came via a meeting with Waterlooville, opposition that had endured a mediocre season and had lost to them 2-0, previously.

Weston finished in fourth position, just outside of the promotion bracket behind Havant, St Leonards Stamcroft and Forest Green Rovers. In total, the team won twenty-one of their forty-two League games, drawing eighteen and losing the remainder.

Robbie was the recipient of two awards from the club. He was voted Supporters Player of the year and Players' Player of the year: accolades that he seemed to procure at every club that he played for. He missed only five of the fifty League and Cup games this season and his spell with the club saw him regarded as a very popular player that the fans were sad to see leave.

With his final season as a player about to commence later in the summer of 1997, Robbie returned to Wales and rejoined Llanelli A.F.C only this time in a new, player-manager role.

Back to Llanelli

"To stay in football, I don't know anything else. I'd like to try coaching or even start in management, with a non-league club. It's been a great life and it only seems like yesterday I started as an apprentice with Swansea."

That was Robbie in an interview with the Cardiff Junior Bluebirds back in 1994. After playing for Barry Town from September 1994 through to the end of the season and their final game on 29 April 1996, Robbie had started for them against Llanelli across the two League of Wales fixtures between the sides that saw thirteen goals. An under-whelming gate of 185 attended the Stebonheath Park game which saw a 3-2 win for the home side Llanelli. In the season before he would sign on as the new player-coach, the Reds had finished third from bottom in the division: so he knew exactly the level of improvement needed at the club but this was his first player-manager role and an exciting, new challenge for the ambitious Welshman. Llanelli being twelve miles west of Swansea and the job also appealed to Robbie as the League was made up of part-timers.

Located a mile to the north east of the town centre, Stebonheath Park, known locally as Stebo Park, is a ground with a capacity of 3,700. This incorporates 1,000 seats but is a far cry from the 1950/ 51 season when games attracted 12,000 spectators (with another figure offered of 49,000). Jock Stein had played for the club against Merthyr Tydfil at Penydarren Park in 1950, years before he would make his mark as Celtic and Scotland manager. He featured as a centre-half and enjoyed a season and a half with Llanelli from the 1950/ 51 campaign onwards. Signed from Scottish club Albion Rovers, where he played as a part-timer, in the 1950/ 51 FA Cup, Llanelli made it through to meet Cardiff City at Ninian Park. It was the one and only time that Jock played at the ground but of course, most of us know of his tragic association with the now-demolished City ground.

Dating back to the early years, by the 1933/ 34 season, Llanelly Association Football Club (*sic*) was looking to gain admission into the Third Division (Southern Section) of the Football League. A promotional booklet proclaimed "the fine playing pitch is splendidly equipped with every accommodation for the public, players and visitors." An impressive 9,000 attended a game against Third Division opposition and were easily accommodated at the ground in the years before stadium safety concerns. The authorities at the club also noted that Swansea Town F.C was the nearest League club within a fifty mile radius. At the time, Llanelly (sic) played in the Welsh League against clubs such as Cardiff City, Swansea, Cardiff Corinthians and Merthyr.

Stebonheath Park had seen some redevelopment in 1990, with £25,000 spent on the ground, including the addition of an athletics track (Barry's Jenner Park has the same facility). Terry Yorath, then manager at Swansea City, was asked by Wales rugby star Phil Bennett to put together a team to mark the reopening of the stadium. This was said to have possibly included Robbie and Alan Curtis but it is unknown if they actually played in any game arranged thereafter.

With the club motto of "Yml Aen" written in Welsh upon its badge, translated it means "Forward/ Ahead". Llanelli hoped that Robbie would contribute to their advancement when he took full charge of team affairs in September 1997.

Ex-Swansea team mates with Robbie, both Dudley Lewis and Wyndham Evans had been working at the club prior to him. Released by the Swans at the end of the 1982/ 83 season, Evans, known as 'Windy' had served the Swans for more than a decade and had a testimonial at the Vetch which featured Robbie against the Liverpool 1974 Cup winners side including Tommy Smith, Phil Boersma, Emlyn Hughes and John Toshack; four of them with Swansea City affiliations. Whilst in his playing days, Lewis was a centre half and like Robbie, gained youth and Under-21 caps for Wales. Another ex-Swan, Glen Letheren, had been keeping goal for them for a time.

Manchester-born and another past Swansea player, Vic Gomersall, was appointed Commercial Manager by new Llanelli Chairman Robert James at the end of January 1997, further enhancing the Vetch lineage, whilst Nigel 'Speedy' Stevenson had played for Haverford West against Llanelli, back in April. Gomersall fulfilled similar duties at the Vetch and would be at Llanelli during Robbie's tenure.

Relegated from the League of Wales in 1996, the following year marked the Centenary of the club with Llanelli then playing in the CC Sport Welsh League First Division.

Appointed by Mr. Jones, himself in his first season as Chairman in 1997, the two had known each other back at Swansea in the early-1980s when Jones had been a leading shareholder at the club.

Robbie had featured in a six-a-side football tournament in July alongside other ex-pros including former Wales winger and team mate Carl Harris and ex-Cardiff / Swansea player-coach Roger Gibbins. And what with their established ties to Swansea, a pre-season friendly at home in early August was arranged with the Swans. Robbie was not in the starting XI for this fixture against Jan Molby's squad who took away a 0-7 triumph. At the time, Llanelli only had four first team regulars in the side, so the result was no surprise and not that important a consideration in the season build-up.

Robbie was in the team, coming on as a second-half substitute that lost 8-0 in another friendly with Swansea but he was said to have been satisfied with the four warm-up matches played as it gave him the chance to survey the players that were available.

Back in July, he had brought in ex-Barry Town target man Francis Ford to bolster the squad

Photo: although not the best quality picture, it shows Robbie in action for his final club. Courtesy Llanelli Star.

263

after the two had played together across the 1994/95 season. Ford, now a manager in the Welsh leagues, also played for Swansea City and Bridgend F.C. He would later play against his former side in October 1998 when Leighton James was player-manager with Llanelli. The Reds had lots of former pros as managers both before and since Robbie's residence. Enjoying varying degrees of success, Leighton Phillips, Wyndham Evans, Eddie May, the aforementioned Leighton James and with one of the most recent being Andy Legg up to 2012. 'Leggy' had been a youngster at Swansea City with Robbie during his second spell at the Vetch in the late-1980s. This long-throw expert, stand back Rory Delap, was one of a number of players to play for both Swansea City and Cardiff City.

However, returning to Robbie, the opening game of the new season on 16 August 1997, a 1-1 at AFC Rhondda, might have ended in a win if it had not been a more self-assured performance by Llanelli. Robbie, who now did a little bit of coaching and was very precise in what he wanted from his lads, had funds promised to him to bring in new recruits and indeed

he would do so. In and out of the team himself, he featured in the Cyril Rogers Cup match with Pontlottyn, a 0-2 away win, and he also turned out in following: a 3-1 against Llanwern, 2-1 with Cilfrew, 5-0 against Cardiff Corries, all in October and a 7-0 home win against Abergavenny. Things were going well and the Corries game was regarded as a good test in gauging where the team stood.

Into November and a 1-1 away at U.W.I.C saw Robbie playing well, as did his team mates. A goal down by half-time, the Reds then went on to defeat Cardiff Civil Service 1-2 before a confidence-boosting 0-9 win at Abergavenny. Robbie missed-out on the pitch for this route, after giving himself a break from playing. Leighton James played for Llanelli, as did Martin James, cousin to a certain Robbie and a youngster at Swansea City when Robbie was an established name there (not forgetting another cousin, Anthony, who also played for the Swans). Martyn, a former Youth Training Scheme trainee, signed professional terms with Swansea in August 1988 but did not feature in any first team matches. Leighton succeeded Robbie as manager at Llanelli. The two had been at Bradford City together previously, with Robbie on the playing staff and Leighton, the coaching.

By December, a year since the club had almost gone bust, an unbeaten run of form took Llanelli to the top of the table. Playing on a Friday evening, in an attempt to encourage new fans to come and watch them, they needed to generate more funds in the quest to return to the League of Wales. An impressive 2-0 success at home against Afan Lido finished with Robbie warning his inexperienced players not to become complacent into thinking promotion was a certainty. Llanelli raced to a seven point gap at the top of the division and a 1-2 victory at Maesteg took them ten points clear of Aberafon-based rivals Lido following a workmanlike team performance which allowed some luck in seeing the club taking the points. Robbie played in that game and in the defeat by Ton Pentre.

In a good 1-0 victory over much-fancied visitors Rhondda, Robbie was back in the home team. A 1-0 away defeat at Pontypool, against Goytre F.C was the club's first away loss of the season. Stepping into the New Year, Llanelli had a ten point lead on their nearest rivals but by the third week of January, it had shrunk back to just three. Robbie selected himself to play in the Goytre game and continued to offer his experience in the next fixture, at home to Port Talbot.

A 2.15pm kick-off saw their third defeat in a month, concluded an impressive run of only a single loss in twenty one games for the Reds. And now it was going to be a real fight if the club was going to take the title. An under hit Robbie back pass to his keeper enabled a Port Talbot player to steal in and poke the ball home during the second half, putting them 1-0 up before a final score of 1-2 to the visitors.

The next spell of games for the fading Llanelli came during a crucial time as Robbie was under intense pressure to win promotion and thus gain entry in to the League of Wales. The games kept coming, with away fixtures at Taffs Well and Grange Quinns before another against lively Cardiff Corries. A poor performance in losing 4-0 to the Corries came from a side seemingly in disarray after seeing a number of players leave the club and finding Robbie needing at least three replacements. Two went to Konica League side Rhyader, managed by ex-Swansea team mate Chris Marustik: the latter collecting six caps for Wales and a graduate of the Vetch youth development policy.

With only a few games remaining, one necessitating another visit to Cardiff, to meet Grange Quins and a home match with Porthcawl, which would be his twenty-fifth of the season, the story was about to play its final scene.

Despite losing 1-0 at Quins, the match showed a marked improvement on the recent 4-0 hammering by Corries, marred only by numerous goal chances during the game not taken by Llanelli: something that all teams are guilty of.

Robbie and Alan Curtis had remained in contact throughout their adult life and the two had arranged to meet up for a drink after the match with Porthcawl Town played on Wednesday, 18 February. Alan had shown his support for his old pal by promoting The Strand pub, formerly the Cornish Mount, which the latter had recently taken over the running of in Swansea town centre. The Llanelli lads had met with their manager there previously, too. Alan and Robbie were going to have a chat before kick-off but car trouble meant that Curtis arrived after the game had already started. Recounting the distressing incident in his autobiography, he recalls seeing Robbie challenge for a ball and subsequently collapse immediately following. Playing as a sweeper, the incident occurred in the first half of the game. Initially he thought that perhaps he had damaged his ligaments before the seriousness of the situation became apparent to everyone. Tony Smolka, on the substitute bench for Llanelli for the game, remembers, "The game kicked-off on a lovely evening at 7.30 pm and I think we were winning 2-1 at the time," recounts Tony of the tragic events unfolding before him. "The ball broke away and Robbie made a half-tackle with a guy, the guy then went on about four or five yards past him before Robbie collapsed. There was no collision. You think the worst straight away at these moments." Tony spent some five years with Llanelli and remembers when Robbie was announced as their new player/manager, "I thought that it was a great appointment," offers the former player, now involved in coaching a team in the local area.

Returning to the Porthcawl game, it was immediately abandoned and despite on-field attempts to revive Robbie by former ambulance paramedic Hugh Roberts and the club physiotherapist, he died. Curt had the unenviable task of informing Robbie's wife, Karen, to make her way to the nearby Prince Phillip hospital and it was whilst gathered there that they were informed that Robbie had died upon arrival. Mr and Mrs James senior, Roy and Jean, who would travel all over to see their son play during his career, were in a state of shock after witnessing first hand the tragic events played out on the pitch. Poignantly, Curt laments the absence of his old pal whenever there is a get-together of ex-Swans.

Regional newspaper the Llanelli Star carried a front page photograph of fans laying flowers on the pitch in tribute to Robbie. Andrew Stephens, then an eighteen-year-old fan, was present at the midweek game. "It was terrible to see. We did not know what was happening, although we knew it was serious," recounted the teenager. Supporters knew that something was wrong, with an anonymous witness adding, "We were all willing him to get up. I have never seen anything so tragic happen on the pitch."

Immediately after his death, West Wales Ambulance NHS Trust commented that there had been some confusion for their attending ambulance crew that arrived at the ground to help Robbie. Some mis-information arose due to the gates to the ground being locked and the crew members improvising by scrambling over a wall to reach him on the pitch. Regrettably, they were given incorrect directions which meant that they arrived at the wrong end of the ground where access was not readily available, whilst club members were awaiting them at a different part of Stebo Park. Robbie passed away aged forty, one month shy of his forty-first birthday, due to a condition called cardiomyopathy, a heart muscle disease (See Scope.org.uk or cardiomyopathy.org for further details).

His funeral took place on Thursday 26 February 1998 at St.Paul's church, Sketty and was then followed by cremation at Morriston Cemetery. The gathering was a virtual Who's Who of past and present sporting names mixed with family members. It must have been difficult as Robbie's second wife attended with Samantha, Luke and Hannah but his first wife, Yvonne did not. Some of his Llanelli players wore club tracksuits and both Leighton James and Curt were involved in the service. Reds Chairman Robert Jones insisted that the playing squad wear club tracksuits at the funeral but many of the players disagreed. The squad met up and agreed that they saw suits, along with club ties, as being a more appropriate way to express their collected respect for their former manager and colleague.

Alan Cork, then Swansea manager, told of plans of meeting with Robbie in the hope of getting him and other former Swans involved in a prospective youth project linked to the club. "He would have been a tremendous influence and a huge asset," offered the former Wimbledon player to the Evening Post. Cork had played against Robbie back in the late-1970s.

Tributes poured in and former Swans and Wales manager Terry Yorath commented to the Star, "The biggest tribute I can pay Robbie is that while he was a gifted footballer on the field, he was a lovely man off it." Yorath also recalled Robbie's dedication as a player, whilst under his management during his second spell at the Vetch. "Robbie was one of the most honest players I had...I never met anyone that trained so hard. I used to tell him to ease up but he never listened because he was so enthusiastic." Interviewed at the time, he added, "Robbie was very strong physically. I don't think he realised how good he was, he would have made any all-time Welsh squad."

Robbie's former playing colleague John Mahoney had recently travelled with him to Spain, as part of a fund-raising initiative on behalf of Newton Village charity team (a part of Swansea where Robbie lived). "He was a caring person with a lot of interests," added the former Swan. Robbie also presented trophies for the Swansea Junior League and was well-known for promoting sport and encouraging youngsters to get involved, as you would have already read throughout this book. John Toshack was compelled to call the local paper to express his thoughts about his former player. "When Robbie was on-song there was no one better...he was quite a deep person and maybe a little inconsistent but I will always have an abiding memory of him picking up the ball in his own half and, ghosting past people and getting in a powerful shot. I would have been happy to have played him in any of my teams...he was one of the finest Welsh players over the last twenty years." Tosh had been at Stebo Park as recently as December 1997, where he had enjoyed a chat and a drink in the bar with his former 'Golden Boys' Robbie and Curt.

A silent tribute was respectfully upheld at Orient where the Swans were playing on the weekend after Robbie's death. Tommy Hutchison added his own touching comments, "He was the ideal pro - the perfect man for all the lads to try to emulate. I was with Robbie at Merthyr as well and he showed the same attitude and spirit there. We were next-door-neighbours. The postman used to get us mixed up and Robbie would play along: he was mischievous and liked a laugh. That's what I will remember him best for. Football has lost Robbie but I have lost a friend." The Swans wore black arm bands as a mark of respect when they faced Exeter at the Vetch on 28 February. The club offered, "Robbie will be fondly remembered by all those associated with him and particularly by those supporters who watched him play with great ability and enthusiasm." At his funeral service, a Cardiff City shirt was also used as part of the tributes paid to him.

A commemorative plaque at Llanelli reads, "Dedicated to the memory of our great friend and player/ manager Robbie who died so tragically whilst playing at Stebonheath."

"Robbie was one of the lads. During one game late in the season, we had to travel to Angelssey to play Camaes Bay, which is in the back of beyond and this necessitated an overnight stay in a hotel." offers Tony Smolka, "So he roomed with two or three of his players, both of whom smoked. This is back in the days when people could do so more freely and in the semi-pro world things weren't so strict, so some lads liked a smoke and a bit of a drink. But Robbie ever being the model pro throughout his career was shocked to discover them smoking in the room and told them that they shouldn't be doing so. The reply from the players was that they didn't care who he was and they continued! "He was great," chuckles Tony, who attends the annual Robbie James Charity Day golf tournament on the Gower, as does Robbie's cousin and Llanelli team mate, Martyn. "That side of him, he really enjoyed it. He was very approachable and a true gent, on and off the pitch. I feel really privileged to have played with him."

Below: media coverage reporting on Robbie's sad death (courtesy of Llanelli Star & South Wales Evening Post).

Robbie the Red Dragon:
The Wales Years

"You could see him grow when he put on a Welsh shirt.
It really meant something to Robbie."
Brian Flynn, S.W. Evening Post, 27 February 1998

Before making the progression up into full international recognition Robbie represented Wales at schoolboy/ youths, under-twenty-one level and on into the full team where he collected forty-seven caps.

At Youth level, he had played in games against almost a dozen nations, including Denmark, Luxembourg, Bulgaria, Malta, Hungary, Poland and Italy in the early-1970s.

By late-1973, he was selected in the under-eighteen squad to play in a three-team qualification group for the International Youth Tournament of U.E.F.A. Also known as the Little World Cup, the finals were being staged in Sweden in summer 1974. Wales found themselves in the tricky group eleven, alongside England

Below: an Under-21 Wales line-up featuring Robbie pictured second right, top row. Next to him is his then-Swansea team mate Alan Curtis.

and the Netherlands. With only the group winners progressing to the finals, they opened proceedings with an away trip in November 1973 and a goal-less draw with the Netherlands. A month later, Wales beat them 3-0 at the Vetch Field. A 1-0 defeat against England in Birmingham was reversed on 13 April 1974 thanks to a Welsh victory in Cardiff. That was enough to see them qualify on five points, although the same as England, Wales had the better goal difference.

Over in Sweden, Wales were put in a group with Denmark, Bulgaria and Luxembourg and played three games in a matter of days. Commencing on 22 May, they lost 3-1 to Denmark in Lomma, beat Luxembourg 5-0 in Eslöve some two days later, and drew 0-0 with Bulgaria on 26 May. Consequently Wales finished in third spot on three points, behind Bulgaria and a single point behind the Danes. The Bulgarians eventually won the tournament on 31 May in the final staged in Malmo.

Robbie featured in the qualifying rounds of the 1975 tournament when Wales found themselves playing the Maltese for the right to advance to the summer tournament in Switzerland. Wales Youth, aka the under-18s, met Malta Youth at Cwmbran on 5 February 1975 with Wrexham keeper Eddie Niedzwiecki, future Stoke City boss and Bristol Rovers opponent, Tony Pulis and David Giles in the line-up with Robbie. Wales won handsomely by 4-0 with one of the goals coming from a young Mr James. That March saw them travel to Malta and win 0-1 in Gzira. Advancing to 9 May, Wales were in Group D along with Italy, Poland and Hungary. A 0-0 opening with Italy was followed by a 4-0 thrashing by the Hungarians on 11 May, before a morale-boosting 3-0 win was earned against Poland, in Lugano, on 13 May. Hungary advanced whilst Wales finished second.

In February 1976, Wales Youth lost 0-1 to their English counterparts in Cardiff but turned around the deficit on 3 March by beating them 2-3 at Manchester City's Maine Road ground although it is uncertain as to whether or not Robbie played. Wales took the qualifying place and advanced to the finals in Hungary in the coming summer.

In a hugely difficult Group A, they found themselves alongside Hungary, Yugoslavia and Italy. Decent wins over the latter two countries, 2-1 and 1-0, respectively, failed to see them through to the quarter finals, as the hosts, who went on to win the tournament, taking top spot. Wales had drawn 1-1 with them but missed advancing due to goal difference.

The Wales squad travelled to Wolverhampton on 15 December 1976 to play England at Molineux, home of Wolves, in a friendly affair to mark the first-ever Under-21 game between the countries. This had come after recent changes made by governing body U.E.F.A. and the creation of a new age bracketing system. A commemorative first day cover was released to mark the occasion, a drab 0-0. Robbie played as centre forward, in tandem with Swansea team mate Alan Curtis, after recently being involved in a fund raising match in aid of the ailing Newport County (against a Man United Select at Ninian Park, Cardiff). He started in alongside Cardiff's John Buchanan, a player forever remembered for a wonder strike at the ground against Robbie's Swansea. Curt was one of the two over-age players allowed to play in the Under-21 side and Glan Letheren, deputy keeper at Leeds and later Swans player, was also in the starting XI. He and Robbie would soon link up at the Vetch but here found themselves competing against youngsters that would make a name for themselves in the game; namely Glen Hoddle and Alan Sunderland. Wales traveled up to Easter Road in

February 1977, for a midweek international meeting with Scotland, in front of a 4,500 crowd. The Scots won 3-2 against a Welsh team that saw Robbie alongside future Swans team mates Letheren and Giles. 'Gilo' signed for Swansea from Wrexham after making a name for himself as a talented youngster at Wrexham, recalls playing for Wales at Under-21 level in a match against Scotland where midfielder Robbie scored the winner. That was in February 1978 in a game played at Sealand Road, home of Chester and watched by 2,500. His goal came from the edge of the penalty area in a move involving the tenacious Mickey Thomas and another team mate. Attending his funeral, David offered his own concise tribute, "He was a fantastic player. I was privileged to play alongside him for Swansea and Wales."

For various reasons, Robbie would not play in every Wales game following his full debut against Malta. For example, he did not feature in any of the 1980 British Home International Championships. But he was often selected in a national team full of outstanding players. His presence added a great deal alongside others of equally-prolific talent in regrettably, various under-achieving Wales teams.

Above: Robbie as an established international player.
He can be found fourth from the left, standing row.

1. Malta v Wales, 25 October 1978, Wrexham, European Championship qualifier.

Robbie's first full cap for his country came in a European Championship Group Seven match played at the Racecourse ground, home of Wrexham. He had joined up with the squad at Llangollen on the day after playing for the Swans in a 2-2 away draw at Hull. Cautioned in the second half of that League match, Robbie picked up a nasty knock on his ankle which saw him end the game limping. However, he recovered in time and was with the squad in readiness for the Malta game.

Consisting of a number of Wrexham and Leeds United players, Robbie found himself stifled in a restricted centre forward role, when he was far better suited to playing in midfield. Both he and fellow debutant striking partner Ian Edwards had scored eleven times for their respective clubs, Swansea and Chester prior to meeting the Maltese part-timers. Conceding twenty-six times in their last three internationals, although against top notch opposition such as West Germany, the visitors were thrashed 7-0 and would again be dispatched in the return fixture in the following June.

The match found Wales wearing a garish yellow away kit. However, the home one, designed by Admiral, had been introduced for the 1976 Wales F.A Centenary match with England, also played at the Racecourse, in March of that year. This now-iconic design, made up of red with a collar and v neck, the Wales badge was confidently counter-balanced centrally, with a two-part yellow and green stripe running down either side of the chest. The pattern continued on to the shorts, also. As a child of the late-1970s, like many youngsters of the time, the author had a replica kit but would have to say that its material was very itchy and whereas the pros had a sewn on badge, our one only had a cheap sticker, as were each of the distinctive picnic-box Admiral logo positioned on the collar and shorts. The tracksuit, an overly busy design, came complete with the same irritable material. Around the same time, Admiral broke in to the professional football league market, providing kits for a number of clubs as diverse as Aberdeen, Coventry City and Southampton. The Coventry strip copied the exact same design as the one utilised on the Wales kit but was in sky blue with white and blue stripes. Their away kit was a strong red with white and blue stripes whilst their third kit was a hideous yellow (but not as ugly as the Wales one). They also produced an alternate kit which was chocolate brown! Poor Terry Yorath, a Wales international stalwart when Robbie arrived on the scene, was a Coventry player and had to wear the kits there. When he was transferred to Tottenham Hotspur, Admiral also supplied the kits but they were far more stylish but still featured a dodgy yellow away design worn by them in a Cup match at the Vetch and a subsequent, pre-season friendly. For the FIFA 2014 World Cup qualifying matches Wales reverted to an Umbro-made kit which echoed the earlier Admiral design, having a thick yellow and slim green strip on the left of the chest.

Returning to Robbie and his international career, over the course of the decade that he represented Wales, they wore a number of kit designs, the most stylish being the Adidas one worn from 1980 onwards. Robbie's player-manager at Swansea, John Toshack, headed the advertising campaign for the new kit. Somewhat controversial in that it featured white sleeves, with the three stripes on each identifying the manufacturer's branding, many would argue that it is the crispest Welsh strip of all time. Upon saying that, there really was something about the Admiral design that lingers.

Back to Robbie and his debut against Malta, goals came from Brighton's Peter O'Sullivan on the nineteenth minute followed by a brace from Edwards, one each from Mickey Thomas and Brian Flynn and a third goal for Chester man Edwards. Robbie got the fourth: a pass from Thomas attacking down the right wing was favourably deflected by a defender straight to him and he tapped it in. Confusingly, some reports do not list him as one of the goal scorers but looking at the match footage, it certainly looks like him scoring during the game. Actually, Robbie could quite conceivably have scored his own hat-trick during the game but his uncharacteristic poor finishing robbed him of this.

Mike Smith, manager at the time, was the first full-time appointment for Wales and exercised a methodical style that was admired by many of his players before ex-Spurs star Mike England later took over.

A gate of 11,475 paid between £4 - £2 to see a Wales starting lineup for Robbie's debut consisting of Davies, Jones, Page, Phillips, M Thomas, B Stevenson, Flynn, Cartwright, Edwards, Robbie, Harris. Phillips would soon join Robbie at Swansea City this season after a transfer from Aston Villa whilst Harris would subsequently face Robbie and his Swansea side on the first day of the 1981/82 season.

2. Wales v West Germany, 02 May 1979, Wrexham, European Championship qualifier.

Robbie came on as a late sub in another Group Seven qualifier played at Wrexham. An impressive crowd of 26,900 saw the skills of a visiting German side that included keeper Sepp Meier, and goal scoring king Rummenigge. A goal in each half for the Germans put the game to bed. Starting lineup: Davies, Page, Jones, Berry, Phillips, Thomas, Mahoney, Yorath, Curtis, Edwards, Harris.

The game provided the debut for future Stoke team mate to Robbie, Berry.

3. Wales v Scotland, 19 May 1979, Cardiff, British Home Championship.

This was to be Robbie's inaugural match in the once-revered British Home Championships whereby Wales, Scotland, England and Northern Ireland would compete in an end-of-season tournament, once a big deal despite coming after a long season for club players. Scheduled across a week each May since 1969, games were usually broadcast on terrestrial television back in the days when the chances of watching a live match were scarce. Rivalry between both fans and players was huge. Wales had been outright winners on seven occasions in the past.

The Scots brought a pretty formidable-looking team to Ninian Park, home of Cardiff City, which featured many of their players at some point making their living in England. These included Souness, Jordan, Dalglish, Burley, Hansen and Hartford. A memorable hat-trick from former City terrace hero player and present Swans player-manager, John Toshack sent the Jock Stein-led Scots packing. Already 2-0 up by half-time, collectively wearing their mega-tight Admiral kit, with yellow socks and shirt numbers, Robbie played at number nine. Tosh, with a point to prove after being dropped for the previous international, scored from a header, left-foot and right-foot strike: showing that he still had it despite his critics at the time saying the opposite. On his former club ground ex-Bluebird Tosh would later return as a Swansea player-manager and years later as the Wales manager checking on possible players and as an invited-guest occasionally spotted seated in the Grandstand. Attended by 20,371, the strong starting line-up for Wales consisted of Davies, Dwyer, Jones, Phillips, Yorath, Mahoney, B Stevenson, Flynn, Curt, Tosh, Robbie.

4. England v Wales, 23 May 1979, England, British Home Championships.

Mike England, who had played against Robbie in the 1975/76 Welsh Cup for Cardiff City, selected an unchanged side to meet a team selected by former West Ham man Ron Greenwood, in front of a huge 70,220 gate. Playing for the 'Three Lions' was a certain Bob Latchford, then of Everton and John Toshack's old Liverpool mate, Emlyn Hughes.

A terrific centre half, Mr England was aged thirty eight when he was appointed Wales manager. Despite having no managerial experience to call upon, he could draw from a wealth of professional football experience gathered from playing with Blackburn Rovers, Spurs, Seattle Sounders, Cardiff City and on more than forty occasions, Wales. Regarded as a good man-motivator, he gave a rousing speech on the eve of the match which worked in galvanizing the squad. Robbie missed the best chance of the match!

5. Northern Ireland v Wales, 25 May 1979, Ireland, British Home Championships.

With the Irish managed by former Spurs star Danny Blanchflower and Wales by their own, in Mike England, Robbie got his second goal as an international, this time coming against decent opponents at Windsor Park. No Welsh side had won there since 1965 but with a Swans 'front row' of Tosh, Curt and Robbie, could they finally succeed?

Arsenal keeper Pat Jennings was their keeper and their midfield included Bryan Hamilton, later to manage Robbie at Leicester City and Sammy McIlroy; a future Stoke team mate, friend and managerial opponent. The Wales equalizer was provided by Robbie, who was enjoying a good game. It came on sixty-two minutes after Wales had fallen behind in the opening sixty seconds. Robbie artfully chested down a Stevenson pass before hitting a twenty-yard shot, that easily beat the efforts of the flailing keeper. He also saw a late shot strike the post.

The match was played only two days after the England fixture and with the same Wales team selection. Its result meant that Wales finished as runners-up for the third consecutive year. Two weeks earlier had seen Robbie and Swansea seal promotion to Division Two via a 2-1 win against Chesterfield at the Vetch.

6. Malta v Wales, 02 June 1979, Malta, European Championship qualifier.

Wales came away form Valetta with a win after a match played on possibly the worst surface ever presented for an international match. Facilitated at the Gzira Stadium, the venue already had a terrible reputation and its pitch was a peculiar mix of grit on top of rock! Special preparations for the safety of the Welsh players involved each of them having their feet protected by bandages woven between their toes; the game was played in sweltering temperatures. At the close of the qualifying period Wales finished third out of four in Group Seven which was won by West Germany. They advanced on to win the Championship played in Italy during summer 1980.

A crowd of 8,358 watched goals by Peter Nicholas and Brian Flynn. The Welsh lineup consisted of Davies, Jones, Phillips, Nicholas, Flynn, B Stevenson, Mahoney, Curtis, Toshack, Robbie, Harris

7. West Germany v Wales, 17 October 1979, Cologne, European Championship qualifier.

The Germans were 4-0 up by half-time, with Alan Curtis scoring a consolation goal in a deflating defeat which marked final caps for both John Toshack and Cardiff's Phil Dwyer, the latter who the Swans wanted to buy during the transfer window in early 1978.

Most of the Welsh players squirmed in embarrassment at the result which came after a run of five recent defeats for the team. Substitutes early on, George Berry had a disaster of a game in defence but did well in the opposition's box before being replaced by Joey Jones. Robbie produced a trio of shots, with one effort producing the save of the match which was watched by 61,000. Alas, only Robbie, Curt and Flynn produced decent performances. The Wales lineup over in Germany was Davies, Dwyer, Jones, Phillips, B Stevenson, Flynn, Nicholas, Mahoney, Curtis, Toshack, Robbie.

8. Czechoslovakia v Wales, 09 September 1981, Prague, World Cup qualifier.

Situated in Group Three, Wales found themselves competing with USSR, Iceland, Czechoslovakia and Turkey for the two qualifying places for the 1982 World Cup finals in Spain. The Czechs were no strangers to Wales as they had already been in the same group for the 1972 European Championship. It was Robbie's eighth cap for Wales, this time in front of a crowd totalling 43,000 at the Strahov Stadion. Wales boss Mike England had been at the Vetch to see Swansea beat Leeds United 5-1 in the recent opening game of the new 1981/82 domestic season; with a view to watching half-dozen Swans players up for possible selection. Robbie was keen to impress but was surprised to be in the squad, prior to the match.

Wales topped the group after five games but fell a goal down by half-time. Robbie was introduced as a replacement for an under-par Mickey Thomas, just after the hour mark.

9. Wales v Iceland, 14 October 1981, Swansea, World Cup qualifier.

A rare start for Robbie in the new Adidas-branded Wales kit in a game played on his club ground, Vetch Field. Due to the condition of the stadium proving previously unacceptable to safely facilitate internationals, major investment had seen improvements to the Vetch which had brought it up to the required safety levels. It was in this same month that his Swansea City side reached the top of the Division One table thanks to victory over Stoke.

Tickets to see the game ranged from £5 down to £3.50 to watch a Wales team that had not scored in its last three international games. This was something which their manager was keen to address and it was clear that the players were adopting a shoot on sight policy as the game progressed. Unfortunately, just before the half-time whistle, the stadium was cloaked in darkness due to the floodlights failing; it transpired that a fire in a nearby electricity box was the culprit and this technical fault resulted in nearly an hour's delay.

On top before then, the break seemed to work against the hosts and by the shrill of the whistle sounding for full-time, the score was 2-2. Robbie had opened the scoring on twenty-five minutes thanks to an Alan Curtis pass being miss-hit by another club team mate, Jeremy Charles, only for Robbie to calmly hit a low shot from all of twenty yards. Now playing in the First Division, Leighton James, Dai Davies, John Mahoney, Jeremy Charles and

Alan Curtis completed the Swansea City connection that had numbered seven in a squad of sixteen and six starting in the match. The other goal came from Curt.

Wales were placed in third spot after playing six games; winning four and drawing / losing the remainder. With a plus-eight goal difference both Russia and the Czechs above them had gathered the same amount of points. So far Wales had beaten both Iceland and Turkey 4-0, defeated the Czechs 1-0 in Cardiff, won 0-1 away in Turkey, drawn in Russia and lost 2-0 to the Czechs, in Prague. However, by the end of the qualifying games, USSR was top of the group, with Wales being beaten to second place on goal difference by Czechoslovakia. The draw with Iceland meant that Wales failed to qualify and did not join England, Northern Ireland and Scotland, who all did. Mike England, a man that did so much during his tenure, had said upon his appointment that his aim was to get Wales through to the 1982 World Cup.

10. Spain v Wales, 24 March 1982, Valencia, friendly.

Robbie scored again for Wales in this friendly match watched by a grizzled crowd of 15,000. His strike came via another of his long-range net busters in a game which saw team mate Gordon Davies seeing a perfectly good goal cancelled out. Dai Davies, Chris Marustik, Ian Walsh and Alan Curtis, all Swans, also played. Robbie started alongside Davies, then making a name for himself with Fulham but it was at Merthyr; a club which Robbie would later play for, that he is remembered.

11. Wales v England, 27 April 1982, Cardiff, British Home Championships.

Wales had met England at Ninian Park back in 1961 with a stupendous team that included Ivor Allchurch, the Charles brothers plus Graham Williams, Swansea Town player Cliff Jones and Swansea-born Jack Kelsey. In 1982, a crowd of 25,284 watched a 1-1 played out. A strong England team included Hoddle, Robson, Wilkins and match-winner Trevor Francis. Familiar Swans team mates included Davies in goal, Marustik and Stevenson in defense and Curt in attack. Not only that, Leighton James came on as a sub,too. The other Mr. James won fifty- four caps for Wales and scored ten times for his country. Retiring from the game in 1989, Leighton went in to coaching and now works in the Welsh media. The starting lineup consisted of Davies, Jones, Ratcliffe, N Stevenson, Marustik, Nicholas, Flynn, Thomas, Curtis, Rush, Robbie.

12. Scotland v Wales, 24 May 1982, Scotland, British Home Championship

A crowd of 25,284 looked-on as the Scots sneaked a goal from Asa Hartford against a Wales side with Robbie and five other Swansea players within it. Both he and Ian Rush caused problems for Alan Rough in the Scots goal but a seventh minute strike for the Scots sealed it.

The Wales team, once more captained by Brian Flynn, was Davies, Marustik, Jones, Nicholas, N Stevenson, B Stevenson, Curtis, Robbie, Rush, Flynn, James.

13. Wales v Northern Ireland, 27 May 1982, Wrexham, British Home Championship.

A shockingly-low crowd of 2,315 attended this Friday encounter which saw Robbie wearing the number eight shirt. Nigel Stevenson, Leighton James and Chris Marustik lined-up beside him again against an Irish side featuring Bryan Hamilton and Sammy McIlroy soon off to the World Cup that summer in Spain. The win saw Wales on two points after three games played, scoring three and conceding two.

14. France v Wales, Toulouse, 1982, friendly.

An Ian Rush goal took the kudos in this friendly encounter between two countries that had not met since 1953. The host's present side included the brilliant Michel Platini. It was the only time that Robbie played against French international opposition. As a Swansea City player he had featured in the side that met Paris St.Germain during an early round of the European Cup Winners' Cup in the 1981/ 82 season. The crowd totalled 26,671.

15. Wales v Norway, 22 September 1982, Swansea, European Championship qualifier.

Not a great team performance by the Welsh but two points collected thanks to a super corner from Mickey Thomas seeing the keeper failing to hold on to the ball and allowing Rush to nod in. A goal line block from Swansea man Marustik was added to by a late shot from the Norwegians which hit the post. It was a pleasing result considering that the Scandinavians had recorded a surprise 2-1 win over England the previous season. Another disappointing crowd of some 4,340 attended the game back in the days when a programme cost 40p. Robbie's second full international played on his home ground, the Vetch.

16. Yugoslavia v Wales, 15 December 1982, Titograd, European Championship qualifier.

"A cracking match, very exciting but played in dreadful conditions." Mike England.

Topping their group before the match, Wales required a win to secure automatic qualification to the European Championships. Holding their hosts 0-0 at half time, prior to the match the Yugoslav manager had dabbled in a little bit of mind games by saying that he did not rate any of the Wales playing squad. An appearance fee of £200 per player saw the team work hard in another physical battle, something that didn't bother Robbie, as he scored the fourth Wales goal, on eighty minutes, to put Wales in the lead. This eight-goal thriller had seen the visitor's two goals down at one stage prior to the match ending 4-4, with three goals conceded by Wales from corners.

Some pressing from Robbie saw his goal come via an indirect free kick from the edge of the 'D' being laid off to him by Flynn and boom: straight in the net from twenty yards! Robbie, whose hard work was noted by his manager, hit the bar with a last minute shot during this game played out on a rain-sodden surface. He also had his header blocked before a rare strike by Joey Jones had reduced the Wales deficit to 3-2. The Welsh also had a shout for a late penalty ruled out.

17. England v Wales, 23 February 1983, Wembley, British Home Internationals.

England manager Bobby Robson saw his side defeat a Wales side 2-1 at home for the first time since 1972. The Welsh had taken the lead with a goal from Rush, thanks to a miss-kick from Robbie causing confusion in the defence. Liverpool midfielder Sammy Lee, a subsequent Q.P.R team mate of Robbie's played for England as did Luther Blissett, who had made his League debut against Robbie's Swansea back in 1976. 24,000 watched the match which featured a Welsh starting lineup of Southall, Jones, Ratcliffe, Price, Thomas, Flynn, Mahoney, Jackett, Davies, Rush, Robbie.

18. Wales v Bulgaria, 27 April 1983, Wrexham, European Championship qualifier.

A decent result 1-0 for Wales in this group four qualifier against an opponent making their first-ever visit to Wales. A match summariser commented that the Wales goal might not have been the best planned strike but it was deserved.

Almost half the team was involved in making it happen, starting with a Brian Flynn cross that was headed down by Joey Jones on to Thomas, who shot from the edge of area before Robbie's attempt was deflected back out by a defender only for Charles to score with the ball going in off the post. The game came when Robbie had recently been made Swansea captain.

19. Norway v Wales, 21 September 1983, Oslo, European Championship qualifier.

Robbie, now earning his living with Stoke City, almost scored the winner with the last kick of the game via a driving shot that produced a fine save from the keeper. Sadly, not a single current Swansea City player was selected for this Group Four match played at the Ullevaal Stadion. The Wales starting lineup was Southall, Jones, Hopkins, Ratcliffe, Price, Flynn, Nicholas, Vaughan, Jackett, Rush, Robbie.

20. Wales v Romania, 12 October 1983, Wrexham, friendly.

A plethora of strikes from the cream of Welsh stars continued with little Mickey Thomas following an early goal from Ian Rush at the Racecourse ground, home of Wrexham F.C. 'Rushy' then with Liverpool, added a second before Robbie joined in with a

sixty-sixth minute strike to put Wales 4-0 up before former Swansea team mate Alan Curtis completed the route after having come on as a replacement for Man-of-the-Match star Robbie. The countries had met back in 1971 when Romania won 2-0 and in more recent times they had beaten Italy and Sweden. Watched by a disappointing gate of only 4,161, the Wales line-up: Southall, Hopkins, Jones, Ratcliffe, Price, Thomas, Flynn, Vaughan, Jackett, Rush, Robbie.

21. Bulgaria v Wales, 16 November 1983, Sofia, European Championship qualifier.

After missing training the day before the match due to ankle problems sustained in his endeavours as a Stoke player battling at the bottom of Division One, it was looking unlikely that Robbie would be fit to play in this game. However, he was and it marked his twenty-first appearance in a Welsh shirt.

With the relevant Football Association of both countries engaged in some tit-for-tat shenanigans at the time, the squad woke up to six inches of snow on the morning of the match. Leading the group at the time, Wales faced a tricky opposition at the Wassil Levski Stadium before a crowd of 8,000. The gate was reduced due to the match being shown live on Bulgarian television. Wales had recorded a 1-0 win back in April 1983 but lost by the same score here. Robbie and his team mates missed plenty of chances in a tense affair.

Shockingly, many of the visiting players received abuse from a dirty opposition that kicked, punched and spat their way through the match.

22. Wales v Yugoslavia, 14 December 1983, Cardiff, Euro Championship qualifier.

A large crowd was in attendance for this match, with qualification possible for Wales providing that they produce a win. Only one team from any of the seven qualifying groups would go through to the tournament finals in France and before the game, Wales sat on top of their group after playing five matches: wining twice, drawing twice and losing once.

Robbie scored on fifty-four minutes in a game which he was joined by his mercurial Stoke colleague Mickey Thomas. Wales' opening goal was thanks to a pass sent from deep in their own half through to an unmarked Robbie who had a one-on-one with the goal keeper on the edge of the penalty box. He took the ball around his man and managed to cut it back before two defenders just missed intercepting it on the line. Robbie celebrated his strike with the fans and you could see in his face the amazement at having being given the opportunity to score: and at Ninian Park! The Yugoslav defenders were ball watching when it sailed passed them and in to his path. However, his goal was eventually nullified in the eightieth minute by a late equalizer. Wales finished the group in second spot, behind Yugoslavia, and missed out on qualification by a point. The Wales starting line-up: Southall, Jones, Hopkins, Ratcliffe, Price, Vaughan, Thomas, Flynn, Jackett, Rush, Robbie.

23. Scotland v Wales, 28 February 1984, Glasgow, British Home International.

Another visit to Hampden Park found Robbie still a Stoke City player, in a game noteworthy not only for his goal but also for the fact that not a single Wales footballer was then playing for any of the four domestic Welsh clubs. For example, Jeremy Charles was at Q.P.R, Mickey Thomas with Chelsea, Kevin Ratcliffe then still an Everton player and Alan Curtis was with Southampton. In comparison, the Scots had all but three players based with domestic clubs.

Robbie was utilised in a much deeper role on the right, to allow the returning Curtis a role in the team. The equalizer for Wales came from Robbie on forty seven minutes in this the ninety-ninth meeting between the Celtic cousins. Wales, who had not won at Hampden since the 1950s, had lots of chances for Robbie and his team mates, in a match attended by 21,542. His goal came after he chased a Mickey Thomas pass before beating Leighton with a superb twenty yard strike.

24. Wales v England, 2 May 1984, Wrexham, British Home International.

A gate totaling 14,250 enjoyed a 1-0 Wales win against an England side incorporating Peter Shilton, Swansea City team mate Ray Kennedy and Sammy Lee, later to sign for Q.P.R when Robbie was there. Current Stoke team mate Mark Chamberlain was also in the England squad.

Wearing the number four shirt, Robbie was joined by debutant Mark Hughes. Then a Manchester United player, 'Sparky' also had his team mate, the tragic Alan Davies, alongside him in the red of Wales. Robbie and Alan later played together at Swansea City and would be involved in an exchange deal between the club and Bradford.

25. Wales v Northern Ireland, 22 May 1984, Swansea, British Home International.

Three weeks since their victory against England, Wales played what was to be their third and final game of the Championship in this mid-week game staged at the Vetch.

Robbie was in a team alongside players selected from Everton, Man United, Watford, Plymouth, Chelsea and Fulham. Sammy McIlroy and Bryan Hamilton again featured for Ireland.

Robbie wore the number six shirt and played in a central midfield role in this eventual 1-1, after Wales had gone a goal up. The Stoke player showed his defensive capabilities by disarming Norman Whiteside in an attacking position and another tackle saw him win the ball against an opponent that ended limping after the encounter! It was the very last British Home International match.

26. Norway v Wales, 6 June 1984, Trondheim, friendly.

A rather disappointing team display in this friendly match arranged as a precursor to World Cup qualification in 1985. It was the first time that the countries had played each other since 1922. Staged at the Lerkendal Stadion in front of a 15,970 crowd with Robbie in a Wales side newly captained by Everton star Kevin Ratcliffe.

27. Israel v Wales, 10 June 1984, Tel Aviv, friendly.

Furious at his team from the previous game with Norway, Mike England was placated with a much better showing in this goal-less draw at the Ramat-Gan National Stadium. A gate of some 3,000 watched a game played out in a muggy atmosphere. The Welsh were without five regular players and the match saw Robbie selected in a centre half role.

28. Iceland v Wales, 12 September 1984, Reykjavic, World Cup qualifier.

In a Wales performance that saw many absentees from the usual crop of players, Mike England defined the 1-0 defeat at the Laugardalsvollur stadium as being "absolutely disgraceful". A decent crowd of some 14,000 saw the humiliation provided by the Scandinavians who were managed by ex-Brit footballer Tony Knapp. Robbie had a good chance cleared off the line and was instrumental in providing another scoring opportunity for Gordon Davies. He also had a goal disallowed due to an infringement.

29. Spain v Wales, 17 October 1984, Seville, World Cup qualifier.

After playing for their club sides, the Welsh squad joined up for this midweek match against an overly-physical Spanish side. The Welsh lads were keen not to respond to any provocation during the game and some changes had been made in selection after a poor run of no wins in eight games for the national side.

A stunning second Spanish goal came thanks to a free kick, with Wales, wearing yellow shirts, were unable to stop a rampant host at the Estadio Sanchez Pizjuan.

30. Wales v Iceland, 14 November 1984, Cardiff, World Cup qualifier.

Many agree that the best national sides usually draw upon one or two clubs for their players and so it was for Swansea at one point. Robbie was one of seven Swans in the Wales squad at this time: joining Dai Davies, Curt, Jeremy Charles, Leighton James and John Mahoney.

The Welsh had played six games and found themselves third in the qualifying group; behind Czechoslovakia and Russia (with Turkey and Iceland below). Wales had recently lost to the Czechs over in Prague and held them to a draw at Wrexham in May 1981. But here at Ninian Park, Wales went 1-0 up thanks to Mickey Thomas and the winner came thanks to a pass from Robbie in centre midfield. It went out to Phillips on the right wing, he then put in a cross nodded down by Thomas and the ball broke eventually to Hughes who took the opportunity to put it away and thus win the match for Wales.

31. Wales v Norway, 26 February 1985, Wrexham, friendly.

Another friendly fixture, this time featuring Robbie in a centre half role, his versatility meant that he was utilised in the national side in defence, midfield and attack: just like Swansea team mate Jeremy Charles. Curt and Alan Davies, also featured. Concluding in a 1-1, both first half goals.

32. Scotland v Wales, 27 March, 1985, Glasgow, World Cup qualifier.

Remarks about the lack of quality in the Wales team by former Manchester United manager Tommy Docherty worked in putting the backs up of the team for this important match. The 'Doc' believed that Wales had only four decent players and that the rest were mediocre. A similarly inflammatory statement would be made by Mickey Thomas in 2013 when Wales again faced the Scots. For the record, the 1985 Wales team seen by a massive 62,424 crowd, consisted of Southall, Slatter, Jones, Jackett, Ratcliffe, Phillips, Robbie, Nicholas, Rush, Hughes, Thomas.

Robbie was now a Q.P.R player and played his part in a marvellous 0-1 win in front of 63,000 spectators at Hampden Park. There was some nastiness involving Graeme Souness towards Peter Nicholas which escalated in to seeing Robbie, Ratcliffe and Joey Jones rush to their team mate's aid! Robbie was a part of a battling Wales side and saw his header easily held.

After retiring, Ratcliffe would move on to providing BBC radio commentary of Wales international matches and domestic League games involving Welsh teams across the 2012/13 season. It was during the Scotland v Wales match, when challenges were flying in and a Scotsman was sent off, that 'Rats' joked that Robbie was the hardest of the lot and that you didn't want to mess with him on the pitch! His comments echoed back to a very physical match between the sides when he and Robbie both played. Kevin and Robbie became team mates at Cardiff across two seasons and would enjoy the promotion/ Welsh Cup winning season.

33. Wales v Spain, 30 April 1985, Wrexham, World Cup qualifier.

Robbie and Wales found themselves in Group Seven of a qualifying pot of three others: Iceland, Spain and Scotland producing mixed results; they lost 1-0 away to Iceland and 3-0 in Spain but won 2-1 against Iceland in November and defeating the Scots 0-1 away in March 1985.

The match transpired to be one of the best ever Wales performances with the second goal being a Mark Hughes wonder strike: hitting the ball from a moving position would become his trade mark. The third goal was created by a header won by Robbie on the half-way line which was nodded to Hughes and Rush completed the move. The then-present Wales squad publicly acknowledged that they favoured playing at the Racecourse rather than at the Vetch or Ninian Park, as the atmosphere was better and worked well in settling them.

34. Norway v Wales, 5 June 1985, Bergen, friendly match.

A friendly fixture between the countries, this time seen by 5,596 at the Brann Stadion. Robbie was still a Q.P.R. man and watched as the Norwegians stormed to being 3-0 up in the opening twenty minutes. The final score was a 4-2 defeat for the Welsh.

35. Wales v Scotland, 10 September 1985, Cardiff, World Cup qualifier.

A crowd close to 40,000 knew that a Wales win would see their first involvement in the finals since 1958. Wearing red, with peculiar horizontal lines across the chest, a strong red dragon squad had already seen off the Jocks at Hampden Park, as well as Spain and when they went 1-0 up thanks to Mark Hughes, things were looking propitious.

Striker Ian Rush was sure that the country could make it to the summer tournament but the Scots only needed to draw to seal their advancement towards a play-off final with Australia.

And as is so often the case when we talk of the national side, with ten minutes remaining, an equaliser came via a penalty. Scored by Davie Cooper, Wales' keeper Neville Southall almost saved it. It was eight years since Scotland had put Wales out of contention for a previous World Cup campaign at Anfield, via a Jordan hand ball and subsequent penalty strike.

Robbie, wearing the number seven shirt, had been seen chatting with Scotland manager Jock Stein prior to kick-off, little knowing the fate for the Celtic legend: tragically, Mr. Stein would die as a result of a heart attack suffered during the match. Most people forget that the big man was a player; such was his heightened managerial status within the game.

Coincidentally, Stein had played for Llanelli AFC many years before and that was a club that Robbie was also fatefully to become associated with. Since the move away from Ninian Park to the Cardiff City stadium, a plaque can be found on the gates of the memorial garden there marking the tragedy.

Jamo was in a Welsh starting XI alongside Rush, Ratcliffe and Thomas. The latter being known by his team mates at Wrexham as 'Noddy' (due to the way his head moved when he ran with the ball). Robbie was subbed on 80 minutes.

36. Saudi Arabia v Wales, 15 February 1986, Saudi Arabia, friendly match.

A rare encounter between the two countries attended by a Dahrain gate of some 20,000 and arranged as a financial booster for the F.A.W. The midweek match was played whilst accompanied by music pumped through the PA system whilst the players were on the field! Robbie was subbed just after the hour mark as Wales advanced to a 1-2 win.

Making his debut in a Wales shirt was David Williams, later to call up Robbie for his final international outing in March 1988.

37. Republic of Ireland v Wales, 26 March 1986, Eire, friendly match.

A friendly arranged for the Irish staged at Lansdowne road ground on a terrible pitch, more used to rugby. The Irish, soon to enjoy success in the World Cup that summer, had a decent side that included Liam Brady, David O'Leary and Ray Houghton. Ray and Eire team mate John Aldridge played against Robbie in the Milk Cup final. Wales team: Southall, Jones, Blackmore, Phillips, Lowndes, Nicholas, Jackett, Davies, Rush, Charles, Robbie.

38. Wales v Uruguay, 21 April 1986, Wrexham, friendly.

A bruising encounter despite being a friendly played on a muddy Racecourse pitch in front of 11,154.

39. Canada v Wales, 10 May 1986, Toronto, friendly.

Staged at the Varsity stadium, this was the first of two fixtures against the Canadians, with the first enjoyed here by a little over 13,000 spectators. Remarkably, they qualified for the Mexico World Cup that summer but their 2-0 home win marked the first time that they had beaten a European team. Playing in white, Wales were sunk by two first half goals.

40. Canada v Wales, 20 May 1986, Vancouver, friendly.

A welcome 0-2 victory for the visitors, on Robbie's fortieth cap for Wales. Staged at the Swansguard stadium, an indoor venue only 9,000 attended, in an arena with a 59,000 capacity.

41. Finland v Wales, 10 September 1986, Helsinki, European Championship qualifier.

Played at the Olympiastadion, Wales came back from a 1-0 first half deficit in this opening match of the qualifying group watched by 9,840. Future Swansea boss Kenny Jackett added to his caps total, as did Dean Saunders, later to become manager of Wales, who acquired more clubs as a player than even Mickey Thomas! The sides had met back in the early-1970s when a young Tosh led the attack .

42. Wales v U.S.S.R, 18 February, 1987, Swansea, friendly.

A 0-0 used as a preparation for the oncoming European Championship qualifiers with Finland and Czechoslovakia. Robbie was with Q.P.R, signing for them in October 1984. Some 17,617 crammed into the Vetch to watch the game.

43. Wales v Finland,1 April 1987, Wrexham, European Championship qualifier.

Robbie featured in the number seven shirt of the new Hummel-manufactured Wales kit. Subsequent group opponents Denmark also had their kits made by them.

Captain Kevin Ratcliffe had plenty of time to put a ball from his own half straight through to the right wing where Robbie ran into the space and managed to whip in a cross for Ian Rush, who put the ball in the net despite being shackled by two Finnish players and having to beat the keeper; much to the delight of the 7,696 crowd. A second goal came when Robbie missed connecting with a cross which went to Rush and subsequently took a couple of strikes at goal before a Glyn Hodges volley made it 2-0.

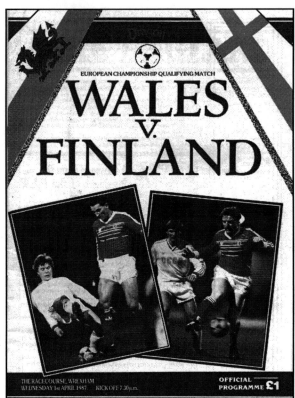

EUROPEAN CHAMPIONSHIP QUALIFYING MATCH

WALES
v.
FINLAND

THE RACECOURSE, WREXHAM
WEDNESDAY 1st APRIL 1987   KICK OFF 7.30 p.m.

OFFICIAL
PROGRAMME £1

Robbie was able to take a long-range punt a little outside the penalty area, low and fast on a greasy surface before a player could attempt to intervene. Wales were aided by some terrible goalkeeping from the keeper and finished 4-0 winners.

44. Wales v Czechoslovakia, 29 April 1987, Wrexham, Euro Championship qualifier.

Late into the second half and the tricky Czechs went 1-0 up via a brilliantly-taken goal before Rush equalised via a pass supplied by Robbie.

45. Wales v Denmark, 9 September 1987, Cardiff, European Championship qualifier.

A very physical Welsh team performance was recorded here, with tackles flying in and Danish players repeatedly hitting the surface of a washed-out Ninian Park pitch. Robbie fulfilled a central midfield role in the match. Again recognisable at number seven, he resembled more a wrestler than footballer; his idiosyncratic rigid running style and stocky frame making him look stiff. Nonetheless, Wales won 1-0 thanks to a move which involved a then-Leicester City Robbie. He put in a smashing, deep cross after receiving a pass out on the left side of the pitch, knocked it back into the area via a perfectly weighted and well-timed header in a well-orchestrated move that Mark Hughes both began and ended. A header from Jones hit the crossbar and quickest to follow-up was Hughes, who put the ball into the net with a diving header. Robbie was booked for an off-the-ball incident which concluded with a Dane being felled and immediately Robbie rushed after the referee only to receive a yellow card. Wales battered their opponents throughout the match and it was not just Robbie dishing out the hammerings either. A surprise result, evident in the smiling faces of the Welsh players at full-time. The match attracted a huge 20,535 and found Robbie substituted for a debuting Barry Horne.

46. Denmark v Wales, 14 October 1987, Copenhagen, European Championship qualifier.

The corresponding fixture found the Danes cheered on by an impressive 44,500 gathered at the Parkstadion. Robbie was substituted during the game which Wales lost 1-0 and along with Hughes, received a yellow card. Wales finished third and in their six games played, they both won and drew twice and lost the remainder; scoring seven to five against.

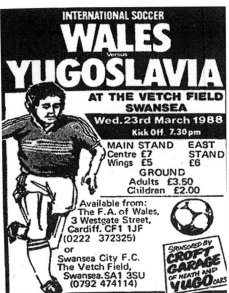

47. Wales v Yugoslavia, 23 March 1988, Swansea, friendly.

Robbie was a Swansea player once more at the time of this match, after having recently re-signed for them in what would be his final outing in a Welsh shirt. The game was played on his thirty-first birthday.

Robbie had featured in a 4-4 with Yugosavia back in a pulsating 1982 European Championship qualifier.

Selected due to an injury to another player, Robbie was asked to give a supporting role to the strikers. Played on a wet and muddy Vetch pitch, the game saw a great goal from Dean Saunders. Son of former Swansea player/ coach Roy, who was at the club when Robbie was a youngster, his strike put Wales 1-0 up. The move commenced with Robbie passing to Blackmore, who in turn put in a cross for 'Deano'. Close to 6,000 saw Robbie bow out of international football just after the hour mark; a decade since his debut against Malta. His ambition was to reach fifty caps but he fell just a little short. Former Wales manager Mike Smith attended Robbie's funeral and had managed him there, offered, "He was a marvelous professional, a superb player for Wales and always gave his best for club and country. Off the field he was a very relaxed and pleasant guy."

A huge thank you to everyone that helped with regards to loans of programmes and much more, including Rich Malcolm. Frank Collict for his illustration and many others.

Swansea 'til I die, A century of supporting the Swans, 2012.
Vetch Field of Dreams & From the Fourth to the First, both by Gary Wharton, Lushington Publishing, 2005.
Eddie May: My Story, Eddie May with Gary Wharton, 2012.
Curt. The Alan Curtis Story, Alan with Tim Johnson & Sturat Sprake, Mainstream, 2009.
Mr Cardiff City, The Autobiography of Phil 'Joe' Dwyer, Dwyer with James Leighton, Fort Pub., 2011
Tommy Smith, I Did it the Hard Way, Arthur Barker Ltd, London, 1980
Ray of Hope: The Ray Kennedy Story, Dr Andrew Lees and Ray Kennedy, Pelam Books, 1993.
The Swansea Evening Post: including John Burgum and Bill Paton's various match reports.
Michael Boon quote from the Swansea match programme, Rochdale, October 1974.
The Home Internationals Soccer Tournament, 1946-1984. A Complete Record. Gary Watson, GW Publications, 2011.

Red Dragons. The Story of Welsh Football, Phil Stead, Y Lolfa publishing, 2012.
Wales: The Complete Who's Who of footballers since 1946. Dean P.Hayes, Sutton, 2004.
Welsh Towns: Merthyr Tydfil, BBC 1 Wales, 2013.
Wales on this Day, Steve Menolry, Pitch Pub., 2010.
Swansea Local Studies Library
Welsh Football Collection, Wrexham.
Barry Town United F.C: Club Secretary, Stuart Lovering.
barrytownfc.com
barrytown.proboards.com
Barry & District News - for their match summaries.
Merthyr Tydfil F.C, compiled by David Watkins, Tempus, 1999.

I looked at many websites, most of which are referenced in the text but also included the following:
rssf.com
sporting-heroes.net
welshgrounds.co.uk
wfda.co.uk
welsh-premier.com
welshicons.org.uk/index.php
11v11.com,
qprreport.proboards.com
footballsite.co.uk
mytampabayrowdies.blogspot.co.uk
Llanelli Star newspaper
Weston Mecury newspaper